Teaching Math in Middle School

Using MTSS to Meet All Students' Needs

Teaching Math in Middle School

Using MTSS to Meet All Students' Needs

by

Leanne R. Ketterlin-Geller, Ph.D.
Southern Methodist University
Dallas, Texas

Sarah R. Powell, Ph.D.
The University of Texas at Austin

David J. Chard, Ph.D.
Boston University
Massachusetts

and

Lindsey Perry, Ph.D.
Southern Methodist University
Dallas, Texas

·P·A·U·L·H·
BROOKES
PUBLISHING Cº ®

Baltimore • London • Sydney

Paul H. Brookes Publishing Co.
Post Office Box 10624
Baltimore, Maryland 21285-0624
USA

www.brookespublishing.com

Typeset by Absolute Services Inc., Towson, Maryland.
Manufactured in the United States of America by
Sheridan Books, Chelsea, Michigan.

Unless otherwise stated, examples in this book are composites. Any similarity to actual individuals or circumstances is coincidental, and no implications should be inferred.

Chapter 17, Implementing MTSS: Voices From the Field, features excerpts from interviews with teachers and other educational professionals. Interview material has been lightly edited for length and clarity. Interviewees' responses, real names, and identifying details are used by permission.

Library of Congress Cataloging-in-Publication Data

Names: Ketterlin-Geller, Leanne R., 1971- author. | Powell, Sarah Rannells, author. | Chard, David, author. | Perry, Lindsey, author.
Title: Teaching math in middle school : using MTSS to meet all students' needs / by Leanne R. Ketterlin-Geller, Ph.D. (Southern Methodist University, Dallas, Texas), Sarah R. Powell, Ph.D. (The University of Texas at Austin), David J. Chard, Ph.D. (Boston University), and Lindsey Perry, Ph.D. (Southern Methodist University, Dallas, Texas).
Description: Baltimore : Paul H. Brookes Publishing Co., 2019. | MTSS, multi-tiered systems of support. | Includes bibliographical references and index.
Identifiers: LCCN 2018056217 | ISBN 9781598572742 (pbk.) | ISBN 9781681253466 (epub) | ISBN 9781681253473 (pdf)
Subjects: LCSH: Mathematics—Study and teaching (Middle school) | Numeracy—Study and teaching (Middle school) | Response to intervention (Learning disabled children)
Classification: LCC QA135.6 .T4245 2019 | DDC 372.7/049—dc23 LC record available at https://lccn.loc.gov/2018056217

British Library Cataloguing in Publication data are available from the British Library.

2023   2022   2021   2020   2019

10   9   8   7   6   5   4   3   2   1

Contents

About the Downloadable Materials

Purchasers of this book may download, print, and/or photocopy the forms provided for implementing multi-tiered systems of support/response to intervention (MTSS/RTI) for professional use. These materials appear in the print book and are also available at http://downloads.brookespublishing.com for both print and e-book buyers. To access the materials that come with the book

1. Go to the Brookes Publishing Download Hub: http://downloads .brookespublishing.com

2. Register to create an account (Or log in with an existing account)

3. Filter or search for your book title

About the Authors

Leanne R. Ketterlin-Geller, Ph.D., is Professor and the Texas Instruments Chair in Education at Southern Methodist University. Her research focuses on the development and validation of formative assessment systems in mathematics that provide instructionally relevant information to support students with diverse needs. She works nationally and internationally to support achievement and engagement in mathematics and other STEM disciplines.

Sarah R. Powell, Ph.D., is Associate Professor in the Department of Special Education at the University of Texas at Austin. Sarah conducts research related to mathematics interventions for students with learning difficulties. Her work is currently supported by the Institute of Education Sciences, National Science Foundation, T.L.L. Temple Foundation, and Office of Special Education Programs of the U.S. Department of Education.

David J. Chard, Ph.D., is Dean ad interim of Boston University's Wheelock College of Education and Human Development and Professor of Special Education. Prior to coming to BU, Dr. Chard served as the 14th President of Wheelock College. He was also founding dean of the Simmons School of Education and Human Development at Southern Methodist University in Dallas, Texas. He is a member of the International Academy for Research in Learning Disabilities and has been a classroom teacher in California, Michigan, and in the U.S. Peace Corps in Lesotho in southern Africa. He served on the Board of Directors of the National Board for Education Sciences for two terms from 2012-2019.

Lindsey Perry, Ph.D., is Research Assistant Professor at Southern Methodist University, Dallas, Texas. Her research focuses on improving students' mathematics knowledge, particularly at the elementary and middle school grades, by better understanding how children reason relationally and spatially. Her work also includes the development of technically adequate assessments that can be used to improve these reasoning skills.

Foreword

All school-age students need to develop a strong understanding of the essential concepts of mathematics to be able to expand professional opportunities, understand and critique the world, and to experience the joy, wonder, and beauty of mathematics. Mathematics learning occurs across grade levels, but an essential period of mathematics development is during middle school as students expand their learning beyond numbers to proportional reasoning which supports thinking algebraically. For some students, mathematics in middle school can be overwhelming and difficult, but school leaders and educators need to ensure that each and every student have access to meaningful mathematics curriculum and high-quality teaching for effective mathematics learning.

In middle school, mathematics teaching, and the process of learning algebraic readiness and proportionality, involve more than just acquiring content and carrying out procedures. At this level, students are expected to represent, analyze, and generalize about patterns. Students should be able to use multiplication and addition to find the relationship between the two sets of numbers and should look at patterns through the use of tables, graphs, and symbolic representation. Over time, with support from teachers, the mathematical practices and processes that students engage in as they engage with algebraic problems deepen their understanding of key concepts while developing procedural fluency.

Algebraic readiness and proportionality provide strong foundations for future mathematics courses. For students to be successful in algebra, it is essential that middle school mathematics teaching and learning provide opportunities to develop algebraic thinking and proportional reasoning. The strategies presented in *Teaching Math in Middle School: Using MTSS to Meet All Students' Needs* provide teachers with research-based ideas that will promote algebraic readiness for all students. Incorporating these concepts will provide students with the opportunity to experience success in middle school mathematics and in algebra.

Specifically, *Teaching Math in Middle School: Using MTSS to Meet All Students' Needs*, provides detailed information about using multi-tiered support systems (MTSS) to effectively teach mathematics to students who may experience difficulty with mathematics. This book is important for educators who need to teach a variety of learners in the classrooms and for school leaders and educators who want to put in place support systems that meet the needs of each and every learner.

Robert Q. Berry, III, Ph.D.
Professor, University of Virginia
President, National Council of Teachers of Mathematics.

Preface

As mathematics teachers, we wear our interest in and attraction to mathematics like badges, proud to tell everyone about how beautiful it is to learn about numbers, how they work, and how they help us understand the world around us. All four of us (the authors of this book) are a little geeky like that. In fact, combined we have more than 80 years of teaching and research interests in how students learn mathematics, how teachers teach mathematics, and how teachers and their colleagues can improve student learning in mathematics. We have all been science and mathematics teachers, teaching a range of topics including chemistry, biology, elementary mathematics, algebra, advanced algebra, trigonometry, physics, and calculus. In addition, we've all pursued graduate degrees focused on improving teaching and learning in mathematics (further evidence of geekiness). As you can see, we've invested a lot of our lives into improving the teaching of mathematics and the science areas that depend on knowledge of mathematics to make sense.

We decided to write this book for several reasons. First, we are struck by the evidence that being proficient in mathematics is key to academic success in life. Second, we believe that academic success should be accessible to everyone. Third, we have all observed our own students as well as others who believe that they are not capable of understanding and doing mathematics. Fourth, teachers who are prepared to teach mathematics well, working together with other education professionals, are the ingredient to ensuring student success in all subjects, but specifically in mathematics. We also believe that systems developed in schools, such as multi-tiered systems of support (MTSS/RTI), are important advances that will help students to succeed. And finally, we wrote this book because we are colleagues and friends who have learned a lot from one another over the years, and we hope that the information we have put in this book will help teachers and their education colleagues to improve their students' learning and confidence with middle school mathematics.

There is a growing body of research that suggests that students' mathematics achievement is an important predictor of later success in life as measured by educational and financial outcomes. Young children often start out in school with measurably different understandings of basic arithmetic, with children of color, children experiencing poverty, or children with disabilities at higher risk for poor mathematics achievement (Berch, Mazzocco, & Ginsburg, 2007; Hanusheck & Rivkin, 2006).

These performance differences are also remarkably stable with early school mathematics performance (K–1st grade) predicting later (5th grade) mathematics performance (Duncan et al., 2007). More recent findings suggest that knowledge of fractions and whole-number division, subjects taught in the intermediate grades, is more strongly related to high school math achievement than knowledge of whole-number addition, subtraction, and multiplication; verbal IQ; working memory; and parental income (Siegler et al., 2012). Taken together, these findings support several important notions about school mathematics: 1) helping students develop an understanding of mathematics early is critical to their later development, 2) development of understanding of rational numbers, in particular, has an important impact on students' later success, and 3) targeted interventions for students who struggle with particular areas of mathematics learning is necessary for their later success.

Because the evidence is abundantly clear that students' understanding of middle-level mathematics concepts (i.e., fractions and division) is critical to their development in higher level mathematics and their overall academic success, we feel it is particularly important that we ensure that all learners have access to high-quality mathematics teaching and the broadest range of instructional supports aimed at promoting their success. To achieve this, we first have to create a culture in schools and at home in which educators and parents believe that mathematics is *useful* and *learnable*. We need important figures in students' lives to promote their understanding of mathematics rather than promoting the idea that "some people are good at it" and "others are not math people." We also have to confront and change some educators' perceptions that some students can't learn mathematics and to recognize that there is evidence to support mathematical development for all students regardless of their background, early learning experiences, or challenges (e.g., Walker, 2007; Steele, 2003; Gersten et al., 2009).

Beyond the initial concern that mathematics is too difficult or too abstract for students to learn, teaching mathematics requires much more. Surveys show that many U.S. teachers at all grade levels have less extensive backgrounds in the mathematics they teach than is recommended by the National Council of Teachers of Mathematics. Still, most teachers feel comfortable with their mathematics content knowledge (Banilower et al., 2013). We would encourage all teachers to take a circumspect approach.

Strive to understand mathematics concepts and principles, be comfortable with your own knowledge, and feel confident that even those aspects of the discipline you find confusing can be learned if you persist in trying to understand. We certainly don't mean to portray this as an easy process. In fact, each of us has faced a time when we experienced our own "ah-hah" moments about a particular idea that we thought we had already mastered. For example, one of the core transitions in understanding that our students make in middle school mathematics is from whole numbers to rational numbers. Many of us experienced learning rational numbers with an approach that was mostly procedural and didn't maximize our understanding. As teachers, we continue to study how rational numbers function. It should not surprise us that we find ourselves asking fundamental questions about such things as dividing fractions, for example. Why is it that when you divide $\frac{1}{2}$ by $\frac{1}{2}$ you get a larger quotient? Rather than simply teaching an "invert and multiply" approach as we may have been taught, how do we encourage students to predict what will happen and then explain *why*?

It is also important that teachers feel competent and confident in doing mathematics and work hard to shrug off the idea that they have to know everything before teaching it. Many successful mathematics teachers deliberately build a culture in their classroom wherein making mistakes is considered necessary for learning. They model this behavior so that students feel comfortable taking risks in their problem solving and don't associate mathematics success with always being right.

In other words, teaching mathematics requires more than being able to do mathematics. Effective mathematics teachers understand how students conceptualize mathematics and how to develop their students' understanding in order to prepare for related concepts and principles that are on the horizon. They also develop their knowledge of common misconceptions students formulate that can disrupt their learning and how to diagnose those misconceptions. It takes experience and professional learning opportunities to develop these knowledge and skills that Ball, Hill, and Bass (2005) have referred to as "mathematics knowledge for teaching." We believe that this knowledge is particularly important when working with students who struggle to learn mathematics. The same survey we mentioned earlier about teachers' preparation in mathematics also reported that the vast majority of teachers do not feel that they have been adequately prepared to work with a diverse array of student needs in mathematics (Banilower et al., 2013).

From our perspective, making middle school mathematics accessible to all learners is a function of knowing your students' learning history, starting where they are, and designing instruction to help them grow in their knowledge and skills, tailoring instruction as needed to ensure that students develop proficiency in big ideas and providing appropriate accommodations when necessary for learners to continue to progress.

Our objectives in this book are to 1) set the context for the importance of supporting all learners in middle school mathematics, 2) share with you our understanding of effective instruction in order to build from a common vocabulary and understanding of the importance of teaching to learning, 3) examine the types of assessment necessary to ensure effective instruction and how different assessments assist teachers to support the full range of learners, and 4) offer ways of thinking about how teachers and other education professionals in a school or school district work collaboratively to optimize the positive impact of an MTSS/RTI approach to teaching mathematics.

HOW THIS BOOK IS ORGANIZED

Our book is structured in four sections. Section I, Building Numeracy in Middle School Students, introduces fundamentals to help math teachers instruct middle school students. Within Section I, Chapter 1, Laying the Foundation for Algebra, discusses the pillars of foundational knowledge middle-school students need to prepare for algebra. Chapter 2, Supporting All Students Through Multi-Tiered Instruction, introduces the widely used MTSS/RTI model. Chapter 3, Supporting All Students Through Differentiation, Accommodation, and Modification, introduces principles for tailoring instruction to meet all students' needs.

Effective implementation of MTSS depends on sound instructional methods and ongoing assessment. Section II of the book, Designing and Delivering Effective Mathematics Instruction, delves into best teaching practices. Within this section, Chapter 4, Aims for Effective Mathematics Instruction, presents overarching principles to guide teachers in planning and implementing lessons. Chapter 5, Evidence-Based Practices for Instruction and Intervention, grounds readers in research-supported teaching practices to use for core instruction in the general education classroom and for instructing students who need extra help. Chapter 6, Instructional Practices to Support Problem Solving, focuses on effective instruction related to problem solving, a common weakness for students with learning difficulties. Chapter 7, Designing Interventions, describes methods for creating and implementing effective intensive intervention. Finally, Chapter 8, Implementing Interventions Within a Multi-Tiered Framework, puts together information from the preceding chapters to explain how middle school math teachers can implement practical interventions and do so with fidelity.

In Section III, Using Data to Make Decisions, we guide teachers in using assessment results to inform instruction within MTSS/RTI. Chapter 9, Why Should We Assess?, provides an overview of the purposes of assessment and the different types of assessments used for each purpose—in essence, what questions we have about students' learning and how assessment helps us find answers. The remainder of Section III expands upon this overview, providing detailed guidance for conducting each type of assessment in Chapter 10, Who Needs Extra Assistance, and How Much? Universal Screeners; Chapter 11, Why Are Students Struggling? Diagnostic Assessments; Chapter 12, Is the Intervention Helping? Progress Monitoring; and Chapter 13, Have Students Reached Their Goals? Summative Assessments.

Successful implementation of MTSS/RTI depends not only on individual teachers' work in their own classrooms, but also on collaboration. Section IV of this book, Implementing MTSS to Support Effective Teaching, is written to help teachers collaborate effectively with other professionals and with parents. Chapter 14, MTSS in Action, guides educators through the details of planning instruction and assessment at each tier of intervention, and Chapter 15, Assessing Your School's Readiness for MTSS Implementation, guides them to analyze strengths and areas for improvement schoolwide as they prepare to implement MTSS. Chapter 16, Collaboration as the Foundation for Implementing MTSS, addresses collaboration between general and special educators, as well as collaboration between teachers and other stakeholders. Finally, Chapter 17, Implementing MTSS: Voices From the Field, offers perspectives from teachers and administrators about the real-life challenges—and rewards—of implementing MTSS/RTI to improve mathematics outcomes in middle school.

We hope that readers find this book a helpful resource in helping all students to succeed in middle school mathematics. Their success has never been more important!

References

Ball, D. L., Hill, H. C., & Bass, H. (2005, Fall). Knowing mathematics for teaching. *American Educator,* 14–46.

Banilower, E. R., Smith, P. S., Weiss, I. R., Malzahn, K. A., Campbell, K. M., & Weis, A. M. (2013). *Report of the 2012 National Survey of Science and Mathematics Education.* Chapel Hill, NC: Horizon Research.

Berch, D. B., Mazzocco, M. M. M., & Ginsburg, H. P. (Eds.). (2007). *Why is math so hard for some children? The nature and origins of mathematical learning difficulties and disabilities.* Baltimore, MD: Paul H. Brookes Publishing Co.

Duncan, G. J., Dowsett, C. J., Claessens, A., Magnuson, K., Huston, A. C., Klebanov, P.,... Japel, C. (2007). School readiness and later achievement. *Developmental Psychology, 43,* 1428–1446.

Gersten, R., Chard, D. J., Jayanthi, M., Baker, S. K., Morphy, P., & Flojo, J. (2009). Mathematics instruction for students with learning disabilities: A meta-analysis of instructional components. *Review of Educational Research, 79,* 1202–1242.

Hanushek, E. A., & Rivkin, S. G. (2006). *School quality and the black–white achievement gap* (NBER Working Paper No. 12651). Washington, DC: National Bureau of Economic Research.

Siegler R. S., Duncan, G. J., Davis-Kean, P. E., Duckworth, K., Claessens, A., Engel, M., . . . Chen, M. (2012). Early predictors of high school mathematics achievement. *Psychological Science, 23*(7), 691–697.

Steele, J. (2003). Children's gender stereotypes about math: The role of stereotype stratification. *Journal of Applied Social Psychology, 33,* 2587–2606.

Walker, E. N. (2007). Why aren't more minorities taking advanced math? *Education Leadership, 65*(3), 48–53.

SECTION I

Building Numeracy in Middle School Students

OVERVIEW: FOUNDATIONS
FOR MEETING ALL STUDENTS' NEEDS

Our goal in writing this book is to provide meaningful resources to you—teachers, instructional coaches, and leaders—as a cohesive and comprehensive tool to support student success in middle school mathematics classes. Section I sets the stage for the remainder of the book. We start by defining algebra readiness in the middle grades in Chapter 1. Next, we describe how instruction and assessment can work together in a multi-tiered system of support (MTSS) to meet students' needs (Chapter 2). In Chapter 3, we illustrate approaches to making instruction and assessment accessible to all students. We hope this section is a useful resource to continue referring to as you make your way through the rest of the book. You will find that we refer to topics introduced in these three chapters throughout the remaining three sections.

The chapters in this section will help you answer the following questions:

1. *What does algebra readiness look like in my middle-school mathematics classroom?* When students work algebraically, they are generalizing their knowledge about numbers and operations to solve problems with unknown quantities. Research on how students learn mathematics highlights three key factors in becoming ready for algebra: 1) procedural fluency with whole numbers, 2) conceptual understanding of rational numbers, and 3) proficiency with rational number operations. In Chapter 1, we describe how students' knowledge and understanding of whole-number concepts and operations lay the foundation for their work with rational numbers. We illustrate how carefully designed instruction can support students' foundational knowledge and help them become ready for algebra.

2. *How can I help all students be ready for algebra?* All students in your mathematics classroom can be ready for algebra. Some students may need more intensive instructional support to reach this goal than others. MTSS is a framework that integrates instruction and assessment to help identify the intensity of instructional support

your students need to be ready for algebra. In Chapter 2, we introduce MTSS and preview the three tiers of instructional support that are typical within MTSS. We discuss how you can use assessment results to help guide your decision making. These concepts are discussed in considerably more detail in Sections II and III of the book.

3. *What is accessibility, and how can I make my instruction and assessments more accessible?* Differentiated instruction, accommodations, and modifications can be implemented to improve the accessibility of your instruction and assessment. In Chapter 3, we describe each of these approaches to improving accessibility, provide examples to help differentiate each approach, and discuss when you might consider using them. An important point to remember from this chapter is that decisions to use these approaches may have different implications for students' opportunities to learn the content. Moreover, accommodations and modifications are typically made by a team of people who are working to support an individual student (e.g., an individualized education program [IEP] team).

CHAPTER 1

Laying the Foundation for Algebra

What do you notice about these problems?

- A boy has 13 apples. Four apples are red. The rest are green. How many green apples does he have?

- There are red and green apples in each basket. The ratio of red apples to the total number of apples is 4:13. If a boy has one basket with 4 red apples, how many green apples does he have?

How are these problems different? How are these problems similar? Why is it that a typical middle school student would have no difficulty solving the first problem (and actually might think it is so easy that there must be a trick) but would struggle to solve the second problem?

The transition from working with concrete objects and scenarios in elementary school (often similar to the first problem) to working with abstract concepts like ratios in middle school (as in the second problem) poses a barrier for many students. For some students, this is when mathematics becomes "magical," not in the sense of fairy princesses making your wishes come true, but more in the sense of casting evil spells. Resilient students usually progress through the content in spite of the evil spell, often relying on their procedural proficiency (instead of their conceptual understanding) to succeed. Less resilient students get mired down in the trickery. This is the beginning of the end of their love of mathematics.

Why is this transition so challenging for some students? In this chapter, we describe the transition from concrete to abstract mathematics and the importance this transition plays in preparing students for algebra. We talk about the critical role of numeracy in helping your students successfully navigate this transition.

PAVING THE WAY FOR ALGEBRAIC REASONING: SETTING THE FOUNDATION IN EARLY MATHEMATICS

Without knowing it, many young students are proficient in working with algebraic concepts. We see examples like the one shown in Figure 1.1.

In the Figure 1.1 example, students are not only making the transition from their knowledge of concrete objects (i.e., the dog bones) to a symbolic representation of the object (the number 3), but also solving for an unknown. In the example shown in Figure 1.2, students are again associating concrete objects (i.e., rabbits and ears)

3 dog bones +   = 7 dog bones

How many bones go in the doghouse to make this true?

Figure 1.1. Sample word problem involving algebraic reasoning (solving for an unknown).

with symbolic representations, but they are also evaluating the relationship between two quantities. Because of the nature of these examples, we as teachers, parents, and tutors sometimes don't recognize the valuable connections these problems have to algebraic concepts.

Simply put, working algebraically means that your students can generalize their knowledge about numbers and operations to solve problems with unknown quantities. When students think algebraically, they can see relationships among quantities without the particular quantities being present in the problem. In the problem with

Complete this table.

1 rabbit = 2 ears	
2 rabbits = _____ ears	
3 rabbits = _____ ears	
4 rabbits = _____ ears	

Figure 1.2. Sample word problem involving algebraic reasoning (evaluating the relationship between two quantities).

the dog bones and doghouse shown in Figure 1.1, the student is being asked to find an unknown quantity. Instead of this unknown being represented with a symbol (as is done with most variables in middle school and beyond), it is represented with a concrete object (the doghouse). However, students are still asked to generalize their arithmetic skills to find the number of bones in the doghouse. Students could find the value of the unknown by any number of means:

$$3 + 4 = 7$$
$$3 + 1 + 1 + 1 + 1 = 7$$
$$3 + 2 + 2 = 7$$
$$7 - 3 = 4$$
$$7 - 4 = 3$$
$$7 - 1 - 1 - 1 - 1 = 3$$

By providing opportunities for young students to think algebraically, we are teaching them to use variables and, as in the rabbit problem, they begin to see covariation among quantities (which serves as a pre-skill to understanding functions).

These examples are concrete in nature and allow students to use their understanding of numbers and operations in a flexible way. However, as soon as we represent the problem abstractly as $3 + x = 7$ and expect students to solve for x in a specific and precise manner, many students begin to stumble and have difficulties. To be more realistic, we understand that most middle school students would have little difficulty with this example. However, given a slightly more complex problem such as the grade 8 item from the 2011 National Assessment of Educational Progress (NAEP) shown in Figure 1.3, many students see no connection between this abstract representation and the concrete representations they worked with throughout elementary school.

The solution appears as impossibly magical as pulling a rabbit out of a hat.

For many students, the leap from concrete to abstract mathematical representations is often the cause of their difficulties with mathematics, and algebra in particular. However, strong numeracy skills can help students transition from working with concrete representations to abstract algebraic reasoning and help them navigate the mathematical magic.

WHAT ARE NUMERACY SKILLS?

In thinking about what skills and knowledge students need to successfully transition from concrete mathematics in elementary school to abstract mathematics in high school algebra, several notable organizations have contributed their perspectives.

12. The point $(4, k)$ is a solution to the equation $3x + 2y = 12$. What is the value of k?

A. −3

B. 0

C. 2

D. 3

E. 4

Figure 1.3. Sample grade 8 item from the 2011 National Assessment of Educational Progress (NAEP).

The National Mathematics Advisory Panel (NMAP; 2008), a presidential panel convened to address issues of mathematics underachievement, identified several foundational skills that support students' algebra readiness, including fluency with whole numbers, fluency with fractions, and particular aspects of geometry and measurement. In this book, we highlight the importance of the first two foundational skills and identify three key areas to support students' readiness for algebra:

1.   Procedural fluency with whole number operations

2.   Conceptual understanding of rational number systems

3.   Proficiency operating with rational numbers

These fundamental skills and knowledge can be seen as a progression that helps students move from concrete to abstract reasoning. First, students develop a conceptual understanding of whole numbers (i.e., 0, 1, 2, 3, . . .) and then they gain skills in adding, subtracting, multiplying, and dividing whole numbers. As they gain proficiency with whole number operations, they are better able to verify the reasonableness of their solutions. Next, they build on and extend their conceptual understanding of whole numbers to develop a conceptual understanding of rational numbers (i.e., any number that can be written as $\frac{p}{q}$, where p and q are integers). Then, students integrate their conceptual understanding of rational numbers with their proficiency in whole number operations to compute with rational numbers. Finally, students combine these skills and knowledge to generalize arithmetic principles learned with whole and rational numbers to solve abstract problems involving symbolic notation. This progression, illustrated in Figure 1.4, helps build a foundation for algebraic reasoning.

These skills combine to contribute to students' overall understanding of numbers, or numeracy. *Numeracy,* often called number sense, refers to a "child's fluidity and flexibility with numbers, the sense of what numbers mean, and an ability to perform mental mathematics and to look at the world and make comparisons" (Gersten & Chard, 1999, pp. 19–20). You might think you have heard numeracy often referenced when talking about young students' development of mathematics skills. You are right. In fact, in the Common Core State Standards in Mathematics (CCSS-M), number sense is referenced as students develop the concept of whole numbers in grade 1 and then begin to understand fractions in grade 5. There is no mention of numeracy or number sense in the middle grades content standards.

However, if you look closer at most content standards, including the CCSS-M, you will see that middle school students are required to flexibly use numbers across number systems (whole numbers, integers, rational numbers). You will also notice that students need to use properties of operations lawfully and understand why they work. Students need to apply their knowledge to problem-solving scenarios to make predictions or solve the situation. You will see that students need to operate proficiently with whole numbers, integers, and rational numbers, and understand, justify, and evaluate outcomes of operations. These skills all relate to students' number sense. What's more, these also all relate to students' development of algebraic reasoning. In other words, even though numeracy is not explicitly mentioned within middle school content standards, it is implicit to students' being able to meet those standards.

This chapter focuses on the three interconnected concepts, listed previously, that support students' transition from concrete to abstract thinking and serve as the foundation for success in algebra: proficiency with whole number operations, focusing

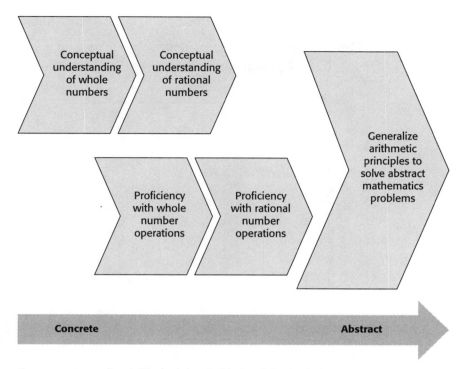

Figure 1.4. Progression of skills that help to build a foundation for algebraic reasoning.

specifically on students' ability to work with properties of operations; conceptual understanding of rational number systems; and proficiency with rational number operations.

Just as pillars support the structure of a building, we can regard these foundational skills as pillars serving to support students' algebraic reasoning. This relationship is illustrated in Figure 1.5. The subsections that follow describe what each pillar "looks like" when students demonstrate these skills in the classroom. Each subsection also highlights core mathematical concepts that middle school teachers can focus upon to strengthen each of the three pillars.

The First Pillar: Developing Proficiency With Whole Number Operations

To develop students' proficiency or procedural fluency with whole number operations, it is important for teachers to understand what is meant by *proficiency* or *procedural fluency*. The examples of Landon and Jailynn described in the following vignette illustrate what this might look like in the middle school classroom.

TWO SEVENTH-GRADERS: LANDON AND JAILYNN

Landon is a seventh-grader who is often referred to as a "math whiz." He has been practicing for the University Interscholastic League (UIL) Number Sense competition, held throughout the state of Texas, and is the best in his club. He can add, subtract, multiply,

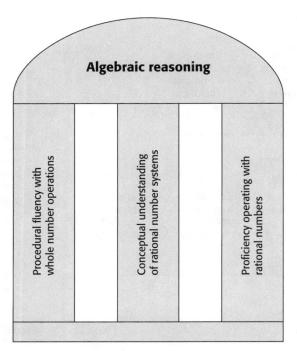

Figure 1.5. The three pillars of algebraic reasoning.

and divide two- and three-digit numbers in his head, but he struggles with word problems. Although he is doing well in his mathematics class, Landon often responds incorrectly to word problems on tests; he gets frustrated when trying to set up the problem and has difficulty deciding how to solve it.

Jailynn is a seventh-grader who does well in her mathematics class but doesn't think of herself as a "math person." She isn't able to execute complex algorithms in her head and is often the last to complete her mathematics tests. She likes word problems and is able to correctly translate the word problem to a symbolic problem and find the solution. She takes her time to complete her mathematics tests because she verifies her answers.

Which student would you say has greater procedural fluency? Although Landon can quickly execute operations and has developed mental arithmetic strategies, when given a mathematics problem in context, he struggles to select the appropriate operation and execute a strategy to solve it. Jailynn, on the other hand, may lack speed and the ability to perform complex mental arithmetic, but she understands the operations in novel contexts, effectively employs the algorithms, and can use different solution strategies to verify her answers. Both students possess unique but important aspects of procedural fluency.

As this vignette illustrates, defining procedural fluency as being able to quickly add, subtract, multiply, and divide is too narrow. In the 2001 publication *Adding It Up,* the National Research Council more expansively describes procedural fluency as the "knowledge of procedures, knowledge of when and how to use them appropriately, and skill in performing them flexibly, accurately, and efficiently" (p. 121).

Being procedurally fluent allows students to devote more of their attention to working out more complex problems, connecting the procedures with concepts, and seeing relationships among quantities. Also, arithmetic skills of upper elementary (Bailey, Siegler, & Geary, 2014; Hecht, Close, & Santisi, 2003) and middle school (Hecht, 1998) students significantly contribute to their ability to perform fraction computation.

Although many people would have said that Landon had greater procedural fluency than Jailynn because of the speed with which he computes as well as the mental strategies he employs, we can see from this definition that he lacks some of the other components of procedural fluency. Jailynn, who many people would have said was not procedurally fluent because she lacks speed and mental arithmetic strategies, has other skills that contribute to her proficiency with procedures. Although proficient in some aspects of whole-number operations, both of these students may encounter difficulties as they make the transition from concrete arithmetic to more abstract algebraic thinking. As a middle school mathematics teacher, you will teach students like Landon and Jailynn, and your task will be to help them both develop a deeper understanding of numbers, or numeracy, in order to strengthen their procedural fluency. Doing so involves working with properties of operations.

For middle school students, advancing their procedural fluency with whole numbers to the point where it will support their algebraic reasoning involves understanding and being able to apply basic properties of operations. The basic properties of operations that support algebra readiness include the distributive property, the commutative and associative properties of addition and multiplication, the identity elements for addition and multiplication, the inverse properties of addition and multiplication, and mathematical equality. Examples of these properties are shown in Table 1.1.

For Landon, understanding these properties of operations will help him understand the relationships among operations to be able to use them more flexibly when solving word problems. For Jailynn, building proficiency with these properties of operations will increase her procedural efficiency so she becomes faster and better able to compute using mental arithmetic strategies. In other words, working with properties of operations strengthens students' conceptual understanding and their procedural fluency.

In their 2008 publication on learning processes for NMAP, Geary and his colleagues described the importance of understanding properties of operations to help

Table 1.1. Properties of operations that support algebra readiness

Property	Example
Distributive	$4(2 + 3) = (4 \times 2) + (4 \times 3)$
Commutative	Addition: $5 + 7 = 7 + 5$ Multiplication: $6 \times 4 = 4 \times 6$
Associative	Addition: $(1 + 3) + 2 = 1 + (3 + 2)$ Multiplication: $(4 \times 5) \times 2 = 4 \times (5 \times 2)$
Identity	Addition: $7 + 0 = 0 + 7$ Multiplication: $7 \times 1 = 1 \times 7$
Inverse	Addition: $5 + (-5) = 0$ Multiplication: $6 \times \frac{1}{6} = 1$

students become procedurally proficient. Students who understand properties of operations can efficiently solve arithmetic problems, identify and correct errors, apply algorithms in contextualized settings, and generalize their understanding to novel situations. Also, as your students get better at using properties of operations to operate with whole numbers, they should be able to transfer their knowledge to solve problems with rational numbers as well as with symbols. This forms the foundation for their ability to lawfully manipulate numbers and symbols to solve algebraic problems.

Because properties of operations have been part of most elementary and middle school content standards for years, you might ask why we are emphasizing the importance of these skills now. Even though these skills are in the content standards, many textbooks and other instructional materials have done little to help students understand properties of operations beyond learning their definitions. In fact, state accountability tests often include items, like the one shown next, that test students' ability to label the property of operation correctly.

Which property is represented by this equation?

$(1 + 4) + 8 = 1 + (4 + 8)$

> A. Associative property
>
> B. Commutative property
>
> C. Distributive property
>
> D. Identity property

However, these items don't assess whether students can use the properties flexibly to solve problems. Two properties are particularly valuable for helping middle school students develop conceptual understanding and procedural fluency: mathematical equality and the distributive property.

Mathematical Equality: The Mortar Between the Bricks   Perhaps the most important property that is often underemphasized in elementary and middle school mathematics is mathematical equality. Many teachers may take this property for granted and provide little instruction to students on its importance. However, students' knowledge and application of this property contributes to their understanding of the lawfulness of mathematics and can affect their ability to solve algebra problems. What is more, if students do not understand mathematical equality, they may continue to think of mathematics as mysterious magic that abides by made-up rules.

Understanding mathematical equality means that students see the equal sign as bridging equivalent relationships between expressions (Baroody & Ginsburg, 1983). Knowing that the equal sign indicates that the quantities are equivalent helps students understand the reasons for rules such as "If you do something to one side, you have to do the same thing to the other side." However, in the elementary school grades, the equal sign is often viewed as an operator symbol that directs students to do something. For example, if a teacher writes "46 – 14 =" on the board, most students would "do" the subtraction and produce the correct answer of 32. In these instances, students learn that the equal sign is a command that directs them to operate. Some students will either directly or indirectly assume that answers to problems such as these have one (and only one) correct answer, and that it must be a number. Solutions such as

Ways to represent 46 − 14

46 − 6 − 8

46 − 10 − 4

(46 + 4) − 14 − 4

(45 + 1) − (15 − 1)

Figure 1.6.   Example of multiple ways to represent the solution to a problem.

46 − 10 − 4 or (45 + 1) − (15 − 1) would be discounted as incorrect. This type of instruction focuses often on what procedure students are to follow when they see the equal sign, rather than on developing students' conceptual understanding of what the equal sign means. This assumption will limit students' ability to think flexibly about quantities and manipulate numbers to solve algebra problems.

As a middle school mathematics teacher, you may find some students come to your classes with these assumptions ingrained in their thinking. They may argue and protest or think you are invoking more mathematical magic when you tell them that there are multiple ways to represent the solution to 46 − 14, as shown in Figure 1.6. To help students see the lawfulness of these solutions, you will likely need to design your instruction carefully to help students identify their misunderstandings and then work to reinforce the meaning of mathematical equality. (See the instruction chapters in Section II of this book for information on the importance of dispelling misconceptions [Chapter 4] and guidance on designing instruction to overcome misconceptions [Chapter 7].) Beginning first with whole number operations and then increasing the complexity by introducing variables, you can demonstrate that the meaning of mathematical equality remains constant when working with concrete to abstract representations. The reward for the hard work of learning this important property of operations will come when students can flexibly work with numbers to solve increasingly complex problems.

Distributive Property: Reinforcing the Pillar   Another property of operations that is indispensable in algebra is the distributive property. Because students are regularly asked to employ the distributive property to solve for x in problems such as $2(3 + x) = 23$, it probably comes as no surprise that we are emphasizing its importance for success in algebra. Although solving these types of problems is important, there are many other reasons for emphasizing the distributive property in your instruction. Specifically, understanding this property can help students like Jailynn perform mathematical operations faster and more efficiently.

As students build their procedural fluency, some students may need additional help in developing strategies to increase their efficiency. For example, Jailynn struggles to carry out operations quickly and is not able to perform complex mental arithmetic. Her inefficiency may become a burden for solving increasingly complex problems in middle and high school mathematics classes. Learning to use the

Table 1.2.   Comparison between the FOIL method and the distributive property

FOIL method	Distributive property method
$(4 + x)(3 + x)$	$(4 + x)(3 + x)$
<u>F</u>irst terms: $(4)(3) = 12$	Distribute the 4 across the second expression: $(4)(3) = 12$
<u>O</u>utside terms: $(4)(x) = 4x$	$(4)(x) = 4x$
<u>I</u>nside terms: $(x)(3) = 3x$	Distribute the x across the second expression: $(x)(3) = 3x$
<u>L</u>ast terms: $(x)(x) = x^2$	$(x)(x) = x^2$
<u>Solution</u>: $x^2 + 3x + 4x + 12 = x^2 + 7x + 12$	<u>Solution</u>: $x^2 + 3x + 4x + 12 = x^2 + 7x + 12$

distributive property may help her turn complex problems into simple arithmetic that she can easily solve in her head. Consider the problem 42 × 63. Using place value and the distributive property, this problem can be written as the sum of two expressions that are much less complex: [(42 × 6) × 10] + (42 × 3). If Jailynn is not ready to compute two-digit by one-digit multiplication in her head, the problem can be further decomposed into single digit multiplication: (40 × 60) + (2 × 60) + (40 × 3) + (2 × 3). Using the distributive property in this way can help students like Jailynn increase their speed in executing algorithms as well as develop strategies for mental computation.

Another important reason for having a thorough understanding of the distributive property is that it demystifies some of the "tricks" students learn to solve problems in algebra. For example, the FOIL method is routinely used to multiply binomials. The FOIL mnemonic represents the steps students take to multiply the **f**irst terms in each binomial, then the **o**utside terms, then the **i**nside terms, and then the **l**ast terms. Although this is technically correct, the FOIL method is nothing more than an application of the distributive property, as shown in Table 1.2.

As teachers clutter the curriculum with tricks like the FOIL method, students become less certain of which actions are lawful and begin to see mathematics as a series of seemingly random rules that are memorized and applied in special circumstances. Visual representations, like the one shown in Figure 1.7, can be used to help

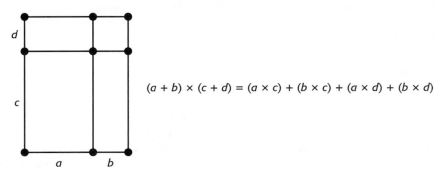

$(a + b) \times (c + d) = (a \times c) + (b \times c) + (a \times d) + (b \times d)$

Figure 1.7.   Example of a visual representation to help students understand how the distributive property works.

students conceptually understand why the distributive property works as it does. Conceptually understanding the distributive property addresses both potential gaps in applying the procedures and improves efficiency. This may be particularly helpful for students who see the distributive property as a set of rules that must be followed in a certain order.

Although we have highlighted mathematical equality and the distributive property here, students' understanding of other properties of operations is an important component of numeracy that will help them develop proficiency with whole number operations and, ultimately, to apply algorithms to solve algebraic problems. As students become proficient in using properties of operations with numeric representations, they can generalize their knowledge to solve increasingly more abstract problems in algebra.

The Second Pillar: Understanding Rational Numbers Conceptually

Young children understand the meaning of numbers from a very young age, and—even without knowing it—they have a firm grasp of concepts such as cardinality ("I got two cookies from Ms. Robinson") and even the ordinal meaning of numbers ("I came in first place in the race"). Quickly, they begin to understand concepts such as quantity ("I have a lot of cookies") and can begin to make quantity comparisons ("No fair! You got more cookies than me"). Soon, an understanding of number as a distance between points develops ("I can jump over three boxes") and distance comparisons ("It is taking forever to get to Grandma's. Are we there yet?"). In each of these instances, children's conceptual understanding of whole numbers is rooted in concrete experiences, objects, or representations.

Once schooling starts, students begin to formalize their understanding of natural numbers and then extend this understanding to whole numbers. They understand that numbers represent quantities with magnitude. They understand that equivalent representations of numbers have the same quantity. Although understanding natural and whole numbers lays the foundation for students to perform operations and then later develop a conceptual understanding of integers and rational numbers, an essential ingredient to this mix is students' understanding of the concept of place value. *Place value* is the value of a digit in a base-10 system and is typically referenced as a shorthand notation for writing numbers. Connections among these different conceptual understandings in mathematics are illustrated in Figure 1.8.

Not only does having a foundational knowledge of place value help students understand basic algorithms and develop greater procedural efficiency, it also serves as a conceptual and procedural link between number systems. Conceptually, students can use their understanding of place value to see how rational numbers are quantities with magnitude. Procedurally, students can use their understanding of place value to help them generalize their knowledge of operations with whole numbers to operations with rational numbers.

Consider the two problems shown in Figure 1.9. Although both items assess the same grade 5 content standard from the CCSS-M that states "read, write, and compare decimals to thousandths" (5.NBT.3), they are tapping into different dimensions of students' understanding. The item on the left assesses students' knowledge of place value vocabulary (hundredths place) and ability to recognize a specific value within a given number. The item on the right assesses students'

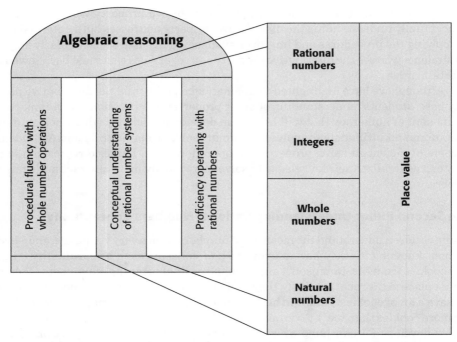

Figure 1.8. Connections among different conceptual understandings in mathematics: natural and whole numbers, integers and rational numbers, and place value.

conceptual understanding of place value by asking students to identify the value of each digit within a given number as well as identify how the digits relate to each other to form the number. Also, the students' knowledge of place value with whole numbers is integrated into their knowledge of place value with decimals. Constructing learning and assessment opportunities that integrate these important dimensions of place value provides the foundation for understanding rational numbers.

As a middle school teacher, you know the struggles many students have when it comes to learning about rational numbers, particularly when learning about fractions. Even for students who have been historically successful in mathematics, learning fractions can be perplexing, vexing, and downright maddening. Students commonly make many generalizations when learning about natural and whole

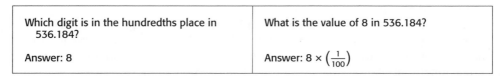

Figure 1.9. Comparison of two fifth-grade test items assessing different dimensions of students' understanding of decimals and related concepts.

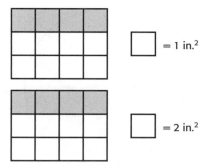

Figure 1.10. Example of a shaded figure used to show that the principle "size always matters" is a misconception.

numbers that can serve as roadblocks for learning fractions—for example, consider the following:

- *Misconception 1:* "Size always matters." Although this is the case for whole numbers, it does not always hold true for rational numbers. With whole numbers, size matters. For example, the area of the two shapes in Figure 1.10 is different because the size of the unit square is different. However, when talking about fractions, the proportion of the two shapes that is shaded is the same.

- *Misconception 2:* "Bigger numbers are bigger." With whole numbers, "bigger" numbers have greater quantity (13 is "bigger" than 2). However, when talking about fractions, "bigger" denominators indicate smaller quantities $\left(\frac{1}{13} \text{ is "smaller" than } \frac{1}{2}\right)$.

- *Misconception 3:* "Multiplying makes numbers bigger." When multiplying whole numbers, the product is a larger number than the factors ($2 \times 2 = 4$). However, when multiplying proper fractions, the product is a smaller number $\left(\frac{1}{2} \times \frac{1}{2} = \frac{1}{4}\right)$.

- *Misconception 4:* "Dividing makes numbers smaller." When dividing whole numbers, the quotient is a smaller number than the dividend ($15 \div 5 = 3$). However, when dividing proper fractions, the quotient is a larger number than the dividend $\left(\frac{1}{15} \div \frac{1}{5} = \frac{1}{3}\right)$.

Each of these overgeneralizations implies that students do not conceptually understand rational numbers. In some cases, students' previous instructional experience with whole numbers or fractions has caused some of the confusion. For example, instruction that overly relies on fraction models such as pizzas or pies can limit students' understanding of the meaning of fractions. Relying too heavily on circular models may cause students to believe that fractions are always shaded parts of circles. Students may not make the connection that the model represents a numerical value unless other representations are presented to them (e.g., number lines). When students conceptually understand rational numbers, they understand that rational numbers represent quantity with magnitude. They understand that rational numbers have multiple representations (including fractions and decimals) but require equal partitioning of a whole or set.

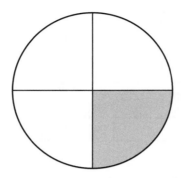

Figure 1.11. Representation of $\frac{1}{4}$ representing understanding of equal partitioning of a whole.

Consider how students develop and demonstrate conceptual understanding of fractions, using the example of $\frac{1}{4}$ to illustrate the progression. Initially, many students would generate a representation like the one shown in Figure 1.11.

Although this representation indicates an understanding of equal partitioning of a whole, it does not represent a full understanding of the meaning of fractions. As students gain greater awareness that fractions can represent equal partitioning of a set, they might represent $\frac{1}{4}$ as shown in Figure 1.12.

Still, to understand fractions conceptually, students should know that fractions are numbers with magnitude that can be used to measure quantities. Representing the fraction $\frac{1}{4}$ using a number line would indicate a deeper conceptual understanding, such as the representation in Figure 1.13.

By representing a fraction as a point on a number line, students recognize a fraction as a quantity, or distance from zero, and see the meaning of equal partitioning of a number line. Students begin to compare the quantity of fractions and further develop and refine the mental number line they constructed for whole numbers in elementary school. They also begin to understand that whole numbers can be represented as fractions and that fractions can be greater than or less than 1, as well as less than 0.

As students understand the magnitude of a fraction, students would represent the fraction $\frac{1}{4}$ using the type of representation shown in Figure 1.14.

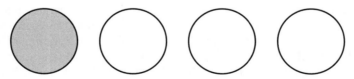

Figure 1.12. Representation of $\frac{1}{4}$ representing understanding of equal partitioning of a set.

Figure 1.13. Representation of $\frac{1}{4}$ representing understanding that fractions are numbers with magnitude that can be used to measure quantities.

As students generate increasingly more sophisticated representations of fractions (as depicted in this progression), they demonstrate deep conceptual understanding that includes recognizing fractions as quantities with magnitude, and they understand the importance of equal partitioning. Students can then integrate their conceptual understanding of rational numbers with their knowledge of natural and whole number systems to increase their flexibility when working with these numbers. For example, students can use composition and decomposition to reason about equivalent fractions, and similarly, decimals. Imagine that a student, Matt, conceptually understands the quantity $\frac{1}{2}$. He should be able to recognize that $\frac{1}{4} + \frac{1}{4} = \frac{2}{4}$ is an equivalent representation to $\frac{1}{2}$ because the magnitude of the representation has not changed even if the quantity is divided into more equal parts. An equivalent fractions chart like the one in Figure 1.15 is often used to teach students about equivalent fractions. Although this chart can be used as a quick reference, students shouldn't need to memorize this chart if they have a solid conceptual understanding of fractions as quantities with magnitude.

In summary, students' understanding of natural and whole number systems—place value, in particular—supports their conceptual understanding of rational numbers. In turn, this conceptual understanding of rational numbers lays the foundation for success in future mathematics. In particular, conceptual understanding of rational numbers has been found to significantly contribute to upper elementary (Hecht et al., 2003) and middle school (Hecht, 1998) students' ability to operate and estimate with fractions as well as students' ability to set up word problems.

The Third Pillar: Developing Proficiency With Rational Number Operations

As we mentioned, many middle school students struggle with fractions. Their limited conceptual understanding is often observed in their confusion with fraction operations. Researchers have found that a strong understanding of foundational fraction concepts predicts fluency with fraction operations. However, we often do not know that students struggle with basic fraction concepts until we get to operations.

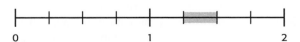

Figure 1.14. Representation of $\frac{1}{4}$ representing understanding of the magnitude of a fraction.

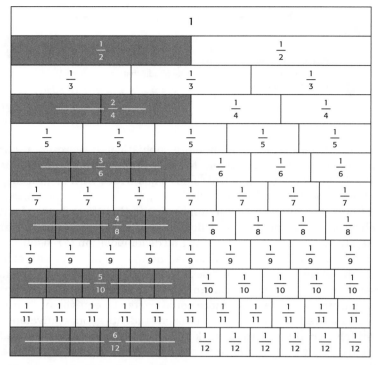

Figure 1.15. Equivalent fractions chart.

Students develop proficiency with fractions in a number of different ways. Hallett, Nunes, and Bryant (2010) found at least five. Some students have stronger conceptual knowledge and weaker procedural knowledge; others have stronger procedural knowledge and weaker conceptual knowledge. Some have average amounts of both, whereas others have strong knowledge of both. This information seems intuitive, but researchers found something interesting when they looked at students' ability to solve fraction problems and reason quantitatively. Students with stronger conceptual understanding of fractions outperformed students with average procedural knowledge, but students with stronger procedural knowledge did not outperform students with average conceptual knowledge. In other words, higher levels of conceptual understanding may help students compensate for average procedural knowledge of fractions, but higher levels of procedural knowledge may not have the same effect on performance.

Conceptual understanding of fractions also extends to conceptually understanding the algorithms that govern operations with fractions. Because operations with fractions may seem counterintuitive to many students, grounding instruction in fraction concepts and the underlying mathematical rationale for the algorithm may help students see through the magic's smoke and mirrors to understand the meaning of the operations. Once students understand the lawfulness of the algorithms, they can begin to see how the procedures can be applied in general. This is an important link to algebra.

Dividing fractions is one of the most vexing of the operations. First, many students (and adults) have a difficult time explaining a situation that involves division of fractions. Textbooks often provide a limited number of situations that can be conveniently modeled using ribbon or string. Although these models help introduce students to the algorithm and provide some context for developing conceptual understanding, they often focus on the measurement model of division (and do little to develop the partitive model or the product-and-factors model) and leave students with an incomplete picture of division of fractions.

Strong conceptual understanding of fractions may compensate for weaker procedural fluency, but the converse may not be true.

To demonstrate how to build conceptual understanding of the meaning of division of fractions, we provide, in Figure 1.16, an example of how teachers can build on students' conceptual understanding of fractions to develop the meaning of division of fractions. This example is not intended to serve as an instructional sequence,

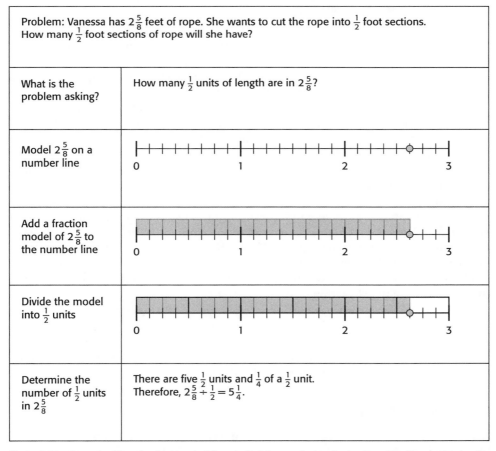

Figure 1.16. Example of how teachers can build on students' conceptual understanding of fractions to develop the meaning of division of fractions.

Table 1.3. Step-by-step discussion of the algorithm for division of fractions

Properties of operations	Algebraic examples	Numeric examples
Division is the inverse operation of multiplication	$M \div N = X \ (N \neq 0) \Leftrightarrow M = X \times N$ $(N \neq 0) \ (1)$	$32 \div 10 = x$ $32 = x \times 10$
Given	Put $M = \frac{a}{b}$, $N = \frac{c}{d}$, and $X = \frac{x}{y}$ $(b \neq 0, d \neq 0, y \neq 0)$	$M = \frac{7}{16}$ $N = \frac{3}{8}$ $x = \frac{x}{y}$
Substitution	$\frac{a}{b} \div \frac{c}{d} = \frac{x}{y}$	$\frac{7}{16} \div \frac{3}{8} = \frac{x}{y}$
Fundamental theorem of fractions	$\xrightarrow{by(1)} \frac{a}{b} = \frac{x}{y} \times \frac{c}{d}$	$\frac{7}{16} = \frac{x}{y} \times \frac{3}{8}$
Identity property of multiplication	$\xrightarrow{\text{multiply both sides by } \frac{d}{c}} \frac{a}{b} \times \frac{d}{c} = \frac{x}{y} \times \frac{c}{d} \times \frac{d}{c}$	$\frac{7}{16} \times \frac{8}{3} = \frac{x}{y} \times \frac{3}{8} \times \frac{8}{3}$
Multiplicative inverse	$\xrightarrow{\frac{c}{d} \times \frac{d}{c} = 1} \frac{a}{b} \times \frac{d}{c} = \frac{x}{y}$	$\xrightarrow{\frac{3}{8} \times \frac{8}{3} = 1} \frac{7}{16} \times \frac{8}{3} = \frac{x}{y}$
If $a = b$ and $b = c$, then $a = c$	$\therefore \frac{a}{b} \div \frac{c}{d} = \frac{a}{b} \times \frac{d}{c}$	$\therefore \frac{7}{16} \div \frac{3}{8} = \frac{7}{16} \times \frac{8}{3}$

Source: Ketterlin-Geller & Chard (2011).

but instead to illustrate the integration of students' conceptual understanding of fractions.

For many students, the second troubling aspect of dividing fractions is the algorithm. Although the algorithm (affectionately called "invert and multiply") is straightforward and easy to execute, many students do not understand why or how it works—further adding to the magic and mystery. Having a conceptual understanding of the meaning of division of fractions is important, but students also need to understand the mathematical rationale for the algorithm and why it is lawful.

To demonstrate the lawfulness of the algorithm, we provide a step-by-step dissection of the algorithm in Table 1.3, along with a numerical example and a generalized example that includes symbolic notation. We have associated the appropriate properties of operations to each step to indicate the lawfulness of the processes. Also, by showing students the properties of operations, teaching this algorithm reinforces to them that the rules of arithmetic generalize from whole numbers to fractions, and that no tricks are being introduced. Again, this is not intended to serve as an instructional guide but should be discussed or reviewed with students to verify their conceptual understanding of the algorithm.

Algorithms for operations with fractions need to be grounded in students' conceptual understanding of fractions but also need to be taught conceptually. Conceptual approaches to teaching the meaning of operations with fractions and the mechanics of the operations may support subsequent fraction problem-solving skills and advanced quantitative reasoning skills necessary for algebra.

BRINGING IT ALL TOGETHER

Although we presented three pillars of numeracy as separate supports to build algebraic proficiency, no pillar can do the job alone. What's more, one pillar cannot be built in isolation from the others. Instead, these three pillars of numeracy need to be taught as integrated concepts to build a deeper level of mathematical proficiency.

Students' development of conceptual understanding begins as they work with number systems, properties, and operations. As students understand and use their numeracy, basic and advanced, it demystifies algebra and allows them to see that algebra is a way of using the knowledge they have learned across the number systems. Foundational understanding of how number systems relate, what lawful properties can be depended on across the systems, and why and how the operations can be used should be developed and strengthened as new number concepts and properties are introduced. This level of numeracy helps students develop algebraic reasoning and supports their lawful application of skills and knowledge to solving abstract problems. Given that algebraic reasoning is essential to college and career readiness, it is critical that students have a solid foundation for algebra.

SUMMARY: THE PILLARS OF ALGEBRAIC REASONING

This chapter identified three pillars of algebraic reasoning: 1) procedural fluency with whole number operations, 2) conceptual understanding of rational number systems, and 3) proficiency operating with rational numbers. These pillars serve as the foundation of algebraic reasoning. We also discussed the importance of mathematical equality and properties of operations. These ideas support the pillars and enable students to be flexible and efficient with numbers. Conceptual understanding is central to all of these ideas.

ADDITIONAL RESOURCES

You may wish to consult the following resources to learn more about the topics discussed in this chapter.

Geary, D. C., Boykin, A. W., Embretson, S., Reyna, V., Siegler, R., Berch, D. B., & Graban, J. (2008). *Chapter 4: Report of the Task Group on Learning Processes*. Retrieved from http://www .ed.gov/about/bdscomm/list/mathpanel/report/learning-processes.pdf

National Mathematics Advisory Panel. (2008). *Foundations for success: The final report of the National Mathematics Advisory Panel*. Retrieved from https://www2.ed.gov/about /bdscomm/list/mathpanel/report/final-report.pdf

Siegler, R., Carpenter, T., Fennell, F., Geary, D., Lewis, J., Okamoto, Y., … Wray, J. (2010). *Developing effective fractions instruction for kindergarten through 8th grade: A practice guide* (NCEE #2010-4039). Washington, DC: National Center for Education Evaluation and Regional Assistance, Institute of Education Sciences, U.S. Department of Education. Retrieved from https://ies.ed.gov/ncee/wwc/Docs/PracticeGuide/fractions_pg_093010.pdf

CHAPTER 2

Supporting All Students Through Multitiered Instruction

In this chapter, we describe a framework for providing appropriate mathematics instruction to all students. This framework combines assessment with instruction to determine whether students are receiving the most meaningful instructional program. We will answer the following questions:

- How many middle school students have difficulty with mathematics?

- Why use an MTSS framework to provide support to students?

- What is the role of instruction and assessment at Tier 1?

- How do instruction and assessment work within Tier 2?

- In Tier 3, how is a diagnostic assessment used? What are common adaptations to instruction in Tier 3?

DIFFICULTY WITH MATHEMATICS: A WIDESPREAD PROBLEM

You are likely reading this book because you know of a student or students who experience difficulty with mathematics. That is not uncommon. According to the 2017 results of the NAEP, only 34% of eighth-grade students perform at or above proficient on a standardized test of mathematics (see Figure 2.1). This means that 36% of students perform at the basic level and 30% of students perform below basic. *Proficient* is described as performing at a level in which the student applies mathematical concepts and procedures consistently to complex problems in all five NAEP content areas (i.e., number properties and operations, measurement, geometry, data analysis, and algebra). *Basic* is described as exhibiting some evidence of conceptual and procedural understanding in the five content areas. Students at the basic level demonstrate an understanding of the operations with whole numbers, fraction, decimals, and percentages.

What these results indicate is that up to 30% of current eighth-grade students are not meeting minimum expectations on a mathematics achievement assessment. According to the National Center for Education Statistics (Kena et al., 2016), however, only 13% of school-age students have an identified disability. The difference between students with identified disabilities and students demonstrating below-basic mathematics performance indicates that schools need to provide a system of mathematics

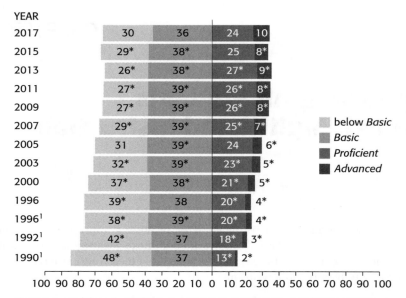

Figure 2.1.   Eighth-grade NAEP data from The Nation's Report Card. (*SOURCE:* U.S. Department of Education, Institute of Education Sciences, National Center for Education Statistics. [2017]. The Nation's Report Card. [Grade 8 data for National Assessment of Educational Progress, Mathematics.] Retrieved from: https://www.nationsreportcard.gov/math_2017/#nation /achievement?grade=8.) (*Key:* *significantly different (*p* < .05) from 2017; [1]accommodations not permitted.)

support for 1) students with an identified disability and an individualized education program (IEP) in mathematics and 2) students with persistent, below-grade-level mathematics performance. One framework for providing appropriate supports to these students is through response to intervention (RTI) or MTSS.

THE FRAMEWORK FOR SUPPORT

In this section, we introduce a framework for support for students with mathematics difficulty. We use the term *mathematics difficulty* to cover both students with a disability (and IEP goals in mathematics) and students not meeting grade-level mathematics expectations. When middle school students with mathematics difficulty receive effective instruction combined with high-quality intervention, mathematics outcomes typically improve (Dennis et al., 2016; Jitendra et al., 2018; Stevens, Rodgers, & Powell, in press). The chapters in Section II provide a comprehensive discussion of instruction and intervention practices used in MTSS, beginning with a definition of effective instruction in Chapter 4.

In addition to instruction, it is important to keep track of student progress as it relates to successful learning from a high-quality intervention (Stecker, Lembke, & Foegen, 2008). An RTI or MTSS framework combines instruction and assessment (Gersten, Beckmann et al., 2009) and provides a system of support that starts in the general education setting but provides more support than what occurs within general education classrooms. (In this book, we use the term *MTSS,* but we realize that some schools may use the term *RTI.* Both terms have similar meanings.) This framework makes frequent use of formative (as opposed to summative) assessment. Whereas summative assessments are intended to measure what students have learned after completing a unit or course of study, formative assessments precede a unit of instruction or occur on an ongoing basis during instruction (see Chap-

An MTSS framework combines instruction and assessment.

ter 9 for a more detailed description of the distinction between formative and summative assessments and Chapter 13 for more information about summative assessments). For example, they may be used early in the school year to identify students who have gaps in math knowledge and skills, or throughout the school year to monitor students' progress. Different types of formative assessments used for these different purposes comprise a system of formative assessments within MTSS. The chapters in Section III provide a comprehensive discussion of the assessments used in MTSS.

A typical MTSS framework includes three tiers of instructional support (e.g., Fuchs, Fuchs, & Compton, 2012; Johnson & Smith, 2011; Turse & Albrecht, 2015). We will present the three-tier framework, but the MTSS Leadership Team (described more in Chapter 15) at your school will work together to determine whether three tiers are appropriate and fit the needs of all of your students. In some cases, an additional tier or two may be added to the MTSS framework. Figure 2.2 presents our framework

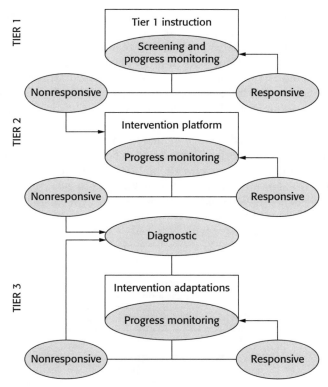

Figure 2.2. The three tiers of intervention typically included in the multitiered systems of support (MTSS) framework.

for MTSS. The sections that follow describe the nature of interventions (and related decision making) that occur at each tier.

Tier 1: Primary Prevention

In Figure 2.3, we show the beginning of the MTSS framework, also called Tier 1. Sometimes Tier 1 is referred to as primary prevention because this is the primary method for providing mathematics support that may prevent further mathematics difficulty. As with all of the other tiers, the two major components of Tier 1 relate to instruction and assessment.

Tier 1 Instruction　　　Within Tier 1, the expectation is that all students are receiving high-quality instruction that has an evidence base. Our expectation is that high-quality instruction comprises evidence-based practices, with the evidence base having been determined through rigorous research (Cook & Cook, 2013). The What Works Clearinghouse (https://ies.ed.gov/ncee/wwc/) or Evidence for ESSA (Every Student Succeeds Act; https://www.evidenceforessa.org/) web sites provide helpful backgrounds on the identification of evidence-based practices for use at Tier 1.

Evidence-based practices may include an evidence-based instruction or intervention or an evidence-based strategy. *Evidence-based instruction or intervention* is a packaged program or curriculum that comes with all components necessary to implement the intervention (e.g., lesson guides, workbooks, manipulatives). For an instruction or intervention program or curriculum to be considered as "evidence-based," developers should provide data that shows the intervention leads to positive mathematics gains for students. An *evidence-based strategy* is not as neatly packaged. It is usually a more general approach to teaching (e.g., explicit instruction), a tool for teaching and learning (e.g., manipulatives), or an activity (e.g., fluency game) that has demonstrated improvement for student mathematics learning. In Chapter 7, we provide more information to help distinguish these levels of evidence. More information about the different types of evidence-based practice is provided in Chapter 5.

In Tier 1, students should receive evidence-based instruction on a daily basis, whenever mathematics instruction is scheduled to occur. Teachers should implement the program, curriculum, or strategy with fidelity (we talk about fidelity later in this chapter and in more depth in Chapter 8). Tier 1 should be of extremely high quality and should use evidence-based practices to ensure that, for the majority of students,

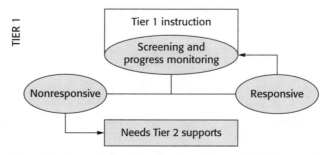

Figure 2.3. Tier 1 of the multi-tiered systems of support (MTSS) framework.

the general education classroom is an effective mathematics environment that contributes to impactful learning. Differentiated instructional strategies (discussed in Chapter 3) can and should be implemented in Tier 1 to meet the varied needs and preferences of your students. School administrators and teachers should review current Tier 1 instructional materials and practices to determine their evidence base. In our experience, many schools could benefit from a careful analysis and revamping of Tier 1 instruction. In Chapter 14, we walk you through a process of examining the Tier 1 instruction at your school.

Tier 1 Assessment   Assessment in Tier 1 occurs in two different ways. First, teachers have to identify which students may have mathematics difficulty. At the middle school level, students may come into a classroom with an already identified disability and IEP goals in mathematics. If so, identification is easy. In other cases, students may have been receiving supplemental mathematics instruction during the previous school year. Again, in these situations, identification is easy. Yet in other cases, students may not have previously demonstrated the need for supplemental mathematics support. To address this situation, teachers can look to the results of universal screeners. Universal screeners help teachers identify which students may need supplemental mathematics support and should be monitored more closely (see Chapter 10 for a thorough discussion about the options for universal screeners and interpretations of the results). Tests that are already administered as part of the regular school routine (e.g., previous end-of-year high-stakes assessment, fall benchmark assessment) (Fuchs, Fuchs, & Compton, 2010) or an additional assessment can be administered for the purpose of identifying students with below-grade-level mathematics performance. In Chapter 17, Kellie, a seventh-grade mathematics teacher, describes the data her school uses to make universal screening decisions.

The second way that assessment is used within Tier 1 is through progress monitoring measures (see Chapter 12 about progress monitoring). Progress monitoring measures are brief mathematics assessments that can be administered regularly (e.g., weekly) to gauge student growth patterns. In Tier 1, a progress monitoring measure is implemented for a few weeks (e.g., 6 to 10 weeks) to determine whether the students identified (with the universal screener) may need supplemental support (i.e., Tier 2). In middle school, progress monitoring measures may assess computation knowledge or more holistic application knowledge (i.e., application of mathematics knowledge across content areas; Lembke, Strickland, & Powell, 2016). Middle-school teachers may also choose to use pre-algebra or algebra progress monitoring measures (Ketterlin-Geller, Gifford, & Perry, 2015).

The progress monitoring measures help teachers understand whether the high-quality Tier 1 instruction is providing the best level of support for a student. If a student, through his or her progress monitoring scores, demonstrates adequate growth (i.e., acceptable and increasing slope) or meets a satisfactory benchmark, then the student should continue to receive mathematics instruction in the Tier 1 setting because we can infer from these data that Tier 1 is meeting the student's needs. As shown by the arrows on Figure 2.3, students demonstrating adequate response remain in Tier 1. If a student does not demonstrate adequate growth or meet a suitable benchmark, this student requires supplemental support in addition to the Tier 1 mathematics instruction. As shown by the arrows on Figure 2.3, students with inadequate response begin to receive Tier 2 instruction. Note that "moving" to Tier 2 does not necessarily mean that students will not continue to receive Tier 1 mathematics instruction. As we describe in the next section, Tier 2 is often provided as a supplement to Tier 1.

Tier 2: Secondary Prevention

In Figure 2.4, which highlights Tier 2, note that the students who are "nonresponsive" to Tier 1 instruction require Tier 2 instructional support. These are students who demonstrated either no response or low response to the instruction provided at the general education level. Tier 2 may also be called secondary prevention, which has two major components: instruction and assessment.

Tier 2 Instruction   Tier 2 often occurs in small-group tutoring. We would recommend that small groups include anywhere from three to eight students, but we realize that some schools may have groups with more than eight. Smaller-sized groups help reach the goals of Tier 2 instruction of providing targeted content that addresses students' persistent misconceptions and errors. In Chapter 17, Kellie talks about the importance of keeping the size of intervention classes small to meet the needs of her students.

In Tier 2, the first step is to develop an intervention platform (see Figure 2.2), so called because it is the jumping-off point for Tier 2 instruction. It is often important to conduct a diagnostic assessment with students to understand their mathematical strengths and weaknesses before developing the intervention platform; doing so helps teachers to really understand what mathematical content needs to be covered. See Chapter 11 for an in-depth discussion of diagnostic assessments.

As you put together the intervention platform, it is important to think about what is going to be taught in Tier 2 and how Tier 2 instruction will be provided. Information gained from a diagnostic assessment and knowledge about the individual students inform the platform's content. In Tier 2, the intervention platform may involve reteaching of foundational mathematics skills or teaching grade-level mathematics content in a different way. It should be appropriately sequenced so that easier mathematics skills are taught before more difficult skills. You may select an evidence-based intervention to utilize as the instructional platform. Unfortunately, in the middle

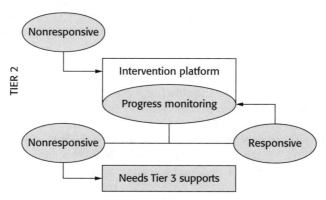

Figure 2.4.   Tier 2 of the multi-tiered systems of support (MTSS) framework.

school grades, teachers may not have access to as many evidence-based mathematics interventions as are available in the elementary grades. Also, some evidence-based interventions may not be appropriate for the intervention platform that you need to deliver (e.g., an intervention focuses on geometry instead of fractions and decimals). In our experience,

> It is important to think about what is going to be taught and how instruction will be provided.

the content of the Tier 2 intervention platform is often a combination of multiple evidence-based strategies integrated together to teach specific mathematics content. In Chapter 17, Melanie, a senior director of curriculum and instruction, reflects on the importance of designing an intervention platform and the challenges it can present to teachers. We address this need by providing guidance in Chapter 7 for designing interventions.

With regard to how Tier 2 is taught, it needs to be a focused effort. Tier 2 instruction must occur regularly during the school week, at least two to three times a week, for a concentrated amount of time (e.g., 30 to 45 minutes). It also needs to last a substantial number of weeks (e.g., 10 to 15 weeks) during the school year. How middle schools schedule Tier 2 varies from school to school. In the best-case scenario, a school will have a designated intervention block that can be used to provide Tier 2. If this is not possible, a school may conduct Tier 2 before or after school. This may sound unrealistic, but it may be the only time in which Tier 2 instruction can be provided. In situations where additional instructional time cannot be provided, Tier 2 instructional support has to be arranged to occur within the general education (Tier 1) classroom. Although this is not ideal, it might be to only way to provide targeted instruction to support students who are experiencing mathematics difficulty. When teachers arrange Tier 2 in this way, it is often through a center or workshop model approach.

If Tier 2 is provided within the confines of the general education classroom, it is important that it is not "more of the same." Based on a careful analysis of student performance data, you have already determined that Tier 1 instruction is not providing the appropriate level of support for the student. As such, Tier 2 instruction that looks and feels noticeably different needs to occur.

Another key point concerning how Tier 2 is taught is that you need to review the evidence-based practices about instructional delivery (see Chapter 5). Most important, you need to use explicit instruction (Gersten, Chard et al., 2009), which involves a combination of modeling and practice. During explicit instruction, you must engage students in meaningful discussion and require students to interact and respond frequently. Explicit instruction should be utilized to deliver all instruction in Tier 2, regardless of whether the teacher is using an evidence-based intervention or a collection of evidence-based strategies. Tier 2 cannot consist solely of extended practice opportunities for students or time on a computer program. Tier 2 has to be intensive, planned instruction in which you teach the students in an engaging and interactive manner.

Tier 2 Assessment   As in Tier 1, instruction cannot be provided without an assessment component. This component is essential to understand whether the instructional platform is meeting your students' needs.

Assessment in Tier 2 should be conducted using progress monitoring measures (see Chapter 12 for a comprehensive discussion). As we introduced in the discussion on Tier 1 Assessment, progress monitoring measures should be reliable and support valid decision making. They should also have alternate forms so that a different measure can be administered each week that assesses similar mathematics content. It is best that the progress monitoring measure is built into the schedule of the intervention platform. For example, in Tier 2 small-group tutoring, you can administer the measure at the same time each week, such as on Fridays at the beginning of the tutoring session.

Progress monitoring data are collected and graphed to understand trends in each student's performance. Many progress monitoring measures do the graphing and interpretation for teachers, but teachers are also able to do their own. Chapter 12 will walk you through the process of creating your own progress monitoring graphs. You can also access a free resource from the National Center on Intensive Intervention to create progress monitoring graphs (https://intensiveintervention.org/resource /student-progress-monitoring-tool-data-collection-and-graphing-excel). Once you start graphing students' progress monitoring data, you will set goals to see whether the intervention platform is effective enough to help students meet their goals. See Figure 2.5 for a sample graph.

Setting goals and evaluating students' progress is an important part of using progress monitoring data within an MTSS system. Typically, three methods may be used to set student goals; we talk about these methods in detail in Chapter 12. On Figure 2.5, the student's goal is marked with an X and an aim line is drawn between the student's scores and the goal.

After determining a goal and drawing an aim line from the student's baseline scores to the goal, you analyze the student's progress monitoring data to determine whether he or she is adequately responding to the intervention platform. Our recommendation is that this analysis occurs every 4 to 8 weeks using the procedures we will discuss in Chapter 12.

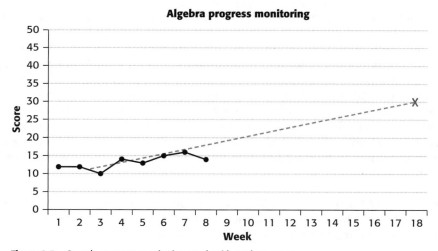

Figure 2.5. Sample progress-monitoring graph with student scores.

As Melanie points out in Chapter 17, you need progress monitoring data to determine your instruction is meeting students' needs. If the student is making adequate progress in Tier 2 (i.e., acceptable and increasing slope, adequate end levels of performance), you may decide to maintain the Tier 2 instructional support. If the student is exceeding expectations and on track for reaching grade-level expectations, you may consider reducing or removing the Tier 2 support. However, if the student is not demonstrating adequate response and you have already intensified the Tier 2 support, you should consider moving the student to Tier 3, in which a more intensive intervention is put in place.

Tier 3: Tertiary Prevention

If Tier 3 support is necessary, you have learned that the current Tier 2 intervention platform is not meeting the needs of a student with persistent learning difficulties. Figure 2.6 shows the important components of Tier 3, which may also be named tertiary prevention. In some schools, Tier 3 instructional support may occur within special education. In the framework that we present, Tier 3 is a more intensive intervention than Tier 2, and this intensity can occur in or outside of special education.

Tier 3 Assessment   Notice that we changed the order of instruction and assessment within this tier's description. That is because a diagnostic assessment should occur as the first part of Tier 3. For students who demonstrated inadequate response to Tier 2 and who therefore require Tier 3, a diagnostic assessment allows for the teacher to make informed decisions about instructional adaptations needed to support the student's needs. Teachers can use a standardized diagnostic assessment (e.g., KeyMath, Diagnostic Online Math Assessment) or use a more informal approach to gathering information about the student's strengths and weaknesses (See Chapter 11 for a comprehensive discussion of diagnostic assessments). In Chapter 17, Kellie talks about the approach her school came up with to design "checkpoints" to help her gather diagnostic information and identify students' learning gaps.

As you will read in the next section, adaptations are made to the intervention platform. As in both Tier 1 and Tier 2, progress monitoring data are collected and analyzed to determine whether the adaptations are adequate for the student (Powell &

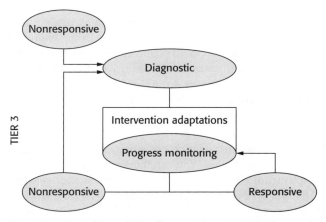

Figure 2.6.   Tier 3 of the multi-tiered systems of support (MTSS) framework.

Stecker, 2014). We recommend that progress monitoring within Tier 3 occur weekly and that the teacher analyze the data every 4 to 8 weeks.

Tier 3 Instruction   If a student requires Tier 3, that means that the Tier 2 intervention platform was not meeting all the student's needs. Rather than throw out everything and start anew, we suggest making adaptations to the intervention platform within Tier 3. There are many types of adaptations that can be made. In this chapter, we highlight six adaptations to mathematics intervention (Fuchs, Fuchs, & Malone, 2017):

1.   Implement the intervention or strategy with greater fidelity (FoI)

2.   Embed behavioral supports

3.   Increase the dosage of the intervention

4.   Adapt the mathematics content

5.   Utilize explicit instruction to the greatest extent

6.   Explicitly teach for transfer of knowledge

Increase Fidelity   One adaptation to consider is to implement the evidence-based intervention or evidence-based strategy with greater fidelity. Fidelity is adherence to the program or strategy (for a more in-depth discussion of FoI, see Chapter 8). You selected an evidence-based practice because it has been shown to improve mathematics outcomes for most students most of the time. If a teacher takes an intervention or strategy and changes it drastically, the results may be skewed either positively or negatively. In our research experience, teachers often do not implement all components of an intervention, so one of the first considerations for an adaptation is to make sure the intervention or strategy is implemented as designed.

Embed Behavioral Supports   A second adaptation to consider is the embedding of behavioral supports. Many students with mathematics learning difficulties also experience difficulty with paying attention to tasks and regulating behavior (Mulcahy, Krezmein, & Travers, 2016; Templeton, Neel, & Blood, 2008). In Chapter 17, Nicole, a district RTI coordinator, points to her experience that students who struggle academically may also develop avoidance behaviors and often struggle with self-regulation. It is important to be aware of this connection and recognize when students may benefit from a simple motivational support system to help them maintain attention and on-task behavior. Motivational systems take many forms, and can include tangible or intangible reinforcers (See Chapter 4 for a discussion about motivation in mathematics instruction). The underlying idea is that when students are paying attention, students are learning mathematics.

Increase the Dosage   A third adaptation is to increase the dosage of the intervention. You can do this in several ways. You can increase the number of minutes within a session—for example, from 20 minutes to 30. You can also increase the number of sessions per week. Instead of meeting with the student(s) twice a week, you can conduct Tier 3 intervention four or five days a week. Finally, you can increase the length of the intervention. Instead of planning for 12 weeks of Tier 3 intervention, you can plan for 18.

Adapt the Mathematics Content   The fourth adaptation, which is specific to mathematics, involves adapting the mathematics content. There are a variety of ways to do so. You could consider revising the student's scope and sequence (see Chapter 7). You could also consider intentionally breaking down complex problems into smaller steps, engaging students in deeper mathematical discourse, or providing worked examples that are examined through discussion. Another adaptation could involve a tighter focus on mathematical language. Perhaps you incorporate mathematics journals or word walls to highlight important mathematics terms. You can also utilize more or different representations to help students see and understand mathematical concepts and procedures (see Chapter 5). You could be more intentional with fluency practice. Fact fluency and computational fluency are often a barrier for many students with learning difficulties. Finally, you may want to provide explicit problem-solving instruction, as students are expected to solve word problems to demonstrate mathematics competency.

Utilize Explicit Instruction   The fifth recommendation is not really an adaptation, but we want to remind teachers to utilize explicit instruction when you design your Tier 2 and/or Tier 3 intervention platforms. We will provide a detailed discussion of explicit instruction in Chapter 5, but as a preview, explicit instruction is the cornerstone to the effective delivery of instruction. If you are not using explicit instruction in Tier 2 or Tier 3 to the maximum level possible, students with mathematics difficulty are missing out on important learning opportunities. Review your modeling to ensure you are providing clear explanations with intentional examples. Review the practice opportunities that you are providing to students and make sure they are engaged in meaningful practice as they work toward independence with mathematics. You should also review your student-level interactions, either via reflection, peer observations, or video, to determine whether you are asking a mix of high- and low-level questions, getting students to frequently respond, and providing affirmative or corrective feedback. Explicit instruction is vital, so adapting instruction to be more explicit is likely a good move.

Explicitly Teach for Transfer   The sixth adaptation is explicitly teaching for transfer. Along the continuum of mathematics learning, students repeatedly use their knowledge for more difficult problems (e.g., 5 – 4, then 25 – 14, then 206 – 176, then $\frac{3}{4} - \frac{1}{2}$, then 5.4 – 3.09). For students with mathematics difficulty, it is not always obvious how something learned in the past relates to current learning or how current learning relates to future learning. Therefore, you need to explicitly teach students how their knowledge about addition, place value, and regrouping for the problem 405 + 16 can transfer to help them solve the problem 4305 + 216. Much of explicitly teaching for transfer involves explicit modeling, practice, and discussion of similar problems.

Tier 3 Decision Making   Many adaptations can be selected. We suggest, however, that you select only a few at a time. You adapt the intervention platform and implement the revised intervention. As the intervention is being implemented, you are continuing to collect, graph, and analyze progress monitoring data. You can apply the same decision rules in Tier 3 as you did in Tier 2, and analyze the data every 4 to 8 weeks to understand whether the selected adaptations are working or need to be adjusted.

For students who demonstrate adequate response to the adapted intervention, continue Tier 3 until a student is on track to meet grade-level expectations. For students who do not demonstrate adequate response, notice the arrows on Figure 2.6 point back up to the diagnostic assessment. You may need to gather more diagnostic data to help you refine the design of your Tier 3 intervention and make additional adaptations based on the new information. Just as before, you will continue administering the progress monitoring measures to determine if you have identified the most effective intervention platform to support your students' needs. The MTSS framework can continue to be used for a single student as long as that student requires supplemental instruction.

SUMMARY: PROVIDING TIERED SUPPORT

In this chapter, we introduced the MTSS framework and the common three-tier model. We described Tier 1 instruction and assessment and emphasized that assessment is an integral component of MTSS. We then focused on Tier 2 and the instruction and assessment that occurs within Tier 2. We described the necessity of using explicit instruction within Tier 2 for the delivery of mathematics content. We also briefly explained how to set goals and determine whether students are on track to meet such goals. Finally, we reviewed Tier 3, which begins with a diagnostic assessment that identifies student strengths and weaknesses. This diagnostic information informs intervention adaptations. As adaptations are put into place, progress monitoring continues to help you determine whether the intervention is working well enough for the student.

CHAPTER 3

Supporting All Students Through Differentiation, Accommodation, and Modification

In this section, we have talked about the development of students' sense of numbers and how to support all learners in a classroom or school by implementing an MTSS framework (the term *RTI* is also commonly used in discussing this framework). In this chapter, we focus on supporting those students who may need extra support during the lesson. This extra support may occur on an "as-needed" basis through differentiated instructional strategies, or it may be more systematic through the use of instructional accommodations or modifications. To help you determine which type of support is needed (and when), we walk through each type and share strategies for changing your instruction to meet students' needs.

LAYERS OF SUPPORT

As our students work hard to learn the content of our mathematics lessons, some will encounter challenges. Some of these challenges might be temporal, meaning that they are fleeting difficulties that can be resolved with some minor adjustments to the instructional design or delivery of lessons. However, some of these challenges might be more persistent difficulties related to learning differences or learning disabilities that require systematic changes in the design and delivery of instruction. As teachers, we need to be "on the lookout" for students who are facing these different types of challenges and know how to respond. This chapter discusses fundamental questions you might ask yourself to ensure students who need extra support receive the right type and amount:

- How do I know if a student is struggling? Is he or she struggling to learn or struggling with the learning environment?

- How do I differentiate instruction to support access?

- Does my student need additional instructional support beyond differentiated instruction?

- What types of changes may be needed?

   How do I know if a student is struggling? Is he or she struggling to learn or struggling with the learning environment? One of the hardest questions we ask ourselves during the learning process is "Are my students struggling to learn the content?" This is a hard question because learning is often a difficult process. How do you know if a student is struggling or just working hard to learn the content?

As we will discuss in detail in Section III of this book, because we want to make decisions during the learning process, we need to look at results from formative assessments. Data from formative assessments can help us determine if students are struggling to learn. First, through administering a universal screener we can identify students who are at risk for failure. Results from this type of formative assessment can point to students who need additional instructional support as well as determine the intensity of the support they may need. Second, we can use results from formative diagnostic assessments to help us pinpoint the areas in which a student is struggling. Third, we can use ongoing progress monitoring data to find out if students are learning at the rate that is expected. As we talked about in Chapter 2 on MTSS, these formative assessments should be viewed as a system of assessments. By reviewing data across these types of formative assessments, we can look for trends in students' performance that might indicate whether the student is struggling with the content.

Administering formative assessments can help determine if there are persistent problems in students' understanding of the content. However, some students may struggle to gain access to the instructional material. In this context, access means the student's ability to understand the way in which the material is being presented (e.g., through reading the textbook, listening to instruction), interact with the information (e.g., through talking

> Whereas some students may have problems understanding the content, others may struggle to gain access to the instructional material.

with others, drawing diagrams of mathematical situations), or demonstrate his or her understanding (e.g., through writing, explaining). When instruction is accessible, the student can fully engage in the instructional process. For some students, however, the instructional environment is not accessible. These students may have trouble reading and/or comprehending the grade-level textbook, expressing their knowledge through writing, or attending to a teacher's lecture, just to name a few examples. To support these students during the learning process, you will need to make adjustments to your instructional design and delivery to improve the accessibility of the learning environment. The intensity and duration of the adjustments will depend on the underlying problems the student is facing.

Is my student struggling with the learning environment? To help us understand how to answer this question, let's consider Lucas, described in the following vignette.

STRUGGLING WITH THE CONTENT OR STRUGGLING TO GAIN ACCESS?: LUCAS

Lucas is a seventh-grade student who likes his math class and earned good grades on most of his assignments last year. When asked what he likes most about math, he says, "I like math because you don't have to read." However, Lucas is starting to struggle on his math assignments. Let us delve a little deeper to determine whether Lucas is struggling with the content or struggling to gain access to the content.

In Grade 5, Lucas was identified as having a learning disability in reading. He struggles to read the textbooks and assignments across his classes. He receives targeted interventions to help support his reading. Lucas has particular difficulty decoding text, which affects his ability to remember the concepts in a large block of text. Also, he has difficulty learning and retaining the meaning of the words. He has recently started using a new strategy to help him comprehend the text: he reads the words aloud under his breath so that he can see and hear the words.

Lucas's sixth-grade math teacher did not assign many word problems, but when she did, the students were allowed to work together to solve the problems. Lucas always managed to overcome his reading difficulties by asking someone to read the problem so they could "get done faster." This strategy seemed to work in Grade 6 but has not been successful in Grade 7. He is struggling in his math class and is earning Cs and Ds on his assignments. Most of these assignments require him to read problems silently during class, use precise mathematical terminology, and write justifications to his answers.

Lucas appears to be struggling with the learning environment. If he is not able to gain access to the content of instruction, he may begin to struggle to learn the mathematics, too. He has difficulty gaining access to the information being conveyed in the learning process. Without addressing his access issues with the learning environment, we will not know if he is also struggling to learn the content. For the rest of this chapter, we discuss how to support students who struggle with the learning environment. In Section II, we will talk about how to support students who are struggling to learn the content.

In this chapter, we highlight the role of differentiated instruction as well as instructional accommodations and modifications. Some of these suggestions will relate to students like Lucas, but others may be designed for students with more significant issues in gaining access to the learning environment. These suggestions should be used only when absolutely necessary so as to maintain the grade-level content expectations for all students.

MAXIMIZING THE ACCESSIBILITY OF YOUR MATHEMATICS INSTRUCTION

As we have already discussed, the goal of instruction is to support student learning. In Section II of this book, we will address best practices in instructional design and delivery to support the goal of student learning. However, even when these practices are put in place, some students continue to struggle. As we will discuss in Chapter 5, providing instructional interventions may help these students learn the content to a greater degree of proficiency. However, some students do not need an instructional intervention to support their learning. These students may be able to learn the content presented in the general education classroom, but they may require a different approach to the instructional design and delivery to reach the learning objectives. These approaches make the learning environment more accessible, and they take the form of differentiated instruction, accommodations, or modifications.

Differentiated instruction, accommodations, and modifications are classifications of different types of changes to the instructional design and delivery of your lessons. The types of changes in these different approaches may be similar but are typically graduated in the level of intensity based on the student's needs. Specifically, differentiated instruction requires the least intensive changes to your instructional design and delivery because the students who benefit from this approach do not need intensive support to gain access to the learning environment. On the other hand, modifications require the most intensive changes to your instructional design and delivery because students who require modifications need the most intensive support to gain access to the learning environment. As these statements imply, deciding

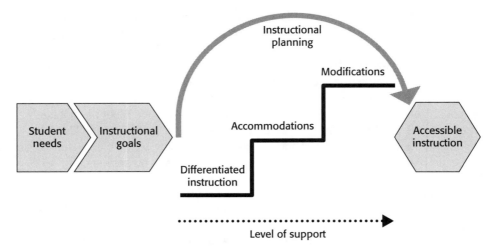

Figure 3.1. Relationship between a student's needs and the level of support required to enhance accessibility. (From Ketterlin-Geller L.R., Jamgochian E.M. [2011] Instructional Adaptations: Accommodations and Modifications That Support Accessible Instruction. In: Elliott S., Kettler R., Beddow P., Kurz A. [eds.] Handbook of Accessible Achievement Tests for All Students, 131–146. Springer, New York, NY.)

whether a student would benefit from differentiated instruction, accommodations, or modifications requires understanding the needs of the student (Ketterlin-Geller & Jamgochian, 2011).

Figure 3.1 shows the relationship between the student's needs and the level of support required for reaching the goal of accessible instruction. As this diagram shows, the student's needs are considered along with the instructional goals to determine the level of support the student requires to make instruction accessible. The least amount of support should be provided to help students reach their goals. As we explain later in this chapter, providing too much unnecessary support may actually reduce the learning opportunities for students as opposed to support them.

THREE LEVELS OF SUPPORT

Deciding on the amount of support a student needs to gain access to instruction may require a bit of detective work on your part. You may know that a student is struggling, but it may be harder to determine if the student is struggling to learn the content or struggling with the learning environment. For some students identified as having a disability, their IEP may already identify accommodations and modifications for you to incorporate into your instructional design and delivery. However, even with these specified adaptations, you may notice other supports specific to mathematics instruction that may or may not have been considered when the IEP was written. As you put your detective skills to work, you can consult with the special education case manager about any recommendations you may have to maximize the accessibility of the student's learning environment.

For Lucas, his previous grades and experiences in prior years indicated that he was able to learn the mathematics content with minimal extra support. However, as the expectations of the class increased in grade 7, he was starting to struggle. The content increased in complexity, and so did the learning environment. Lucas was expected to read and respond to problems silently during class. Also, he was expected to use precise mathematical terms and explain his answers in writing. These tasks posed a challenge for Lucas. Differentiated instruction, accommodations, or modifications may be needed to help Lucas overcome these challenges. These three levels of support, and questions related to each level, are discussed below.

Differentiated Instruction

How do I differentiate instruction to support access? Many books have been written about differentiating instruction to support student learning. Although we briefly describe the process of differentiating instruction in this chapter, we cannot do this topic justice in just a few paragraphs. If you would like to learn more about differentiating instruction, we highly recommend that you consult a book such as *Teaching Mathematics Meaningfully: Solutions for Reaching Struggling Learners* (Allsopp, Lovin, & van Ingen, 2018) or other resources not specific to mathematics such as *Modifying Schoolwork: Teachers' Guides to Inclusive Practices* (Janney & Snell, 2006).

Differentiated instruction is a process of intentionally changing the design and/or delivery of your instruction to support students' access to the learning environment (and, ultimately, their learning of the content). The content expectations do not change when you are differentiating instruction; all students are expected to learn the same mathematics content to the same depth and breadth, but they may take different roads to get there. This process requires attention to what types of changes individual students in your classroom might need to support their learning. For example, some students might have deeper background knowledge on a particular topic than others. Knowing this information as you are planning your instruction can help you design and deliver differentiated instruction.

When differentiating your instructional design and delivery, you are personalizing instruction based on the unique individuals you have in your class. To better understand these individuals, it is useful to consider their background knowledge, readiness for the current topic, language skills and abilities, preferences, and interests (Hall, 2002). This information can be gathered throughout the year using a variety of strategies, including informal observations, pretests of the content, preference surveys, and interest inventories. As you collect this information, you may find it helpful to have a system for recording it for quick reference. An example of how this data may be organized is shown in Table 3.1.

Table 3.1. Example of table organizing student data

Student name	Interests	Working preferences	Areas of difficulty	Background knowledge and access skills	
				Unit 1: Fractions	Unit 2: Decimals
Brad	Computer games Playing piano Favorite subject: science	Likes working in small groups Gets easily distracted when working with friends	Consistently using precise mathematical vocabulary	Understands meaning of numerator and denominator Proficient at finding common denominator	Identifies whole number place values
Isabel	Volleyball Camping Favorite subject: history	Likes working with a partner Prefers to sit near the front of the room	Working on quick recall of multiplication facts	Simplifies fractions easily Adds and subtracts fractions with like denominators	Writes a decimal as a fraction

Once information about students' background knowledge, access skills, and preferences is gathered, stored, and updated as needed, you can continually refer to this information during your instructional planning. Approaches to differentiating your instruction may include changes to the design and/or delivery of your instruction that encompass an array of teaching approaches, learning and assessment activities, and varied resources designed to help support each student in reaching the learning goals (Tomlinson, 1999).

Thinking back to Lucas, he struggled to learn and apply new mathematical language necessary to learn the content. To differentiate instruction for students like Lucas, you may decide to preview the vocabulary for an upcoming unit or lesson. For example, in the CCSS-M in Grade 7, new vocabulary is introduced around concepts of geometry (e.g., supplementary, complementary, vertical, adjacent angles). For students who may struggle to learn and use mathematical terms such as these, you can help them create an ongoing personalized mathematical dictionary that includes the mathematical term, definition written in their own words, and a visual representation. An example of this type of support can be seen in Figure 3.2. This self-made resource can serve as a reference point as they work to apply the terminology.

Another approach to differentiation may involve varying the complexity of the instructional models used depending on the students' background knowledge. For example, in grade 6, if the lesson objective is to create a visual fraction model to represent the quotient (CCSS-M 6.NS.1), some students may model the quotient using fraction tiles to incorporate the use of concrete manipulatives. Other students may be able

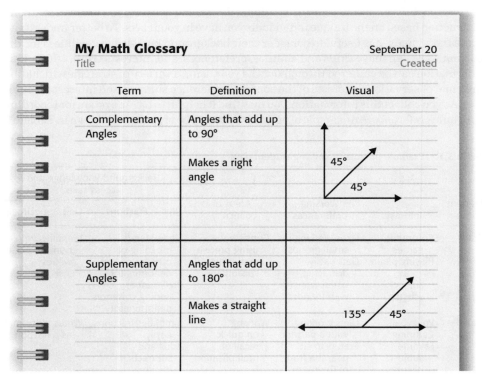

Figure 3.2. Sample math glossary.

Table 3.2. Integrating students' background knowledge with differentiated instructional strategies

Learning goal	Students' background knowledge	Differentiated activity
Interpret and compute quotients of fractions and solve word problems involving division of fractions by fractions (e.g., by using visual fraction models and equations to represent the problem) (CCSS-M 6.NS.1)	Student is developing a conceptual understanding of fractions. Student grasps fraction concepts using manipulatives. Student struggles to draw models of division. Student is continuing to develop proficiency working with abstract representations.	Model the quotient using fraction tiles.
	Student understands the concept of division of whole numbers and can draw relevant and accurate area models. Student is able to execute the algorithm for dividing fractions but is developing conceptual understanding.	Model the quotient using area models.
	Student conceptually understands fractions. Student can compute quotients of fractions using the algorithm and is developing a conceptual understanding of division of fractions.	Model the quotient on a number line.

to model the quotient using area models, and still others may be challenged to model the quotient on a number line. Table 3.2 illustrates how you can integrate students' background knowledge with differentiated instructional strategies.

However, it is important to remember that all students are expected to learn the content to the same depth and breadth when differentiating instruction. If changing the instructional models alters these expectations, then another approach should be taken.

To support students with varying levels of readiness for learning a new concept, you may consider varying the level of scaffolding provided during teacher-directed modeling. For example, when teaching students to find a percentage of a quantity as a rate per 100, some students may be able to quickly generalize their understanding of proportional relationships to understand that 23% of 90 is the same as $\frac{23}{100}$ multiplied by 90. However, other students may need additional models (such as a double number line) to understand this relationship.

Other strategies for differentiating your instructional delivery include varying the composition of groups to provide peer support during the learning process. These groups may be formed based on similarities or differences in relevant characteristics. For example, if you want to incorporate peer tutoring or mentoring, you may elect to create heterogeneous groups that vary based on students' understanding of the content. However, you may want to group students based on common areas of interest so you can provide tailored application tasks. Such tasks may increase students' motivation by relating the content to their personal experiences.

You may implement differentiated instructional strategies after careful planning or based on immediate and direct observations of student learning. In addition, the instructional strategies may change from lesson to lesson, depending on students' needs. However, some students need consistent and systematic changes to the instructional design and delivery to support access to the learning environment—changes that often involve additional support beyond that provided through differentiated instruction. These supports are called accommodations and modifications. The distinctions between these two levels of support, questions related to each one, and types of accommodations and modifications are discussed in the next subsection.

Accommodations and Modifications

Does my student need additional instructional support beyond differentiated instruction? For some students, differentiating instructional design and delivery will not provide enough support to increase access to the learning environment. For these students, additional changes such as accommodations or modifications may be needed.

IEP teams assign accommodations and modifications based on the specific needs of individual students. During IEP team meetings, content-area teachers can provide input on the types of supports the student needs during instruction. It is important that the student's mathematics teacher attend these meetings to help determine which supports in mathematics instruction the student needs. Because IEPs are legal documents, the accommodations and modifications identified on a student's IEP must be systematically applied throughout the learning process. However, if during your investigative work, you identify additional supports that may be needed, you can discuss your observations with the student's special education case manager to determine if the IEP can be amended. In most states, you cannot provide an accommodation or modification without documentation on the student's IEP.

Instructional accommodations and modifications are changes in the presentation, setting, timing or schedule, and response mode of instruction. Whereas accommodations do not change the underlying instructional objective, modifications do. For example, an instructional accommodation may change the time a student is provided to learn the content, but an instructional modification may change the depth to which the student is required to learn the material. This important distinction affects the student's opportunity to learn grade-level material. Students who receive instructional accommodations are expected to learn the same content—that is, the same mathematics content standards, with the same depth of cognitive complexity, to the same degree of difficulty—as students who do not receive instructional accommodations. Just as when you differentiate your instruction, there should be no differences in these students' opportunity to learn grade-level content. However, students receiving instructional modifications are learning the content to a different level of depth, breadth, and/or proficiency than other students. Instructional modifications have been assigned to these students because they allow them to have the learning environment that is best aligned with their needs. Most often, these students have more significant intellectual disabilities and are receiving a substantial amount of instructional support from a special education teacher.

> Differentiated instruction and accommodations do not change the depth, breadth, or difficulty of your instructional objectives. Modifications do.

What types of changes may be needed? Accommodations and modifications are typically classified into four categories: presentation, setting, timing and scheduling, and response mode.

Changes to Presentation   Changes to the presentation of instruction or assessment are often provided for students who have physical, sensory, or cognitive difficulties that affect their perception of visual or auditory stimuli (Thompson, 2005). Presentation accommodations change the way in which instructional material or assessments are disseminated to students. For example, some students may have

Table 3.3. Some examples of presentation changes

Accommodations	Modifications
• Audio- or video-record a lesson instead of taking notes • Read the directions and/or problems aloud to the student • Increase the font size (e.g., enlarge text, use a magnification device) • Increase the contrast or differentiation of information included in visual representations (e.g., use color to help students identify corresponding sides on similar figures) • Increase white space on assignments • Reduce the number of items on a page • Allow the student to use a screen reader • Provide tactile prompts such as physical guidance or raised-line paper • Allow the student to use highlighters • Provide the student with a copy of notes or class presentations before the lesson begins • Allow the student to use a dictionary that does not include mathematical terms	• Allow the student to read shorter versions of the mathematics textbook that may not contain grade-level vocabulary • Shorten story problems by reducing the number of relevant mathematical steps needed to respond • Reduce the reading expectation for word problems (e.g., removing irrelevant information) • Allow the student to use a dictionary on tests that includes mathematical terms

visual impairments that make it difficult to perceive written materials. Accommodations to support access for these students may include the use of large font on printed materials, magnification devices, or materials with high contrast. In some cases, the student might benefit from the use of tactile prompts such as raised-line paper or raised graphics.

As we learned with Lucas, some students may have difficulty comprehending written material that is presented in textbooks or on word problems. Students with these difficulties might gain access to the material by having it read aloud to them, either by you, by another adult or peer, through audio or video recordings, or by using screen readers. All of these changes are classified as accommodations because they do not change the mathematics content expectations for the student; they require the student to learn the mathematics to the same depth, breadth, and level of proficiency as all other students.

Some students with more significant physical, sensory, or cognitive difficulties may need modifications to presentation to gain access to the mathematics content. For example, a student who has difficulty understanding the concepts presented in the grade-level text (beyond an issue with reading comprehension) may need an abridged version of the text. A modification for this student may involve reducing the number of concepts he or she is expected to learn. Because they change the depth, breadth, and/or level of mathematical proficiency of the learning objectives, these changes are modifications and should only be provided with guidance from the IEP team.

Table 3.3 presents examples of accommodations and modifications that involve changing the way mathematics content is presented.

Changes to Setting Changes to the setting of instruction or assessments are most beneficial for students who are easily distracted by routine classroom interactions or who need support to make the learning environment physically accessible. Other students might have personal characteristics or use other accommodations or

Table 3.4. Some examples of setting changes

Accommodations	Modifications
• Change the location where the student is completing the assignment • Provide a separate location for the student to complete the assignment • Allow the student to use a physical device to reduce distractions (i.e., headphones or study carrel) • Allow the student to complete an assignment in a small group or in a room with fewer students • Use specialized lighting or acoustic devices	• Allow the student to work with a partner on a task that is intended to be completed alone

modifications that are distracting to other students. For example, Lucas talks to himself as a reading strategy when trying to decipher word problems. Such a student (and the students around the child) may also benefit from changes to the setting of their instruction or assessment.

Setting accommodations are changes to the conditions or locations of instruction or assessment. Some setting accommodations that can be implemented to support these students include changing the seating and/or grouping for the child, such as sitting near the teacher or away from doors or windows, or using specialized equipment. Providing instruction in small groups may help to minimize distractions. In some cases, students may need to receive instruction or take a test in a separate location to help them concentrate; however, to allow the child to spend most of his or her learning time in the general education classroom, this option should be used only when necessary. Other students may benefit from using headphones or a study carrel to focus their attention. Because these changes to the setting of instruction or assessments do not change the mathematics content expectations, these are classified as accommodations. Even though some students might benefit from these setting accommodations at different times during instruction, students with disabilities who have been assigned one or more of these accommodations must be provided with the accommodation on a regular basis.

Setting modifications can be considered for students with more significant characteristics that affect their ability to attend during instruction or when taking assessments. These students may need to spend more time outside of the general education classroom to receive individualized instruction. Other students may need to work with a partner on a task that was originally intended for individual students to demonstrate independence or mastery. Because these changes alter the depth, breadth, and/or level of proficiency of the mathematics content expectations, these should only be provided when specified on the student's IEP.

Table 3.4 presents examples of accommodations and modifications that involve making setting changes.

Changes to Timing or Scheduling   Timing or scheduling accommodations change the amount of time a student has to engage with an activity or the way in which the time is organized. Changes to the timing or scheduling of instruction or assessments are often used to support students who process information slowly (i.e., student reads at a slow rate), have a physical disability that affects their ability to complete a task (i.e., student has difficulty with fine motor control and so takes

Table 3.5. Some examples of timing or scheduling changes

Accommodations	Modifications
• Provide longer time for the student to complete an assignment, as needed • Allow the student to take multiple breaks while completing an assignment • Allow the student to take a test at a certain time of the day (e.g., first thing in the morning)	• Provide more time for the student to respond to an assignment or test that is intended to be timed (e.g., allow twice as much time as intended) • Extend the number of sessions a student has to complete an assignment or test that is intended to be timed (e.g., allow the student to take a test over 2 days)

longer to write), or use another form of instructional accommodation or modification that requires additional time (i.e., student uses a screen reader to decode text). Accommodations to support students' access to the learning environment include providing extended time to complete a task, building in multiple breaks to avoid too much fatigue, or breaking a task into smaller parts. Because accommodations do not change the mathematics content expectations, these changes should be applied only when timing is not part of the learning objective. However, when timing is important (i.e., timed test of fluency with operations), these changes may not be appropriate.

If a student needs these types of timing and scheduling changes for all tasks, including tasks that would be timed for all other students, these changes would be classified as modifications. Because the mathematics content expectations would be altered, these modifications should only be applied when stated on the IEP.

Table 3.5 presents examples of accommodations and modifications that involve making changes to timing or scheduling.

Changes to Response Mode
Response mode accommodations and modifications are changes to the way students express their knowledge and skills. These changes may support students who have difficulty expressing themselves in a specific mode due to either language difficulties or motor difficulties. Some students with these difficulties might benefit from being able to express themselves in a specific manner (i.e., writing, typing, or orally presenting their responses) or from using different communication modes such as sign language.

Still other students who may benefit from changing the response mode are those who have difficulty organizing their thinking. Some response mode accommodations that support these students include allowing them to use a visual/graphic organizer to organize their thinking, use manipulatives to generate their answer, or write their responses directly on the assignment (as opposed to filling out an answer sheet). Because these changes do not alter the depth, breadth, or level of proficiency, students receiving these accommodations should be held to the same mathematical content expectations. However, some students have more significant needs that require modifications to the response mode. Some modifications include reducing the number of mathematics items the student needs to complete (i.e., assigning fewer homework or classwork problems) or reducing the depth of the explanation required to justify his or her response. A modification to the response mode for multiple-choice tests may involve reducing the number of answer choices from which the student can choose. These modifications reduce the depth, breadth, and/or level of proficiency of the mathematics content expectations.

Table 3.6.   Some examples of response mode changes

Accommodations	Modifications
• Allow the student to write responses to assignments instead of speaking them aloud • Allow the student to speak responses to assignments instead of writing them • Allow the student to use a communication device • Allow audio recording of teachers' presentations • Use a scribe • Use concrete objects and manipulatives • Use a graphic organizer to organize one's thoughts • Use a calculator or multiplication chart on an assignment that *does not* assess computation	• Require fewer items on an assignment or fewer assignments • Reduce the number of answer options on a multiple-choice assignment • Describe one's thinking (i.e., explanation, justification) at a reduced depth • Use a calculator or multiplication chart on an assignment that *does* assess computation • Have material scored using a different rubric or level of expectations than other students

Table 3.6 presents examples of accommodations and modifications that involve changing the response mode.

IMPLICATIONS FOR PROVIDING ACCOMMODATIONS AND MODIFICATIONS

Several implications should be considered when recommending instructional accommodations and modifications to improve access to mathematics instruction:

1. Providing a modification to a student may change the student's future opportunities to learn mathematics content. For example, consider the CCSS-M content standard in grade 3 that requires students to fluently multiply and divide within 100 and know from memory all products of two one-digit numbers. If a student received a modification in grade 3 that reduced the expectation that the student know from memory all products of two one-digit numbers by, for example, allowing the use of a calculator or a multiplication chart, subsequent application of this skill will be limited.

2. Providing an accommodation or modification should not preclude the student from receiving instruction in this area. For example, if a student needs to use a calculator on a computation test (a modification), the student should still receive instruction to build his or her computational fluency.

3. Providing an accommodation or modification in instruction should be accompanied by the same accommodation or modification during assessment. For example, if a student is permitted to use a custom dictionary that defines all nonmathematical words (an accommodation) during instruction, the student should be allowed to use the custom dictionary during assessment.

As you work with the special educators in your building (see Section IV) to determine the best supports for all students in your mathematics classes, keep in mind that none of these changes precludes the others. A student who is receiving an accommodation (e.g., provision of extra time) may also benefit from differentiated instructional strategies (e.g., additional teacher modeling). Similarly, a student who is receiving a modification (e.g., reduced number of classwork, homework, and assessment problems) may also benefit from receiving an accommodation (e.g., having the items read aloud).

Table 3.7. Integrated instructional supports for Lucas

	Possible adaptations to instruction
Differentiated instruction strategies	Preview new vocabulary with Lucas before the lesson. Work with Lucas to create a customized mathematical dictionary. Support and incorporate Lucas's background knowledge to build on his prior success in mathematics. Include opportunities for Lucas to work with his peers or in small groups to complete assignments.
Accommodations	Structure independent reading tasks so that Lucas has someone to support his reading (partner, adult). Read aloud the directions and expectations for assignments. Allow Lucas to sit by himself when completing independent tasks so he can read the text aloud. Teach Lucas comprehension strategies so he can identify key elements of the mathematics text, including word problems.
Modifications	Allow Lucas to use his customized mathematical dictionary on tests or assignments that require independent application of mathematical vocabulary. Remove irrelevant information from word problems. Reduce the number of text-heavy items on assignments and tests.

Just as we saw with Lucas, he benefited from differentiated instruction and the use of accommodations. Table 3.7 shows how these instructional supports can be integrated to support Lucas's needs.

It is important to consider which instructional changes align with the specific needs of the student. Although assignment of accommodations and modifications is beyond the scope of this chapter, carefully considering the student's needs and the instructional expectations will help you determine how best to support his or her access to the instructional environment.

SUMMARY: DIFFERENTIATION, ACCOMMODATION, AND MODIFICATION

In this chapter, we focused on supporting students through differentiation, accommodation, and modification. We shared strategies about how to determine what type of support is needed for each student and ways to provide this support. Students may need different levels of support, including as-needed support or more systematic accommodations or modifications. These levels of support can be integrated to provide students with the support they need.

SECTION II

Designing and Delivering Effective Mathematics Instruction

OVERVIEW: TEACHING BASED IN EVIDENCE

In this section, we focus on important instructional considerations for use within an MTSS framework. In Chapter 4, we identify why it's important to provide effective mathematics instruction. We discuss the role of motivation within instruction, how to engage students in learning, and how to provide precise and accurate instruction for students with learning difficulties. In Chapter 5, we outline essential evidence-based practices that should be used when designing an intervention platform to address students' needs. We describe, in detail, the use of explicit instruction, multiple representations, and precise mathematical language. We also highlight, in Chapter 6, the importance of providing effective problem-solving instruction. In Chapter 7, we describe how to plan the scope and sequence of mathematics interventions, and we provide resources for identifying evidence-based practices. We wrap up this section on instructional practices with a look at instructional examples within the tiers of MTSS in Chapter 8.

Across these five chapters, our intention is that the information will help you answer the following questions:

1. *What are the evidence-based practices to use in Tier 2 or 3 instruction?* In Chapter 5, we start with explicit instruction, which should be the foundation of instructional delivery for Tiers 2 and 3. We describe how to use multiple representations within mathematics instruction and why our mathematical language should be precise when delivering instruction and practicing mathematics with students with learning difficulties. We also emphasize the need to build fluency with students and help students become effective problem solvers. Problem solving is so important that we devote an entire chapter (Chapter 6) to effective word-problem practices.

2. *How do I design effective instruction within MTSS?* It is important to develop an appropriate scope and sequence of mathematical content for students with learning difficulties, and we provide detail about the development of a scope and sequence for intervention in Chapter 7. Once the scope and sequence is developed, we provide insight on identifying evidence-based practices, either interventions or strategies. These interventions or strategies should be delivered with the practices described in Chapter 5.

3. *How do I ensure my instruction is effective?* It is necessary to understand whether you are implementing evidence-based interventions or strategies with fidelity (Chapter 8). It is also necessary to combine instructional efforts with assessment efforts (see Section III of this book—Chapters 9 to 13) to determine whether students are making adequate progress with the intervention platform or whether instructional adaptations need to be made.

CHAPTER 4

Aims for Effective Mathematics Instruction

In this chapter, we describe reasons for providing effective mathematics instruction. This chapter sets up the other chapters about mathematics instruction in Section II of this book by providing a description of the foundational ideas behind impactful instruction. It is important for teachers to reflect upon the reasons for putting in the effort to provide better mathematics instruction for students with mathematics difficulty. We answer the following questions about effective instruction:

- Why does instruction need to motivate students?

- What are some ways to motivate students during mathematics instruction?

- How are mathematical ideas taught precisely and accurately?

- How does instruction dispel common mathematical misconceptions?

- How can you engage students in meaningful ways during mathematics instruction?

- What are ways to meet the needs of all learners in the mathematics classroom?

WHAT EFFECTIVE INSTRUCTION NEEDS TO ACCOMPLISH

Much has been made of effective instruction since about 2000 as schools have increasingly been held accountable for academic outcomes in critical areas such as mathematics. Before the era of setting content standards, very few people talked about whether a teacher's instruction was effective. In fact, whether students learned what you were planning to teach them was largely attributed to the student. Some students were considered "good" at mathematics, whereas others were considered "average" or "below average." Some teachers never thought that a student's success in learning mathematics might have as much or more to do with the effectiveness of our teaching. Yet, there is ample evidence that student achievement is dependent, in part, on the degree to which we are able to design and deliver instruction that is engaging and relevant to the learner and focuses on high standards in mathematics (Jitendra, 2013). Before we dive in to the details of how to design and deliver effective instruction, it is a good idea to define what we mean by *effective instruction*.

Effective instruction has to accomplish many things (see Figure 4.1). It has to motivate students, introduce mathematical ideas precisely and accurately, dispel

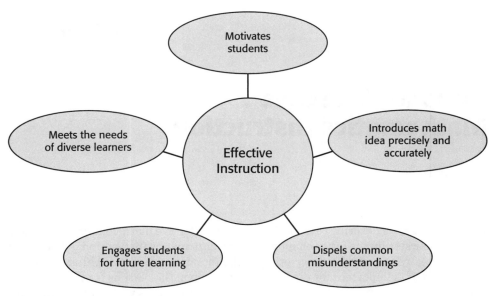

Figure 4.1. Accomplishments of effective instruction.

common misunderstandings, engage students in using the new information in a way that will ensure that what they learn is accurately integrated with what they already know, and meet the needs of diverse learners. In addition, the instruction has to be planned and delivered in such a way that it can be used in future experiences, either to learn more information or to solve problems. It is worth our time to discuss each feature noted here so that we have a common understanding of how your planning and teaching affect your students and their understanding of mathematics.

MOTIVATE STUDENTS

We're all looking for students who love to learn what we are teaching them, persevere when they are challenged, and are interested in mastering new skills and acquiring new knowledge. In reality, it has never been that easy. Motivating students to do mathematics is an ongoing challenge and is a topic that receives a considerable amount of discussion and thought. After all, if students aren't motivated, can they really benefit from the experiences they have in and out of the classroom? Motivation is largely about students' beliefs in their ability to accomplish what they are working on. If they have a history of what they believe to be failure in mathematics, they are less likely to want to persevere in using mathematics to solve problems. On the other hand, if they have a history of success in mathematics, students are more likely to see math as a tool for problem solving.

The Institute of Education Sciences (IES) practice guide about teaching mathematics to students with learning difficulties (Gersten, Beckmann et al., 2009) suggested that using motivational strategies in the classroom may improve students' mathematics performance. The authors identified three recommendations for incorporating motivational strategies into instruction. First, teachers should reinforce or praise students for their effort and for attending to and being engaged in the lesson. Praise should be specific to students' actual effort and not generic. Praise should also be immediate, taking place as students are engaged with the lesson. Second, teachers should consider rewarding student accomplishments. Rewards, both verbal and material, can be given based on students' completion of, and performance on, tasks. Third, teachers should allow students to chart their progress and set goals for improvement. This encourages students to take responsibility for their learning and allows them to set and track their own learning goals.

In addition to these strategies, we recommend three more, described in detail in the following subsections.

1. Address students' negative beliefs about mathematics.

2. Get their attention and keep them interested.

3. Build a mastery-oriented culture in your classroom.

Address Negative Beliefs About Mathematics

It is essential to be aware of your students' learning histories, their previous performance in mathematics classrooms, and their beliefs about their abilities to use mathematics successfully. As you get to know your students, listen for comments about mathematics that might suggest that students do not believe they can be successful. They will often attribute their struggles to bad luck, lack of effort on their part, the difficulty of the problems you are asking them to solve, or their incomplete knowledge of the strategy necessary to solve the problems (Dowker, Sarkar, & Looi, 2016). Perhaps what is most concerning about these kinds of beliefs is that if students do not experience success, they develop into adults who also don't believe they can use mathematics successfully. Students and adults describe themselves as not being "math people."

It may be important, especially at the beginning of the school year, to survey students' motivation to learn mathematics. There are lots of different surveys about motivation; the survey created by Ersoy and Oksuz (2015) is an example of one that might be helpful to use. On this motivation scale, students mark whether they agree, slightly agree, or disagree with different statements, such as "mathematics is easy," "mathematics is boring," or "mathematics can be used in daily life." You may not want to use all the questions, or you may want to write some of your own questions. After administration, you can gauge each student's motivation to learn mathematics and be an active learner in your mathematics classroom. You may find it useful to add some of these details to the table you create about your students' needs and preferences (see Table 3.1 in Chapter 3).

Students who have negative beliefs about their ability to do mathematics need learning opportunities that demonstrate that they can be successful. This will likely come through effective instruction, designed and delivered by you. Designing instructional experiences for students that provide a strong foundation of mathematics learning will begin to provide self-confidence to students about the learning of mathematics and motivate students to learn more (Ramirez, Chang, Maloney, Levine, & Beilock, 2016). To help students who think of themselves as failures in mathematics, we have to focus as much on their effort to find a strategy to use to solve a mathematics problem as we do on the solution itself.

Get Students' Attention—And Keep Them Interested

Many students are not intrinsically motivated to learn mathematics, even if they have been successful or even moderately successful in the past. In addition to helping those who believe they are not good at math, you need to 1) capture all students' interest and 2) keep their interest so that they are motivated to learn more. Capturing students' interest involves finding creative ways to establish the relevance of what you are teaching to their life, their families' lives, and their future. Certainly, not all topics are immediately relevant to the life of school-age students. There are, however, ample examples of ways in which mathematical concepts can be illustrated using topics that are of interest to your students. There are lots of engaging hands-on tools (i.e., manipulatives) that students can use to learn about mathematics concepts and procedures. For every hands-on tool, there is likely a virtual tool that can be used on tablets or computers. For example, instead of utilizing a real geoboard with rubber bands flying around the classroom, there are several free geoboard apps that can be downloaded and used for free. The National Library of Virtual Manipulatives (http://nlvm.usu.edu/) is a great web site to find hundreds of virtual mathematics tools. In addition, there are also many excellent videos about mathematics topics, and many of these videos have interesting characters and memorable songs.

Not all mathematics instruction needs to be immediately relevant. Sometimes it helps to be honest with your students about the importance of learning to reason mathematically so that it will help them solve problems in the future. In addition, sometimes it is important to let your students know that what you are teaching them is a tool that can be used later to solve important problems. In our experience, striving for relevance is very important, but when we contrive relevance, students tend to see through our efforts, and motivation is once again a problem.

Beyond ensuring that students see how mathematics can help them think about their world and about when it can be useful, keep in mind that you are more likely to maintain students' interest when they perceive themselves being successful with the content. This means that you need to be sure that they are mastering the knowledge and skills taught and used in your classroom and that they are moving at a pace and with the types of supports necessary to be successful. Both content mastery and pace of instruction will be discussed a bit later in this chapter.

Build a Mastery-Oriented Classroom Culture

By about the second grade, students are becoming increasingly motivated by getting the "right" answer, competing with their peers, and using their speed and accuracy to compare one to another. Some researchers have referred to this as an ego-oriented approach to learning (Meece, Blumenfeld, & Hoyle, 1988; Schenke, Ruzek, Lam, Karabenick, & Eccles, 2018). We have two concerns with encouraging this type of orientation to mathematics learning. First, if one person is rewarded continuously for being "right" and "fast," all others in the classroom perceive themselves as being less worthy than the student who finishes first. Research suggests that by about fourth grade, if students have been taught in a consistent environment of competitiveness, they begin to hide their errors and not share their ideas about how to solve problems (Ashcraft & Moore, 2009). Unfortunately, this is about the time that mathematics gets both complicated and interesting, and teachers may have given many students the impression that they are not going to be able to keep pace with the best students in class.

Consider the two approaches to teaching the same content in a sixth-grade mathematics classroom—ego-oriented and mastery-oriented—shown in Figure 4.2.

Rather than encourage a competitive approach to learning mathematics in which someone (perhaps most everyone) loses, we recommend encouraging students to

Ego-Oriented Classroom	Mastery-Oriented Classroom
WHAT IT LOOKS LIKE	
• Focuses on total number correct • Provides feedback based on the final answer • Emphasizes learning as an individual process	• Focuses on students' reasoning • Provides feedback based on students' thought process • Emphasizes learning as a collaborative process
WHAT IT SOUNDS LIKE	
• "What did you get for this problem?" • "Check your answers with a partner." • "You did not simplify the fraction correctly." • "Try to do as many problems as you can."	• "How did you approach solving this problem?" • "Compare with a partner how you solved the problem." • "You did a great job finding equivalent fractions. Share how you simplified the fraction." • "Try to come up with innovative ways to solve these problems."

Figure 4.2. Comparison of ego-oriented and mastery-oriented classrooms.

collaborate in solving problems, sharing solution strategies, and providing feedback on the process for finding a solution rather than on the solution itself. The mastery-oriented approach shown on the right in Figure 4.2 supports students' efforts to persevere at a problem, considering it from multiple perspectives and trying multiple ways to get at a solution. It also encourages students to look carefully at their reasoning for approaching mathematical problems in a particular way and whether that reasoning is mathematically lawful (Cerasoli & Ford, 2014).

Does this mean that you shouldn't have any competition in the classroom? On the contrary, we believe there is room for healthy competition in mathematics classrooms. In fact, we all have memories of competitions in school where we worked hard as a group to learn new ideas and how to apply them. We would suggest that you consider competition where students work in teams to use their mathematical knowledge and skills to solve important problems. Here are some guidelines to consider as you think about how to structure such competitive activities:

- Recognize groups that exhibit strong teamwork in addition to groups that find correct answers.

- Strategically arrange students so that all groups have an equal opportunity to "win."

- Emphasize the mathematical task and positive teamwork more than the reward.

- Choose rewards that are intangible (e.g., praise) instead of prizes that give "winners" a real advantage over "losers" (e.g., homework passes, extra time at recess).

- Limit the length of the competition to prevent groups from becoming discouraged over time.

- Change groups regularly so that students have the opportunity to work with other students and to prevent one group from winning repeatedly.

Motivation, as we have discussed it here, really involves both effort and interests. Research suggests that as students develop through the elementary years of school, they think differently about how to be successful academically (Park, Gunderson,

Tsukayama, Levine, & Beilock, 2016). Young children assume that if they work hard enough at something they'll be rewarded. As they grow older, they begin to shift that thinking and believe that their success is due, at least in part, to their ability. By about third grade, their domain-specific self-efficacy beliefs (i.e., whether they think they are good at a subject) significantly influence their decision to invest effort in the domain. In other words, students who believe they are good at mathematics are willing to invest more time in improving their knowledge and skill and vice versa (Simzar, Martinez, Rutherford, Domina, & Conley, 2015). Even more troubling is that those students with lower self-efficacy in the particular subject tend to use efforts that are not effective or efficient. For example, they often read and reread a page or problem without developing a plan or they stare at the problem, unsure about what steps to take to solve it.

As we have discussed, it is very important to understand each of your students' learning histories in order for you to determine what kind of motivational support you will need to provide. In general, we recommend an approach that emphasizes effort, provides feedback on that effort, and makes getting the correct answer a product of the effort. We also highly recommend that you strive to keep the mathematics you are teaching as relevant as possible to your students. As we have noted, it is important to keep in mind that relevance can be too contrived. It's okay to tell your students that not everything seems relevant when you learn it and they will use these skills as they progress in mathematics. Finally, when you know your students' learning histories in mathematics, it will be critical to tailor your feedback to their needs. Encouraging them to self-assess, providing incremental and regular positive feedback on their effort to solve problems, and developing their own sense of positive self-efficacy in mathematics is part of effective instruction.

INTRODUCE IDEAS PRECISELY AND ACCURATELY

Mathematics is a tool and a language that allows us to model natural phenomena in our world using numbers and symbols that we can communicate to others. These tools and language have been developed over centuries and have precise meanings. It is important to keep in mind as we teach mathematics to our students that we need to ensure their future success by assuring that their mathematics knowledge and skills reflect the precision and lawfulness of the domain.

Specific steps teachers can take toward this goal include the following:

1. Strengthen our own knowledge of mathematical ideas.

2. Build students' knowledge on a strong foundation of conceptual understanding and procedural fluency.

3. Develop powerful models (concrete, pictorial or visual representation, and abstract).

4. Use precise but developmentally appropriate vocabulary.

These steps are discussed in detail in the subsections that follow.

Strengthen Our Own Knowledge

Given our busy schedules, it is easy to forget that the quality of our teaching depends on the strength of our own knowledge. Mathematics is a very complicated domain; even what we consider basic skills such as simple operations can involve challenging ideas. Let's try an exercise to make this point clear, and let's think briefly about

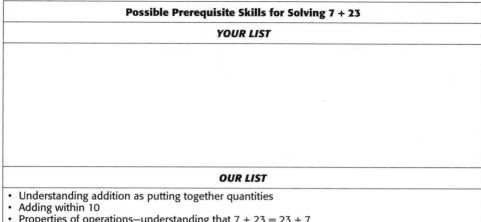

Possible Prerequisite Skills for Solving 7 + 23
YOUR LIST
OUR LIST
• Understanding addition as putting together quantities • Adding within 10 • Properties of operations—understanding that 7 + 23 = 23 + 7 • Recognizing a number as groups of tens and ones • Symbolic notation for addition • Composing and decomposing numbers—recognizing 7 + 23 = (7 + 3) + 20 • Regrouping 10 ones for 1 ten

Figure 4.3. Prerequisite skills for adding.

elementary mathematics. Look at the top part of Figure 4.3. Without looking at the bottom half, make a list of all the things we need to know to fully understand how to find the sum of 7 and 23 (an expectation of students in second grade according to the CCSS-M). Once you've created your list, compare it to our list that we developed.

This is a simple illustration of why it is essential that, as teachers, we continue to expand what we know about mathematics. This may seem daunting, but many resources can assist us in deepening our understanding of core concepts and principles that we need to know when we teach. These resources help us plan our instruction and can also help us think through the layers of knowledge and skills that are prerequisites to understanding what we are teaching. That way, if a student is struggling with an idea, we are more likely going to be able to pinpoint how to support them in overcoming their obstacles to learning.

One of our favorite resources is a textbook about teaching mathematics that is used in a number of preservice teacher preparation programs: *Elementary and Middle School Mathematics: Teaching Developmentally* (Van de Walle, Karp, & Bay-Williams, 2015). This book delves into mathematics topics with a heavy emphasis on the concepts of mathematics. There are many other excellent textbooks and books on the market. Many good publications come from the National Council of Teachers of Mathematics (NCTM; https://www.nctm.org), although some of these resources are more student-centered than designed for teacher learning. Other good resources include attending professional learning conferences, like the NCTM annual meeting or regional conferences; attending high-quality professional development organized by your school district or state; or completing online modules about effective mathematics teaching. The National Center on Intensive Intervention (https://intensiveintervention.org) has helpful modules about teaching mathematics to students with mathematics difficulty that may be of interest to many readers of this book. Nicole, district RTI coordinator interviewed in Chapter 17, also referenced the value of the IRIS Modules from Vanderbilt University for learning about evidence-based mathematics interventions.

Build Students' Knowledge on a Strong Foundation

There is common agreement that one source of difficulties students face as they move from grade to grade in mathematics is that they failed to develop a deep understanding of basic concepts and principles before they were expected to demonstrate computational fluency. The National Research Council, in the seminal text *Adding It Up* (2001), described conceptual understanding and procedural fluency as two of five interconnected strands of mathematical proficiency. *Conceptual understanding* involves the comprehension of mathematical concepts, operations, and relations. *Procedural fluency* is interpreted as skill in carrying out procedures with flexibility, accuracy, efficiency, and appropriateness. (For those of you keeping track at home, the other three strands of mathematical proficiency include strategic competence, adaptive reasoning, and productive disposition.) Note that both conceptual understanding and procedural fluency are also highlighted in the *Principles to Actions* of the NCTM (2014).

For students in the middle grades, strong mathematics performance depends on whether they had a solid foundation of instruction in whole number concepts. Let's use an example to illustrate how establishing a strong foundation can work. Consider the following algebraic expression:

$$\frac{2}{3}x\left(10 - 3y + 2\right) + 2xy$$

If we want students to be able to lawfully manipulate terms in an algebraic expression such as this in order to simplify it for use in solving a problem, there are many number concepts embedded in this work that will aid in their understanding. In Figure 4.4, we have worked through the simplification so that you can see the number concepts and properties that students need to understand in order to complete this task.

If you determine that your students are missing critical foundational information they need to understand and do the mathematics you are planning to teach, they will not benefit by moving forward with the grade-level content. The idea that mathematics is learned along a continuum was one of the reasons for the introduction of the CCSS-M. The standards provide a cohesive picture of mathematics learning across grade levels. Therefore, gaps in critical mathematics information will contribute to inadequate learning in later grades.

Develop Powerful Models

Contributing to students' strong conceptual understanding is the development of models, ways to illustrate how physical phenomena can be represented mathematically.

Step	Concept or property
$\frac{2}{3}x(10 - 3y + 2) + 2xy$	(Original expression)
$\frac{2}{3}x(12 - 3y) + 2xy$	Order of operations, commutative property of addition
$\frac{2}{3}x(12) + \frac{2}{3}x(-3y) + 2xy$	Distributive property
$8x - 2xy + 2xy$	Multiplying rational numbers
$8x$	Combining like terms

Figure 4.4. Concepts and properties related to algebra.

These models reinforce with students the fundamental idea that abstract mathematical expressions and symbols are a way to communicate about things that are real. There is a strong literature on the importance of using various models or representations of mathematics: concrete, pictorial, and abstract (Butler, Miller, Crehan, Babbitt, & Pierce, 2003; Witzel, 2005). Concrete models are hands-on tools or manipulatives that students can touch and move around. Pictorial models, or visual representations as they are often called, are two-dimensional images presented on paper or using virtual manipulatives. Abstract models involve solving mathematics problems with numbers and symbols, along with reading the words of mathematics.

One challenge with using concrete models in our teaching is that we want to find powerful models that reflect accurately what we are trying to teach. As teachers we find that we improve in our selection of powerful models with experience, so don't worry if you try one that doesn't work so well. Let's take a seventh-grade standard from the CCSS-M and determine a way to teach it using concrete models (see Figure 4.5).

Almost every time we teach something new to students in the middle grades, it is important to consider whether concrete models would benefit their conceptual understanding. In some cases, you may determine that you've developed students' understanding adequately to move on to modeling the mathematics abstractly using language, numbers, and symbols. However, it bears repeating, you may need to step back and use concrete models or visual representations if their understanding is not supporting their procedural fluency.

You might ask, "How would I know if students' understanding isn't sufficient to move forward?" Let's go back to the example in Figure 4.5 with finding equivalent expressions. Figure 4.6 lays out the same example with a series of questions that, when asked, would help you determine whether students understand why they can do what they are doing. You can see from the questions accompanying the model that this gives you lots of information about a student's understanding of the properties of number illustrated in this model.

Research recommends providing students with multiple representations (such as the blocks and balls from Figure 4.6). Multiple representations help students see mathematics in multiple ways and understand the concepts of mathematics at a deeper level. Many researchers and teachers call these multiple representations the Concrete, Representational, Abstract (CRA; Witzel, 2005) or the Concrete, Pictorial,

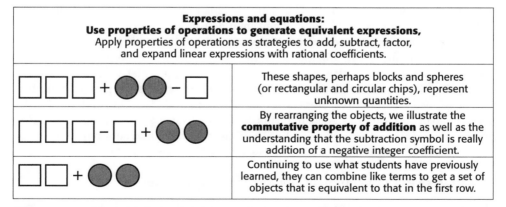

Figure 4.5. Concrete models for learning about expressions. (© Copyright 2010 National Governors Association Center for Best Practices and Council of Chief State School Officers. All rights reserved.)

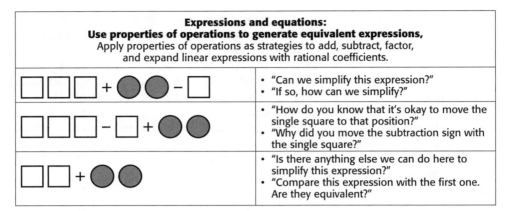

Figure 4.6. Questions to help students learn about expressions. (© Copyright 2010 National Governors Association Center for Best Practices and Council of Chief State School Officers. All rights reserved.)

Abstract (Miller & Hudson, 2006). In later chapters, we will refer to these as concrete models, visual representations, and abstract notation.

When using multiple representations, there is overlap among all the components of the concrete models, visual representations, and abstract notation (i.e., numerals, symbols). Also, there isn't a defined order (e.g., concrete, then visual representation, then abstract notation). In our intervention work, we realize that using multiple representations is kind of messy. Representations are used when necessary or sometimes not at all. Concrete models and visual representations should always be presented alongside the abstract notation. A concrete model may be used for a few days and then not used again for a week or two. The use of multiple representations depends upon each student's needs. (See Chapter 5 for more information about the use of multiple representations within effective mathematics instruction.)

As you consider enhancing the models you use for instruction, especially the concrete models and visual representations, here are a few planning guidelines. First, if you are introducing a new manipulative or virtual tool, such as Algeblocks or plastic clips, let students "play" with the tool for several minutes. This will give students time to make the log cabin (with Algeblocks) or necklace (with plastic clips) that they want to make before starting to use the "toys" as "math tools." Speaking of toys, although it is fine to allow a few minutes for students to explore the hands-on materials, do not call any hands-on materials "toys." They should be called "tools" or referred to with their proper name (e.g., "algebra tiles," "geoboards," or "polydrons").

Plan ahead for an organizational method for manipulatives or tablets. We often use a lot of plastic bags with an appropriate number of manipulatives in each bag. For example, students only need to have 18 AngLegs (i.e., different-sized plastic sticks that can be clipped together to create two-dimensional shapes) to do a quadrilateral activity instead of 100 AngLegs. Also, in terms of organization, develop a method for passing out materials and collecting materials. This way, your instructional time can be spent teaching mathematics instead of passing out the tools to learn mathematics.

Use Precise But Developmentally Appropriate Vocabulary

As human beings, we naturally communicate with words. The words we use and when we use them play an important role in our mathematics teaching. Only recently has

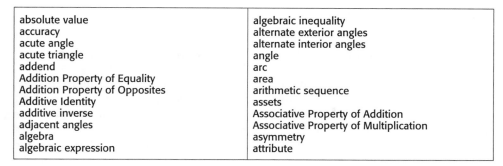

absolute value	algebraic inequality
accuracy	alternate exterior angles
acute angle	alternate interior angles
acute triangle	angle
addend	arc
Addition Property of Equality	area
Addition Property of Opposites	arithmetic sequence
Additive Identity	assets
additive inverse	Associative Property of Addition
adjacent angles	Associative Property of Multiplication
algebra	asymmetry
algebraic expression	attribute

Figure 4.7. Seventh-grade vocabulary terms that start with *a*.

academic vocabulary received the sort of attention it deserves (Schleppegrell, 2012). Unfortunately, there is very little research on specific practices that relate to teaching vocabulary in mathematics. There is, however, a substantial knowledge base about teaching vocabulary in other areas (Riccomini, Smith, Hughes, & Fries, 2015).

Perhaps one of the most important principles to keep in mind is to use words that are accurately applied to the relevant mathematics (Powell, Stevens, & Hughes, in press). In our experience, it is common to hear teachers refer to the "number on the bottom of a fraction" rather than the *denominator*. Likewise, frequently we hear teachers use euphemisms or slightly less accurate terms to describe particular mathematical ideas. For example, rather than using the term *measures of central tendency* to refer to mean, median, and mode, we have observed teachers repeatedly saying "mean, median, and mode." We believe using less than accurate terms or avoiding terms is a result of teachers' concerns that the difficult vocabulary actually contributes to students' difficulty with the mathematics. See Chapter 5 for more information about the importance of using precise mathematics vocabulary.

We believe that in most cases, mathematically accurate terminology actually supports student learning. For example, the term *measures of central tendency* actually tells the student what mean, median, and mode do in terms of summarizing data. The number of mathematics vocabulary terms that are included in middle school textbooks is typically around 500 different terms (Hughes, Powell, & Lee, in press). That's a lot of words! See Figure 4.7 for a list of seventh-grade terms that start with the letter *a*. Because there are so many terms, teachers have to be thoughtful about which words to introduce and how to reinforce their meanings in such a way that students will use them frequently and, therefore, increase the likelihood that they will use them in their mathematics discussions.

DISPEL COMMON MISUNDERSTANDINGS

Closely linked to the importance of strengthening our own knowledge of fundamental mathematics is the notion of mathematics knowledge for teaching (Hill, Rowan, & Ball, 2005). The idea here is that beyond just understanding mathematics, effective teachers need to know how mathematical thinking develops, where misconceptions start, and how to track back with a student to determine where the student's understanding went wrong. Typically, if we can account for students not being chronically absent, misunderstanding is a consequence of the student misperceiving something we teach or something they see us do. In the following subsection, we use an example about rational numbers to illustrate.

Example 1: Rational Numbers

It is common for students with mathematics difficulty, and even some who do not typically struggle, to perceive fractions as quantities rather than as *representations* of quantities. In addition, they often stipulate that fractions can only be quantities between whole numbers (Schumacher & Malone, 2017). So, to be more specific, they conceive of $\frac{1}{3}$ as a valid fraction because it is less than 1. However, they don't fully understand that $\frac{3}{3}$ or $\frac{9}{3}$ are also fractional representations of quantities. This misconception is not because they are unable to think of a quantity as having more than one name (way of representing it); after all, most of us have more than one name and, in some cases, additional nicknames. Rather, they struggle with the concept for several reasons.

First, students often are not taught the relationship between systems of numbers (Ni & Zhou, 2005). Figure 4.8 illustrates how whole numbers relate to rational numbers. Specifically, every whole number is a rational number; therefore, fractions and decimals can be used to represent the quantity typically represented by a whole number $\left(\text{e.g., } \frac{6}{3} \text{ or } \frac{9}{3}\right)$.

Second, we typically teach students that some representations are more valid than others. For example, in a recent conversation with a colleague, he insisted that we couldn't teach fraction operations $\left(\text{e.g., } \frac{3}{11} + \frac{15}{11} = \underline{\hspace{1cm}}\right)$ unless we used a mixed number $\left(\text{i.e., } 1\frac{4}{11}\right)$. This sends students the message that mixed numbers are somehow more valid representations of quantities than fractional representations where the numerator happens to be larger than the denominator. It also contributes to the misconception that whole number representations of a quantity (e.g., 3) are somehow more acceptable than an equivalent fractional representation $\left(\text{e.g., } \frac{45}{15}\right)$. Again, this misconception erodes mathematical thinking.

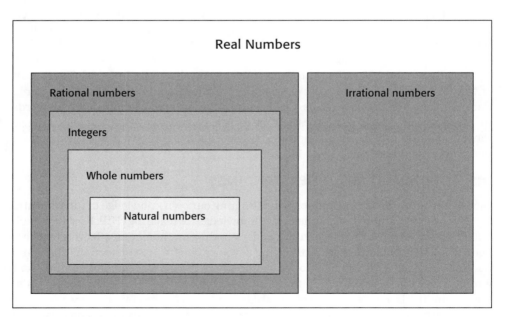

Figure 4.8. Relationships among real numbers.

Example 2: Proportional Reasoning

Let's try another example, this time discussing proportional reasoning. What often happens when we teach proportions is we demonstrate that we can solve for an unknown value in the proportion by cross multiplying. Consider the following problem:

Sarah runs 2 miles in 14 minutes. How many miles can she run in 21 minutes?

Typically, we would set up the solution strategy to this problem as a proportion:

$$\frac{2}{14} = \frac{x}{21}$$

Now, if we have taught students the process for solving for the unknown quantity and have students practice this while adequately discussing why it is mathematically lawful to take each step, the shortcut to cross multiplication becomes obvious. In addition, efficiencies like cross multiplication—that have developed to speed up our computation—need to make sense to us and to our students, not be mysterious. These mysteries and misconceptions lie at the heart of ineffective instruction.

ENGAGE STUDENTS FOR FUTURE PROBLEM SOLVING

One of the most important expectations of effective instruction is that it teaches students how to solve problems. The primary goal of mathematics instruction, of course, is to teach students to solve problems. Research over the past several years has provided lots of valuable evidence of how to effectively teach students to problem solve. We will discuss a specific part of problem solving—word-problem solving—in Chapter 6. For now, we focus on the big idea that effective mathematics instruction helps students reason and become problem solvers in mathematics (NCTM, 2014).

Historically, many of us were taught all the tools we needed to solve problems (e.g., mathematical concepts, language and symbols, and computation skills) but were not actually taught how to translate and represent problems mathematically or to reason, strategize, explain, and justify our approaches and our answers. Consequently, like many students in our classrooms today, we often didn't understand that problem solving required persistence and a willingness to try an approach that may or may not work. With few exceptions, the focus was only on the answer, and we were almost never asked to explain how we arrived at the answer or to justify our decisions. This approach has the tendency to give students the impression that the answer is more important than the process; this couldn't be further from the truth in school mathematics. The purpose of teaching problem solving is to build habits or dispositions in students to keep working at a problem until you solve it, not to find the answer.

MEET DIVERSE LEARNERS' NEEDS

Perhaps one of the greatest challenges in teaching is being able to accommodate the wide range of needs that students bring to our classrooms. This is likely one of the reasons that you are reading this book. Our classrooms have always been diverse; that is not a new phenomenon. What is new is that as teachers we are now held accountable for our students' performance as a way of determining the effectiveness of our instruction (e.g., Every Student Succeeds Act of 2015, PL 114-95). Now everyone knows when our students are not achieving the learning objectives. Recent research on meeting the needs of struggling learners as well as high achievers in the classroom provides important guidance on how to determine the teaching practices that will enhance our effectiveness in teaching mathematics. Gersten, Chard et al. (2009) suggest the following, based on their analysis of research about students with mathematics difficulties. These recommendations form much of the content of this book:

- Screen all students to identify those at risk for potential mathematics difficulties (see Chapter 10). Provide interventions to students identified as at risk.

- Instructional materials for intervention should focus intensely on in-depth learning of whole numbers (through grade 5) and rational numbers (in grades 4 through 8).

- Instruction during intervention should be explicit and systematic (see Chapter 5). This includes providing models of proficient problem solving (see Chapter 6), verbalization of thought processes, guided practice, corrective feedback, and frequent cumulative review.

- Interventions should include instruction on solving word problems that is based on common underlying structures (see Chapter 6).

- Intervention materials should include opportunities for students to work with visual representations (see Chapter 5). Interventionists should be proficient in the use of visual representation of mathematical ideas.

- Interventions should devote time in each session to building fluency retrieval of basic arithmetic facts (see Chapter 5).

- Students' progress should be monitored (see Chapter 11).

- Interventions should include motivational strategies (see Chapter 5).

The topic of meeting the needs of diverse learners extends beyond one teacher's classroom. In Section III, we discuss how to integrate the findings from your assessments to determine what instructional design decisions you need to make in order to meet the needs of all learners. In Chapter 15, we'll discuss how a school can create a system of instructional supports that will maximize the instructional effectiveness in your classroom and across the school.

SUMMARY: CORE INSTRUCTIONAL AIMS

In this chapter, we focused on the aims of providing effective instruction. Effective instruction needs to accomplish multiple aims. It must motivate students, and to do so, teachers must address students' negative beliefs about mathematics, get and keep students' interest, and strive to build a mastery-oriented classroom culture. Another aim of effective instruction is to introduce mathematics ideas precisely and accurately, which requires teachers to strengthen their own knowledge base as well as that of their students, develop powerful models, and make thoughtful use of mathematics vocabulary. Effective instruction also aims to dispel students' common misunderstandings and build the skills and engagement needed for future problem solving—all while also meeting diverse learners' varied needs. In the next few chapters related to instruction, we dive deeper into many of these ideas.

CHAPTER 5

Evidence-Based Practices for Instruction and Intervention

In this chapter, we focus on recommended evidence-based practices that support students with learning difficulties during mathematics instruction that is provided within an MTSS framework. If students require additional mathematics support through MTSS, it is necessary for your instruction to rely on interventions or strategies that have an evidence base. We answer the following questions:

- What are the different settings for mathematics instruction within MTSS?

- What does the research say about effective mathematics instruction?

- How is explicit instruction used in an MTSS framework?

- How can multiple representations enhance mathematics instruction?

- Why is it important to use precise and concise mathematical language?

- How should procedural fluency be incorporated into mathematics intervention?

- Why is it important to consider a motivational component within intervention?

SETTINGS OF MATHEMATICS INSTRUCTION

Students with learning difficulties often receive mathematics instruction in two settings: the general education classroom and small-group intervention outside the general education setting. Chapter 2 described in detail the settings, instruction, and assessment used within the MTSS framework. To briefly recap, the majority of students receive Tier 1 instruction or primary prevention within the general education classroom. General education teachers provide whole-class mathematics instruction, ideally using evidence-based practices, that follows a scope and sequence designed to help students meet end-of-year grade-level mathematics expectations. They may provide additional small-group or individual instruction and may also utilize technology to differentiate instruction. All students should be screened in order to identify which students may need additional support (Johnson & Smith, 2011). (See Chapter 10 for more about universal screeners in mathematics.)

When results from universal screeners identify students who may be at risk (i.e., those who are not on track to meet grade-level expectations), these students often require systematic supplementary instructional support that goes beyond differentiated instruction. The first line of support, often called Tier 2 or secondary prevention, is provided in small groups—sometimes within the general education classroom, but more often in a separate, quieter setting elsewhere in the school—and students with similar mathematics needs are grouped together. Tier 2 is most effective when provided by a teacher with a strong understanding of mathematical concepts who can explain mathematics in different ways and make decisions about students' progress on an ongoing basis. Tier 2 instruction occurs regularly and often (e.g., three times a week for 30 minutes each session). If students do not show adequate response (i.e., do not demonstrate adequate growth or meet end levels of performance), schools may utilize a more intensive intervention, referred to as Tier 3 or tertiary prevention, provided within small groups of students with similar needs or to individual students.

It is important in both Tier 2 and Tier 3 instruction that the mathematics instruction is not more of the same kind of instruction that was delivered in Tier 1. If students are having difficulty learning mathematics concepts and procedures taught in Tier 1 and struggling to make adequate progress, then Tier 2 and Tier 3 intervention should be substantially different in terms of the quality and quantity of instruction provided. At these tiers, students require teachers who can appropriately model mathematics concepts and procedures, explain them in different ways, and provide remediation when necessary. In this chapter, we focus on evidence-based practices for Tier 2 and Tier 3 intervention that have emerged from the research as being beneficial for students with learning difficulties. This is by no means a comprehensive list. Instead, we focus on the evidence-based practices that have been demonstrated time and time again to be helpful for students with learning difficulties.

WHAT WORKS

To understand which evidence-based practices are important to emphasize in Tier 2 or Tier 3, we synthesized the research conducted by notable researchers on what works best for middle school students with learning difficulties. We briefly review the research in the next two subsections.

Synthesis of Tier 2 and 3 Interventions

In our synthesis, we examined the effects of mathematics interventions conducted across 25 years of research. We conducted a systematic search of the literature for students, and we located eight studies that targeted middle school students with learning difficulties in grades 6 through 8 (Stevens, Rodgers, & Powell, 2018). Across these studies, conducted between 1990 and 2015, the participants included students identified with a mathematics disability (i.e., a school-identified learning disability) or mathematics difficulty. The participants were identified as having mathematics difficulty if 1) teachers or administrators determined students needed intervention to address mathematics performance deficits, 2) students had mathematics goals on their IEPs, or 3) students performed below the 40th percentile on a mathematics assessment. Overall, 311 participants were included in these studies, with a range of 6–89 participants per study and a mean of 39 students.

Within the interventions provided to the students with learning difficulties, two focused on improving outcomes related to operations (i.e., addition, subtraction, multiplication, and division; Manalo, Bunnell, & Stillman, 2000). In one study, students learned to use stories and mnemonics to learn procedures for computation.

In the other, a teacher used explicit instruction (i.e., the teacher demonstrated steps to solve a computation problem, students imitated those steps, and then students practiced independently). Students in both studies demonstrated improved computation scores when compared to students who did not receive the intervention after receiving instruction for 6 or 8 weeks. These findings suggest that teachers should provide explicit instruction with strategies when students experience difficulty with computation.

Four interventions focused on improving outcomes for word-problem solving (Bottge, 1999; Bottge, Rueda, LaRoque, Serlin, & Kwon, 2007; Walker & Poteet, 1990; Xin, Jitendra, & Deatline-Buchman, 2005). In two of the studies, students worked in small groups to solve word problems presented in a contextualized, video-based format. This instruction, rooted in problem-based learning, was compared to business-as-usual word-problem-solving instruction in which students solved textbook word problems using a standard approach (i.e., read the problem, paraphrase, visualize, hypothesize, estimate, compute, and check your work). Another study compared word-problem-solving instruction using representations (i.e., graphic organizers) to a more traditional approach emphasizing keywords. The final study examined word-problem instruction rooted in understanding word-problem schemas versus general word-problem strategies. (See Chapter 6 for more detailed information about problem-solving schemas). Students in both groups used a problem-solving approach (i.e., read the problem, draw a picture to represent the problem, solve, and check), but the schema-based group also learned to identify a specific word-problem structure and use that structure in their world-problem representation and solution. Across all four studies, students who received the specialized problem-solving interventions outperformed those receiving standard word-problem-solving instruction or business-as-usual instruction on researcher-developed measures of problem solving.

Finally, two studies investigated fraction interventions (Butler, Miller, Crehan, Babbitt, & Pierce, 2003; Scarlato & Burr, 2002). One study compared equivalent fraction instruction using a Concrete, Representational, Abstract (CRA) sequence to instruction that used only a Representational, Abstract (RA) sequence. Both groups received explicit instruction in identifying equivalent fractions, but the CRA group learned about fraction equivalence initially using concrete models or manipulatives. The students in the CRA group performed better on fraction outcomes than those in the RA group. Please note, we refer to CRA as using multiple representations. In the other study, students received explicit instruction about fractions and decimals (i.e., modeling, guided, and independent practice with corrective feedback) compared to students receiving instruction from a traditional textbook. Students receiving the specialized fraction instruction outperformed students not receiving such instruction.

Across studies, students received instruction from a special education teacher or a researcher. This suggests school-based personnel can effectively implement focused math interventions. Seven of the studies provided between 5 and 25 sessions, with a range of 2.1 to 23.3 total hours of intervention; one study, however, provided an extensive intervention of 100 sessions for a total of 75 hours of instruction. Five studies reported small-group instruction ranging from three to seven students, and two reported larger groups of more than eight students.

From this synthesis, we learned of common intervention features and practices that may benefit middle school students with learning difficulties in mathematics. First, students may benefit from systematic and explicit instruction, which uses effective teacher-guided modeling and gives students repeated opportunities for practice with high-quality feedback. We discuss explicit instruction in more detail later in this chapter. It is important that instruction emphasize conceptual understanding rather than focus solely on rules or procedures. For example, teachers might consider ways to present mathematics using multiple tools (e.g., video or CRA). Students may also benefit from instruction in problem-solving schemas, or word-problem types, so that students can approach problem solving with existing structures in mind. See Chapter 6 for more information about word-problem schemas.

Additional Research

In addition to our synthesis, other key studies and research guides have identified important instructional components necessary for teaching mathematics to middle school students with learning difficulties. For example, Gersten, Chard et al. (2009) identified explicit instruction as an essential component of effective mathematics instruction for students who are struggling. Another essential component was the use of visual representations, because representations help students understand mathematical concepts and procedures. Gersten, Chard and colleagues also suggested that teachers encouraged students to talk about mathematics in addition to teachers providing effective feedback to students.

Siegler et al. (2010) emphasized the following related to rational numbers content within mathematics instruction (i.e., fractions, decimals, percentages): First, students must understand sharing and proportionality. Students must interpret fractions as numbers and learn how fractions can be represented on a number line. Teachers must provide explicit instruction about why procedures for computation make sense. Finally, students must develop a conceptual understanding of problems related to ratio, rate, and proportions. Similarly, Star et al. (2015) identified important areas of mathematical content related to algebra. Teachers should use worked examples and help students understand the structure of algebra representations. Students should also be permitted to use different methods when solving algebraic problems.

In addition to individual research studies, practice guides put together by the Institute of Education Sciences (IES) provided a focus for intervention that is based on evidence. For example, Woodward et al. (2012) identified that both routine and nonroutine word problems need to be a focus of instruction. Teachers should also help students monitor and reflect during the problem-solving process (see Chapter 6 for more information on attack strategies). Students should use visual representations to represent word problems, and teachers should help students make sense of the notation that can be used to represent word problems (e.g., equations).

EVIDENCE-BASED PRACTICES

We used the information from our own research review, the reviews of others, and our experiences working with middle school teachers and students to compile a list of evidence-based interventions or practices with the strongest evidence for use in Tier 2 or Tier 3 intervention. An intervention or teaching practice that is evidence based has been demonstrated in scientific research to show consistent positive results for students who are similar to the ones receiving the intervention. Use of evidence-based interventions or practices is required by federal laws (Every Student Succeeds Act of 2015, PL 114-95; Individuals with Disabilities Education Improvement Act [IDEA] of 2004, PL 108-446). In this section, we describe evidence-based practices that are important in terms of delivery of Tier 2 or Tier 3 intervention (i.e., explicit instruction, using multiple representations, and using formal mathematical language). We also discuss evidence-based practices that should be incorporated within Tier 2 and Tier 3 interventions (i.e., fact and computational fluency activities, effective problem-solving instruction, and motivational tools).

Use Explicit Instruction

We start with explicit instruction, which is often described as the core of effective mathematics instruction for students with learning difficulties (Hudson, Miller, & Butler, 2006; Jitendra et al., 2018; Witzel, Mercer, & Miller, 2003). Explicit instruction may also be referred to as direct instruction. Note that there is a formalized program titled Direct Instruction (Stein, Carnine, & Dixon, 1998) and a broader instructional approach called direct instruction; our focus is on the instructional approach, which we will call explicit instruction. There are many interpretations of explicit instruction, so we will present our interpretation, but we realize that others may present slightly different models. Our interpretation aligns with recommendations from the National Center on Intensive Intervention (https://intensiveintervention.org). Figure 5.1 provides an outline of explicit instruction.

MODELING	PRACTICE
Clear explanation	Guided practice
Planned examples	Independent practice

during MODELING and PRACTICE

Ask high- and low-level questions

Elicit frequent responses

Provide immediate affirmative and corrective feedback

Maintain a brisk place

Figure 5.1. Explicit instruction outline.

There are two primary components to explicit instruction: modeling and practice. Modeling is conducted by you (the teacher), and practice is organized by you (the teacher). First, let's focus on modeling.

Modeling   Modeling happens when you provide a clear explanation of a mathematical concept or procedure. For example, you may model how to multiply fractions with fraction bars or how to solve a two-step linear equation. With the clear explanation, you use precise mathematics language and present information in a step-by-step fashion. As part of modeling, you have planned which example(s) to use. Examples may be open-ended, or you may use worked examples (i.e., previously solved problems). Within worked examples, you could use worked examples that are answered correctly or incorrectly. During modeling, you are doing the work and students are watching. Even though students are watching, the students are still active participants, as we describe in the next few paragraphs.

As modeling occurs, you must attend to the components listed at the bottom of Figure 5.1. That is, ask students a mix of high- and low-level questions during modeling. High-level questions encourage deeper thinking and reasoning. These questions often begin with "Why?" or "How?" or "Explain" or "Describe." Low-level questions require simpler answers and are helpful for checking procedural understanding. Examples of low-level questions may include, "What is 6 times 7?" or "If you add 2 to the left side of the equal sign, what do you have to do to the right side?" By asking a mix of questions, you can gauge student learning and understanding and ensure that all students are paying attention and on task. Asking different types of questions also supports active engagement.

Also during modeling, you elicit frequent responses. Our typical rule when designing interventions is to elicit student responses at least every 30 to 60 seconds. Responses may address the high- or low-level questions, but teachers also elicit responses when they ask students to make a thumbs-up or -down, write something on a whiteboard, draw something on a worksheet, update a vocabulary term on a word wall, provide a choral response, talk to a partner, solve a problem, or check the work of a problem. There are many response methods beyond the few listed here. When you are modeling, it is essential that students are participating—this is where the idea of eliciting frequent responses comes into play. If you have been modeling and talking for 60 seconds without involving students in the lesson in some manner, then students begin losing focus and less mathematical learning is occurring. In our experience, the combination of asking questions and eliciting frequent responses is often misunderstood within modeling. Some teachers believe that modeling is only teacher demonstration and teacher talk. This is not the case. Effective modeling is more of a dialogue between you and your students. Even though you are leading (i.e., modeling), the students are actively participating.

When students provide responses during modeling, you must provide specific affirmative and corrective feedback. This feedback should be provided immediately as often as possible. Affirmative feedback is more effective when students receive specific feedback about concepts or procedures. For example, "Yes! This problem compares the miles to hours" or "I like

> When designing and implementing interventions, teachers should elicit student responses at least every 30 to 60 seconds.

how you used the balance scale to solve that equation." Corrective feedback should not only communicate that the student made a mistake or misunderstood the task at hand, but should also provide specific information on how to complete the task correctly. One thing we sometimes see in schools is the teacher calling on another student to provide corrective feedback to a student who answered incorrectly. This makes the student with the mistake feel defeated and does not help that student. Instead, teachers should ask questions to understand the root of the mistake and provide modeling about correcting the mistake. You could say, "Tell me how you came to that that conclusion." or "Explain the steps you used to solve the problem." When pausing and focusing on a student's mistake, often other students learn from the mistake and correction as well. This also allows you to provide specific information about which steps the student performed correctly and which steps need to be revisited to correct the mistake.

Finally, during modeling, teachers should maintain a brisk pace. Organize the lesson in terms of materials and technology. Plan for seating arrangements and movement within the classroom prior to the start of the lesson. Be knowledgeable about the material and ready to provide effective modeling. When you teach at a brisk pace, students pay attention and focus on the instruction.

Here's an example of modeling from a teacher's lesson about multiplication of fractions. As you read the modeling, look for the elements discussed earlier: clear explanation with well-planned examples; a mix of high- and low-level questions; frequent opportunities for students to respond; affirmative and corrective feedback; and a brisk pace used throughout.

Teacher: Look at this problem. [Writes $\frac{1}{2} \times \frac{3}{5}$ via projector.]

Teacher: Let's read this problem together.

Students: One half times three fifths.

Teacher: Today, I want to talk about what multiplication means when we multiply fractions. In this problem, we are multiplying fractions. What symbol shows you that we are multiplying?

Students: The times sign or multiplication symbol.

Teacher: Yes. The multiplication symbol [points] indicates that we are going to multiply. When we multiply fractions, I interpret the problem as one half of three fifths. Say that with me.

Students: One half of three fifths.

Teacher: This problem is one half of three fifths. That means I will find one half of three fifths. Let me show you how this works. I'm going to find one half of three fifths. So, I show three fifths. What fraction?

Students: Three fifths.

Teacher: Who can come to the front and draw three fifths with the fraction bars?

Student: [Draws a whole divided into 5 equal parts; shades 3 parts. See Figure 5.2.]

Figure 5.2. Pictorial representation of three fifths.

Teacher:	So, we have three fifths. What fraction?
Students:	Three fifths.
Teacher:	Our multiplication problem asks us to find one half of three fifths. I can do this a few different ways. Let me show you one way. I can divide each one-fifth piece into halves and shade one half of each one-fifth piece. Watch me. To divide each one-fifth piece into half, I draw a line down the middle of each one-fifth piece. I do this for the shaded pieces and the nonshaded pieces. (See Figure 5.3.)
Teacher:	What did I do first?
Students:	Divide each one-fifth piece into halves by drawing a line down the middle of each one-fifth piece.
Teacher:	Now I have a fraction with a denominator of what? How many equal parts in the whole?
Student (Hui):	5!
Teacher:	Hui, tell me why you said 5.
Student (Hui):	I said 5 because the fraction is in fifths.
Teacher:	That's correct, Hui, the original fraction that we drew was in fifths. But after determining we need one half of each one-fifth piece, I divided each one-fifth piece into two equal parts. So now we have— count with me—
Student (Hui):	1, 2, 3, 4, 5, 6, 7, 8, 9, 10.
Teacher:	We have 10 equal parts. How many equal parts?
Students:	10.
Teacher:	Yes, we have a fraction with a denominator of 10. Three fifths is the same as six tenths. Now, I only need one half of each of the one-fifth pieces. I'll shade in one half of the first one-fifth piece. [Shades.] I'll shade one half of the second one-fifth piece. [Shades.] And, I'll shade one half of the third one-fifth piece. Explain what I just did.
Students:	You shaded one half of each one-fifth piece.

Figure 5.3. Pictorial representation of three fifths with each one-fifth piece divided in half.

Teacher: Why didn't I shade these two one-fifth pieces? [Points to one-fifth pieces not originally shaded.]

Students: Because those pieces aren't part of the fraction three fifths.

Teacher: Yes! We were focused on finding one half of three fifths, not one half of five fifths. That would be a different problem.

Teacher: So, how many pieces did I shade? Let's count together.

Students: 1, 2, 3.

Teacher: I shaded 3 parts of . . . what's the denominator again?

Students: 10.

Teacher: The denominator is 10. So, one half of three fifths equals three tenths. Let's say that together.

Students: One half of three fifths equals three tenths.

Notice in this example that the teacher provides a clear explanation of multiplication with fractions. The example ($\frac{1}{2} \times \frac{3}{5}$) was determined before the lesson. During the modeling, the teacher is leading the conversation with the students and requiring students to respond frequently. The teacher asks lower-level questions, but higher-level questions are interspersed with the content. When a student responded incorrectly, the teacher took time to help the student understand the mistake and correct it. In addition, although it is not easy to interpret in reading the teacher and student dialogue, this lesson is organized and moving along at a brisk pace.

Practice The other primary component to explicit instruction is practice. During practice, students are provided with multiple opportunities to practice the mathematics concepts or procedures that were modeled by the teacher. Guided practice is practice in which you and your students practice together. That is, you work through a problem alongside your students; they are solving the same problem you are working on. This scaffolded support helps students with learning difficulties and provides a gradual release of responsibility from modeling to independent practice. Guided practice is often best with a teacher and students, but it can also be conducted among small groups of students or pairs of students working together on the same problem.

Independent practice is practice that students do independently, but you continue to provide feedback and answer questions once students complete the task at hand. Independent practice helps show you whether students understand the mathematics concepts or procedures that were targeted by the lesson. As much as possible, it should be conducted under the teacher's supervision. Assigning independent practice as homework does not ensure that students are receiving the level of support necessary to understand or complete different problems.

Similar to modeling, you must attend to the components listed at the bottom of Figure 5.1. When students are engaged in guided and independent practice, continue to ask higher- and lower-level questions, elicit frequent responses, provide affirmative and corrective feedback, and move students along at a brisk pace. Effective practice continues as a dialogue between you and your students. Ineffective practice encourages students to work alone without your support.

To complete the picture of modeling and practice for the problem $\frac{1}{2} \times \frac{3}{5}$, a teacher would have likely modeled two or three additional problems. Then, the teacher would ask students to write a problem on their own paper or whiteboard as he or she wrote the same problem on the projector. Then, the teacher and students would simultaneously draw pictorial or visual representations of fractions to practice multiplication of fractions. Maybe the teacher and student would do three problems using guided practice. Finally, the teacher would encourage independent practice with another three problems. The problems would be presented via the projector; students would write the problems on their own paper or whiteboard, work on solving each problem, and receive teacher feedback.

Use Multiple Representations

Another evidence-based practice supported by research is the use of multiple representations. Figure 5.4 displays a graphic organizer related to the different types of representations. In this chapter, we describe multiple representations a little differently from the way in which representations are described in a sequence (e.g., Flores, Hinton, & Strozier, 2014; Witzel, Riccomini, & Schneider, 2008). We present a framework for multiple representations, in which the abstract, concrete, and pictorial forms of mathematics work together to help students understand mathematics at a deeper level.

The abstract form of mathematics is mathematics presented with numbers, symbols, and words. This is often how we view mathematics (e.g., 56 + 179 = 235). In many cases, the abstract form of mathematics is the student's destination, but teachers use the concrete and pictorial or visual representations to help students understand concepts and procedures. The concrete form of mathematics is mathematics using three-dimensional, hands-on materials to show different concepts and procedures. Hands-on materials may be formal manipulatives such as fraction

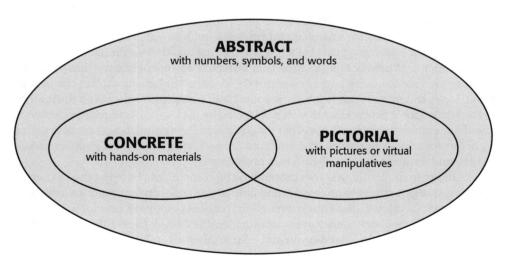

Figure 5.4. Multiple representations.

bars, algebra tiles, tangrams, geoboards, or two-color counters; they may also be less formal (e.g., straws for measurement, paper clips for place value, or shoeboxes for three-dimensional figures). The pictorial form of mathematics is mathematics represented with two-dimensional pictures or virtual manipulatives, and is often referred to in this book as visual representations. In many cases, the pictorial is called the representational, but because all three forms are representations, we will use pictorial or visual representations to describe this part of the multiple representations framework. Pictorial images may be presented within textbooks or workbooks or teacher and student drawings (see Figures 5.2 and 5.3). Pictorial representations may be graphic organizers that help students understand mathematics concepts (e.g., Jitendra & Star, 2012). The pictorial may also be presented with technology. There is likely a virtual manipulative for every hands-on manipulative that is used in classrooms, and many of these are free or provided at little cost. A geoboard can be represented with a concrete, hands-on tool, a virtual representation, or a pictorial representation provided on paper. Examples of the first two types of geoboards can easily be found through an online search. A pictorial example is shown in Figure 5.5.

Together, the concrete models and pictorial or visual representations help support explanation of mathematics concepts and procedures. When using the concrete models or the pictorial or visual representations, the abstract form of a problem should also be displayed and discussed. For example, if using algebra tiles to solve a one-step linear equation, you should also write an equation (e.g., $x + 4 = 10$) on the board. If encouraging students to draw fractions (similar to Figures 5.2 and 5.3), the abstract form of the problem (i.e., $\frac{1}{2} \times \frac{3}{5}$) should be displayed for all to see. The same would be true if using a digital geoboard to show how fractions and decimals are related (e.g., $\frac{3}{5}$ is the same as 0.60). The concrete model and pictorial or visual representation support students' conceptual understanding; as such, it is important that you use these representations in conjunction with the abstract notation so that students develop deeper understanding of mathematics rather than solely procedural understanding.

As mentioned, some researchers describe these multiple representations as being sequential (i.e., introduce the concrete, then the pictorial, then the abstract forms).

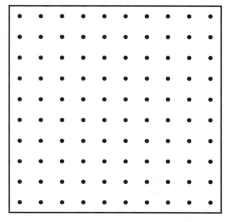

Figure 5.5. Pictorial representation of a geoboard.

In our work with students with learning difficulties, we observed that different students need different levels of support. Some students may need more practice with concrete models, whereas other students may not benefit from such exposure. In this way, we recommend designing instruction with the abstract notation in mind and using the concrete models and pictorial or visual representations to support deeper levels of understanding. Sometimes we use both the concrete and pictorial forms. In other cases, we use only one or neither. It all depends upon the students and their needs. Use of the three forms of representation can even change from small group to small group and year to year. If using the concrete and pictorial forms to emphasize the abstract form, teachers may need to intentionally fade the use of the concrete or pictorial forms so students do not come to rely on representations that may not always be available to them.

With multiple representations, it is important to note that you cannot provide different representations without using explicit instruction to explain and practice with the representations (van Garderen, Scheuermann, & Jackson, 2012). In this way, explicit instruction is essential for all mathematics instruction, including instruction that uses concrete models and pictorial or visual representations.

> Design instruction with the abstract in mind and use concrete and pictorial representations to support deeper levels of understanding.

Use Mathematical Language Thoughtfully

In addition to using explicit instruction and multiple representations, it is important to use formal, consistent, and concise mathematical language when teaching middle school students with learning difficulties. The complexity of mathematical language cannot be overestimated. For example, as we noted in the previous chapter, there are about 500 distinct mathematics terms that seventh-grade students are expected to know (Hughes, Powell & Lee, in press), including a couple of dozen terms for the letter *a* alone, such as *absolute value, accuracy,* and *acute angle*. Notice that many vocabulary terms include multiple words (e.g., *acute angle*). Students are not only interpreting one word; students are interpreting multiple words and making connections between words. What's more, the number of mathematics vocabulary terms that seventh-grade students are responsible for is likely even more than 500. The examples we just provided came from an analysis of several popular seventh-grade mathematics textbooks. However, students are also responsible for knowing vocabulary terms introduced at earlier grades that are not the focus of seventh-grade instruction (e.g., *above, addition, after, algorithm, alike, apex, approximate,* and others).

Mathematics vocabulary terms are problematic for students with learning difficulties for a number of reasons (Rubenstein & Thompson, 2002). First, many terms have multiple meanings in English, some of which are not mathematics-related. For example, a *foot* is 12 inches but students also have a *foot* on their body. Second, some terms have multiple meanings within mathematics (e.g., a number can be *squared* [4^2] and a shape can be *square*). Third, some mathematics terms, like *some* and *sum*, sound the same but have different meanings. This can be quite confusing when teachers are talking and students are learning from oral language. Fourth, some vocabulary terms have multiple meanings. Consider the term *base*, which can refer to the base of an exponent, the base of a three-dimensional shape, a base versus an acid in chemistry, or the bases in baseball. The term *degree* has multiple meanings within mathematics and outside of mathematics. It is easy to see how students become confused with mathematical language.

We recommend that you follow these four guidelines, further explained in the next subsections.

1. Use formal mathematics terms (i.e., rather than informal or catchy phrases).

2. Use similar or related terms correctly and precisely.

3. Plan for such language use prior to instruction.

4. Hold students accountable for using mathematical language correctly.

Use Formal Mathematical Terms

Let's consider first the importance of using formal mathematics terms. For example, you may ask students to solve an equation by writing the answer. Even though *answer* is a commonly used term and can be used when students solve a range of equations, the term does not represent the mathematical operations required to solve each equation. On the other hand, however, using the formal mathematics terms *sum, difference, product,* or *quotient* reinforces the calculations that students will perform to solve the problems, thus supporting the conceptual understanding of such terms. Furthermore, students will encounter the formal mathematics terms on high-stakes assessments; it is important for students to be exposed to these terms in preparation for such assessments. Consider another example related to fractions and decimals. You might refer to a fraction as having a *top number* and *bottom number*. This language may hinder students' understanding of fractions because it suggests a fraction consists of two separate numbers (i.e., top number and bottom number) rather one number. Instead, use the terms *numerator* and *denominator*, and expect students to use these terms regularly as well.

Use Similar or Related Terms Correctly and Precisely

In addition to formal mathematics terms, it is important for you to be precise and specific when using closely related mathematics terms (Powell, Stevens, & Hughes, 2019). For example, teachers may use the terms *factor* and *multiple* interchangeably, but these terms have distinct meanings. Using these terms interchangeably may cause confusion for students. *Factor* refers to all of the whole numbers by which you can divide a number with no remainder (e.g., the factors of 6 are 1, 2, 3, and 6), but *multiple* refers to the number obtained after multiplying 6 by another whole number (e.g., 6, 12, and 18 are multiples of 6). Each number has a fixed number of factors (i.e., there are four factors for the number 6), but many possible multiples (e.g., $6 \times 1 = 6, 6 \times 2 = 12, 6 \times 3 = 18$).

Plan for Language Use Prior to Instruction

Using formal, specific mathematics language is challenging; we recommend that teachers consider their language use (as well as students' language use) when planning for mathematics intervention within Tier 2 or 3. We have observed that teachers limit the mathematics language used within intervention or try to make the language easier (i.e., use informal mathematics language instead of precise mathematics vocabulary). You should use formal language but provide explicit instruction about the meaning of mathematics terms. You may also need to provide support about similar terms (e.g., *parallelogram, trapezoid, rhombus, rectangle, square,* and *kite*) and how the terms are the same and different. For Tier 2 and 3 instruction, we recommend that teachers focus mathematics language on terms that support conceptual understanding. The use of consistent and precise language will support students' long-term learning and mathematical understanding.

Hold Students Accountable for Using Mathematical Language Correctly

You also need to plan opportunities for students to speak and write about mathematics using proper mathematical language in addition to listening to the language of mathematics. Without practice with listening, speaking, writing, and reading in mathematics, students will not develop a strong lexicon of mathematics language. Most information about mathematics is gained through listening (i.e., listening to teachers or peers talking about mathematics) and reading (i.e., reading text online or in a textbook), whereas most learning occurs through speaking and writing. Learning mathematics concepts and procedures must be the focus of intervention, and language is a big part of this learning.

Practice Fluency With Facts and Computation

Explicit instruction, using multiple representations, and employing precise mathematical language are evidence-based practices necessary for the delivery of Tier 2 and Tier 3 instruction. In the next few sections, we highlight evidence-based strategies that should be used within these tiers. We focus on bolstering knowledge related to fluency and problem solving and the incorporation of a motivational component.

In our work with middle school teachers, one comment we hear time after time is that students with learning difficulties have trouble with mathematics because of a lack of fluency with facts or computation. There are 390 addition, subtraction, multiplication, and division facts that are foundational to much of mathematics. Figure 5.6 displays the different types of facts.

For students with learning difficulties, teachers should provide brief fact practice (if necessary) on a daily basis; 1 or 2 minutes a day is sufficient. Facts can and should be practiced using a variety of games, activities, songs, and worksheets. When practicing facts, it is helpful for students to monitor and graph their scores to see how their proficiency is improving. Facts can be practiced by operation (e.g., all multiplication facts), within families (e.g., $4 \times 6 = 24, 6 \times 4 = 24, 24 \div 4 = 6, 24 \div 6 = 4$), within combinations (e.g., $4 \times 0, 4 \times 1, 4 \times 2, 4 \times 3, 4 \times 4, 4 \times 5, 4 \times 6, 4 \times 7, 4 \times 8, 4 \times 9$), or in other ways. Students should receive focused practice with mathematics facts (i.e., by operation) and

Addition	Subtraction	Multiplication	Division
1–digit addends, 1– or 2–digit sum	1– or 2–digit minuend, 1–digit subtrahend, 1–digit difference	1–digit factors, 1– or 2–digit product	1– or 2–digit dividend, 1–digit divisor 1–digit quotient
$3 + 6 = 11$	$9 - 6 = 3$	$4 \times 6 = 24$	$56 \div 8 = 7$
5 + 3 8	14 − 7 7	1 × 6 6	5 5)25

Figure 5.6. Mathematics facts.

cumulative practice across mathematics facts (i.e., practicing all 390 facts—although never in one sitting!).

Beyond mathematics facts, students should develop fluency with computation (i.e., multidigit addition, subtraction, multiplication, or division). You can use explicit instruction to model and practice different computation algorithms. To develop fluency with whole number computation and rational-number computation, students must have a multitude of practice opportunities. With computational fluency, the goal is not memorization of answers but, rather, efficiency with computational procedures. If a student can add 144 + 396 in 20 seconds instead of 90 seconds, everything in mathematics will be that much easier for the student.

Fluency practice may also go beyond mathematics facts and computation. For example, we have observed teachers practicing fluency with generating multiples, which helps with determining common denominators between fractions. You may ask students to generate fractions equivalent to $\frac{1}{2}$, which would help with understanding benchmark fractions when comparing or ordering fractions. Students may develop fluency with adding, subtracting, multiplying, or dividing positive and negative integers. In a similar way, you may want students to develop fluency with solving one- and two-step linear equations or writing equations in slope-intercept form. Fluency with calculating area, volume, or surface area would help students with geometry and measurement.

Teach Problem Solving

In middle school, almost all students demonstrate mathematics knowledge through problem solving. That is, students read mathematics problems and answer questions posed in the problems. For students with learning difficulties, problem solving is often an overwhelming task because of the multiple steps necessary to solve problems. We dedicate Chapter 6 of this book to problem solving and how teachers can provide effective problem-solving instruction.

Include a Motivational Component

Although motivation is not directly related to mathematics, strong Tier 2 and Tier 3 interventions include a motivation component to keep students on task and motivated (Fuchs, Seethaler et al., 2008). We introduced the importance of incorporating motivational components into instruction in Chapter 4. Motivation components may involve tangible (e.g., prizes) or intangible (e.g., praise) rewards for students. In some interventions, you may use a motivation component that checks on student behavior at regular intervals (e.g., every 5 minutes) or irregular intervals (e.g., first 3 minutes, then 9 minutes, then 5 minutes). You may also utilize a motivational component that checks whether students complete each activity within an intervention session.

In our experiences, many teachers tie an existing motivational component already used within the classroom into Tier 2 or Tier 3 instruction. We do not have a preference as to the type of motivational component that a teacher uses. The most important thing is that a motivational component is in place so that students attend to mathematics learning and maximize the instruction provided within Tier 2 or 3.

SUMMARY: EVIDENCE-BASED INTERVENTION PRACTICES

In this chapter, we focused on several essential evidence-based practices related to mathematics instruction within Tier 2 or Tier 3. First, we focused on necessary components related to the delivery of Tier 2 or 3 instruction. We described explicit instruction as a combination of modeling and practice. We explained how during both modeling and practice, teachers need to ask a combination of high- and low-level questions, ask students to respond frequently, provide specific affirmative and corrective feedback, and move teaching along at a brisk pace. We then discussed the importance of using multiple representations to help students understand the abstract (i.e., numbers, symbols, and words) of mathematics. You should also focus on the language of mathematics and provide explicit instruction related to the hundreds of mathematics vocabulary terms that students may hear, see, or speak within mathematics. In addition to delivery components, we discussed strategies that should be embedded within effective Tier 2 and 3 instruction. That is, you should help students build fluency with both whole and rational number operations, provide effective problem-solving instruction, and include a component to help with student motivation.

CHAPTER 6

Instructional Practices to Support Problem Solving

In Chapter 5, we described effective instructional strategies that should be included within Tier 2 and Tier 3 mathematics instruction for students with learning difficulties. In this chapter, we focus on effective Tier 2 and Tier 3 instruction related to problem solving. We describe problem solving within a separate chapter because problem solving is how students show their mathematical competency and it is often an area of difficulty for many students with learning difficulties. In this chapter, we will answer the following questions:

- Why is problem solving an essential focus for Tier 2 and Tier 3 mathematics intervention?

- Why is an attack strategy useful and what are some examples of different attack strategies?

- What is a schema and how does it support problem solving?

- What are the additive schemas and how are these taught?

- What are the multiplicative schemas and how are these taught?

- Which ineffective problem-solving practices should you avoid?

OVERVIEW: PROBLEM SOLVING IN SCHOOLS

In middle schools, students are asked to demonstrate mathematics knowledge both formally (e.g., chapter tests, high-stakes assessments) and informally (e.g., exit slips, discussion, homework). In this chapter, we focus on standardized assessments and the types of problems they typically present. On chapter and unit tests, students often solve computation problems and word problems. On standardized summative assessments (e.g., state accountability tests), students almost exclusively solve word problems that require them to apply mathematical knowledge in real-world contexts. A word problem is a scenario presented with words and numbers in which students must interpret the prompt or question and provide a response. Because a word problem requires an understanding of reading and language along with the concepts and procedures of mathematics, many students have difficulty with solving word problems. This is especially true for middle school students with learning difficulties (Jitendra & Star, 2011; Krawec, Huang, Montague, Kressler, & de Alba, 2012; Xin et al., 2005).

Directive	Routine	Non-routine
Which expressions are equivalent to $3(2x - 2y)$?	A brownie recipe requires $\frac{1}{3}$ cup of sugar for every batch of brownies. How many batches of brownies can be made with 2 and $\frac{2}{3}$ cups of sugar?	Three containers have capacities of 2.5 gallons, 3.5 gallons, and 5 gallons. How can you use these three containers to measure exactly 9 gallons of water?
Rotate the shape 90° counter-clockwise around the origin.	On July 1, the value of a stock was $37.40. On July 31, the value of the stock changed by a gain of $12.75. What was the value of the stock at the end of July?	

Figure 6.1. Examples of directive, routine, and non-routine word problems.

Students are typically asked to solve three different types of word problems: directive, routine, and non-routine. See Figure 6.1 for examples of each type. In a directive problem, students are given directions to do or find something. Many directive word problems relate to algebra, geometry, or measurement. Most often, students solve routine word problems, which may involve one or two steps. Routine word problems present numbers within the problem (or within a chart or graph), and the prompt or question encourages the student to manipulate the numbers to answer it. Although less common, students may solve non-routine word problems. Non-routine problems usually have multiple answers or multiple ways to solve the problem. They involve creativity and thinking outside the box.

The majority of standardized summative assessments items are either directive or routine. We will focus on these two types of problems within this chapter, but many of the instructional strategies may be helpful in teaching students how to approach non-routine word problems, too.

EFFECTIVE PROBLEM-SOLVING STRATEGIES

Because of the importance placed on problem solving within middle school mathematics, a strong research base exists to help teachers understand how to provide effective word-problem instruction. First, students need to learn an attack strategy to help guide the process of problem solving (Jitendra & Star, 2012; Montague, 2008; Xin & Zhang, 2009). Second, students need to recognize and solve word problems according to the schema of the word problem (Jitendra, DiPipi, & Perron-Jones, 2002; Jitendra & Star, 2012; Van de Walle, Karp, & Bay-Williams, 2013; Xin & Zhang, 2009). As part of appropriate schema-based instruction, teachers need to use appropriate mathematical language to help students understand the mathematical meaning of words within each problem.

Attack Strategies

An *attack strategy* is an evidence-based practice that students can use to structure their thinking before and during the solving of a word problem. An attack strategy is grounded in metacognitive strategies and commonly uses a mnemonic or acronym so students can remember it easily. Attack strategies often include self-regulation components, whereby students ask themselves questions and monitor their performance as they solve a word problem. Attack strategies, in general, follow the outline of problem solving introduced by George Pólya (1945): understand, plan, carry out, and look back. Specific to students with learning difficulties, Montague (2008) outlined seven cognitive processes helpful for solving word problems: 1) read the problem, 2) put the problem into one's own words, 3) draw a schematic representation, 4) hypothesize or set a plan, 5) predict the answer, 6) solve, and 7) check.

Figure 6.2 provides sample attack strategies used in middle school. When selecting an attack strategy (and students only need one), choose one that should work with routine word problems and be helpful for attacking directive and non-routine word problems.

A frequently used attack strategy, adapted from Pólya (1945), is called UPSCheck. The students are led through the word problem by being asked to understand, plan,

Understand
Plan
Solve
Check

Adapted from Pólya (2009)

Find the problem
Organize information using a diagram
Plan to solve the problem
Solve the problem

Jitendra & Star (2012)

Search the word problem
Translate the words into an equation or picture
Answer the problem
Review the solution

Gagnon & Maccini (2001)

Detect the problem type
Organize the information using the conceptual model diagram
Transform the diagram into a math equation
Solve for the unknown quantity and check your answer

Xin & Zhang (2009)

Read (for understanding)
Paraphrase (your own words)
Visualize (a picture or diagram)
Hypothesize (a plan to solve the problem)
Estimate (predict the answer)
Compute (do the arithmetic)
Check (make sure everything is right)

Montague (2008)

Figure 6.2. Sample attack strategies. (*Sources:* From Pólya, G., & Conway, J. H. [2014]. *How to Solve It.* New York, NY: Ishi Press; adapted by permission. From Jitendra, A. K., & Star, J. R. [2011]. An exploratory study contrasting high- and low-achieving students' percent word problem solving. *Learning and Individual Differences,* 22, 151–158; reprinted by permission. From Joseph Calvin Gagnon, J. G., & Maccini, P. [2001]. Preparing students with disabilities for algebra. *Teaching Exceptional Children,* 34[1], 8–15; reprinted by permission. From Xin, Y. P., & Zhang, D. [2009]. Exploring a conceptual model-based approach to teaching situated in real word problems. *The Journal of Educational Research,* 102[6], 427–441; reprinted by permission. From Montague, M. [2008]. Self-regulation strategies to improve mathematical problem solving for students with learning disabilities. *Learning Disability Quarterly* 31[1], 37–44, reprinted by permission.)

solve, and check the answer. First, through teacher modeling and practice opportunities, students learn what it means to understand the problem. Understanding involves giving the problem a careful reading and asking, "What is the problem mostly talking about?" Next, students learn to plan. When planning, students focus on the underlying schema of the word problem (see the next subsection). After making a plan, students solve the problem using a computational strategy of their choosing. Lastly, students check their answer. Students use self-regulation skills to ask themselves, "Does this answer make sense, and why?" The other attack strategies presented in Figure 6.2 are also useable across the middle school grades. As with any attack strategy, students will need explicit instruction (i.e., teacher modeling and practice opportunities) to learn how to apply it to different word problems.

When problem solving is the focus of instruction, attack strategies must be modeled regularly and practiced by the students. An attack strategy poster displayed on the wall of the classroom is only helpful when you refer to such a poster during modeling and guided practice, and students utilize the attack strategy when solving problems. At some point, some students rely less on the attack strategy as the problem-solving process becomes ingrained and self-motivated. However, until all students in your class understand and use the attack strategy, you should continue to model and use the attack strategy during instruction.

Focus on Schemas

A *schema* is a framework for solving a word problem (Powell, 2011). Many students with learning difficulties have trouble setting up and solving word problems. Students have a hard time identifying the relevant information necessary for solving the problem (Krawec, 2014). Students also have difficulty selecting the operation to use for computation or performing the computation (Kingsdorf & Krawec, 2014). To alleviate some of these difficulties, Tier 2 and Tier 3 instruction should emphasize schemas for solving word problems. Teachers can help students focus on the underlying schema of a word problem and provide practice identifying relevant information, using equations and graphic organizers to organize that information, and solving the problems. In the next two subsections, we provide an overview of additive and multiplicative schemas used within middle school.

In schema instruction, students are taught to recognize a given word problem as belonging to a schema (i.e., problem type) and employ strategies to solve that word-problem type. Research on schema instruction has highlighted the benefit of teaching this strategy to students with learning difficulties (Fuchs, Fuchs, & Prentice, 2004; Fuchs, Seethaler, et al., 2008; Jitendra, Griffin, Haria, et al., 2007). In traditional word-problem solving, students may be taught to identify key words to solve word problems. Often, however, students scan for key words only and do not understand the problem's underlying structure (Griffin & Jitendra, 2009). Surprisingly, almost all routine word problems that students see and solve in elementary and middle school fall into one of seven different schemas: total, difference, change, equal groups, comparison, ratios or proportions, or combinations. In the next few sections, we explore these schemas in greater depth. We start first by exploring additive schemas.

Additive Schemas   The three additive word-problem schemas include total, difference, and change. Additive schemas involve word problems in which addition or subtraction may be used for solving the problem. The operation, however, does not

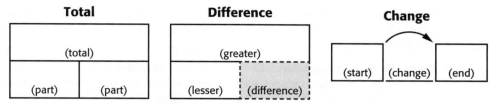

Figure 6.3. Additive graphic organizers.

define the word problem—the schema does. For each of the following additive schemas, we discuss the definition, provide sample equations and graphic organizers that help organize the information, and supply examples of each schema. See Figure 6.3 for examples of the additive graphic organizers.

Total   In total problems, two or more separate parts are combined for a sum or total (Kintsch & Greeno, 1985; Fuchs et al., 2014). Total problems may also be referred to as combine or part-part-whole problems. They require an understanding of part–whole relationships (i.e., the whole is equal to the sum of the parts; Jitendra, Griffin, Deatline-Buchman, & Sczesniak, 2007). In total problems, the unknown may be the total or one of the parts. After determining that a word problem adheres to the total schema, it is helpful for students to use an equation (e.g., P1 + P2 = T) or graphic organizer to organize word-problem information. In some total problems, there may be more than two parts, which means an adjustment of the equation (i.e., P1 + P2 + P3 = T). Determining how to translate the numbers from the word problem and use them appropriately is often difficult for students with learning difficulties; therefore, an equation or graphic organizer helps make this task easier. Figure 6.4 shows an example of a total problem. In this example, the student underlined the focus of the problem (i.e., yards). The student also crossed out the irrelevant information. After determining that this was a total problem because the question asks about the total number of yards of ribbon that Mona bought, the student wrote a total equation (i.e., P1 + P2 = T) to organize the numbers from the word problem. The student then identified P1 as $\frac{1}{3}$ and P2 as $\frac{3}{4}$. The student used a question mark to represent the unknown. In this example, the unknown was the total. The student then added to determine the total as 1 and $\frac{1}{12}$. Finally, the student labeled or added units to the numeric answer.

Mona bought $\frac{1}{3}$ of a yard of red ribbon and $\frac{3}{4}$ of a yard of blue ribbon. ~~She also bought 12 buttons.~~
How many <u>yards</u> of ribbon did Mona buy?

$$P1 + P2 = T$$

$$\frac{1}{3} + \frac{3}{4} = ?$$

$$? = 1\frac{1}{12} \text{ yards of ribbon}$$

Figure 6.4. Sample total problem.

Here is a sample dialogue of a teacher working with students in Tier 2 or Tier 3 instruction to solve the total problem in Figure 6.4. This dialogue also models using the UPSCheck attack strategy.

Teacher: Look at this problem. It's a mix of numbers and words—a word problem. Every time we see a word problem, let's use our attack strategy of UPSCheck. What strategy should we use?

Students: UPSCheck!

Teacher: The first part of UPSCheck is the *U. U* means we need to *understand* the problem. What does U stand for?

Students: Understand the problem.

Teacher: Let's understand the problem by reading it. "Mona bought one third of a yard of red ribbon and three fourths of a yard of blue ribbon. She also bought 12 buttons. How many yards of ribbon did Mona buy?" What do we have to find in this problem?

Students: The number of yards of ribbon that Mona bought.

Teacher: Yes! We have to find the total number of yards that Mona bought. Let's underline *yards* so we focus on the numbers that are about yards of ribbon.

Teacher: Now, let's focus on the *P* of UPSCheck. *P* means we need to make a plan. What do we need to do?

Students: Make a plan.

Teacher: Let's make a plan by determining the schema of the word problem. What type of problem is this?

Students: Total problem.

Teacher: Why is this a total problem?

Students: We have to combine the red ribbon and blue ribbon to find the total.

Teacher: Let's write our total equation to help us solve this total problem. The total equation is P1 plus P2 equals T.

Teacher: Now, let's do the *S* of UPSCheck. Let's *solve* the problem. What should we do?

Students: Solve the problem.

Teacher: Let's go back to the beginning and determine which numbers we need in our total equation. "Mona bought one third of a yard of red ribbon...." One third is a number. Is this a number we need to solve the problem?

Students: Yes!

Teacher: Does one third tell about one of the parts or the total?

Students: One of the parts.

Teacher:	One third tells us about one of the parts. Let's write one third under P1. Now, let's keep reading. ". . . and three fourths of a yard of blue ribbon." Three fourths is a number. Is this a number we need?
Students:	Yes.
Teacher:	Does three fourths tell about one of the parts or the total?
Students:	Parts!
Teacher:	Three fourths tells us about one of the other parts. Let's write three fourths under P2. Now let's keep reading. "She also bought 12 buttons." Twelve is a number. Do we need this number to solve the problem?
Students:	No.
Teacher:	Why don't we need 12 to solve the problem?
Students:	Twelve talks about buttons and not yards.
Teacher:	Great. Let's cross out 12 because it's irrelevant information.
Teacher:	Now, let's put in the signs and solve. What's one third plus three fourths?
Students:	One and one twelfth.
Teacher:	And what's a good label for that answer?
Students:	Yards of ribbon.
Teacher:	Finally, let's do the *check* of UPSCheck. Does that answer make sense? Why?

Difference　　In difference problems, students compare an amount that is greater and an amount that is less to find the difference. The unknown could be the amount that is greater, the amount that is less, or the difference. Difference problems can also be called compare problems. Several different equations can be used for difference problems. The first and most commonly used is: B – S = D, where B is the bigger amount, S is the smaller amount, and D is the difference (Fuchs et al., 2014). Another equation, however, is more aligned with how teachers discuss amounts in mathematics: G – L = D, where G is the greater amount, L is the lesser amount, and D is the difference. In addition to the difference equations, students could also use a difference graphic organizer (see Figure 6.3).

Figure 6.5 shows a worked example of a difference problem. This problem shows a graph that must be interpreted to solve the problem. Before starting with an attack strategy, the student labeled all the parts of the graph to make understanding the information easier. When students have to stop in the middle of solving a problem and determine amounts from a graph, it may leave more room for error. In this problem, the student determined that the problem was a difference problem and used the difference graphic organizer to organize the information from the word problem. Then, the student wrote an equation and used "M" to mark the unknown number of miles.

Change　　Change problems usually begin by presenting an initial quantity and then describe something that happens to increase or decrease that quantity. In change problems, the start amount, the change amount, or the end amount can be the unknown.

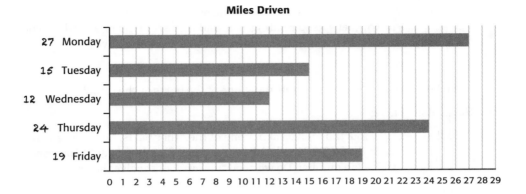

Miles Driven

How many <u>fewer miles</u> did Dan drive on Friday than Monday?

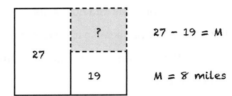

Figure 6.5. Sample difference problem.

A common change equation is ST ± C = E, where ST is the start amount, C is the change amount, and E is the end amount. See Figure 6.3 for a change graphic organizer.

Change problems have a few unique features. First, to solve the problem accurately, the student must determine whether the change amount increases or decreases the end quantity. For example, if the student is given the following word problem, he or she will need to decide whether the change amount increases or decreases the end quantity: *Jan had $42. Then, her dad gave her more money to go shopping. Now, Jan has $65. How much money did her dad give her?* In this example, the student would need to determine that the change amount increases the overall end amount in order to use the correct equation (e.g., ST + C = E). Also, change problems can include several change amounts within the problem that either increase or decrease the end quantity. For example, consider this problem: *Jan had $42. Then, her dad gave her $23. Jan then spent $50 on shoes. How much money does Jan have now?* In these cases, the change equation can be altered (e.g., ST + C – C = E). Figure 6.6 shows an example of a change problem.

Now that we have reviewed the three additive schemas, let us focus on the four multiplicative schemas most commonly seen in middle school.

Multiplicative Schemas   There are four multiplicative schemas that are common in problems in middle school mathematics: equal groups, comparison, ratios or proportions, and combinations. Multiplicative schemas involve word problems in which multiplication or division may be used to solve the problem. Just like the additive schemas, the operation (i.e., multiplication or division) does not describe the word problem; instead, the schema does. For each of the following multiplicative schemas, we provide the definition, sample graphic organizers, and sample worked examples.

In May, a tomato plant was 6.5 inches tall. By July, the tomato plant was 24.75 inches. How many <u>inches</u> did the tomato plant grow between May and July?

$$ST + C = E$$

$$6.5 + ? = 24.75$$

$$? = 31.25 \text{ inches}$$

Figure 6.6. Sample change problem.

Equal Groups   In equal groups problems, students have a group or unit that is multiplied by a specific number or rate to compute the product (Xin & Zhang, 2009). Equal groups problems may also be referred to as vary problems (Jitendra, DiPipi, & Perron-Jones, 2002). In equal groups problems, the unknown may be the groups or the unit, the number within each group or unit, or the product. The schema is still the same with groups or units. For example, an equal groups problem with groups and a number within each group would be *Molly buys 3 boxes of crayons with 12 crayons in each box.* An equal groups problem with units and rate would be *Molly buys 3 sweaters that cost $29 each.* See Figure 6.7 for a worked sample equal groups problem. In this problem, the student uses a graphic organizer to organize the equal groups information (Xin & Zhang, 2009).

The equal groups schema is typically introduced as students learn multiplication and division in the elementary grades. Similar to the additive problems, students use an attack strategy in combination with focusing on the word problem's schema. The attack strategy helps students work through the major steps of the word problem, whereas the schema helps students develop a deep understanding of the word problem.

Comparison   Another multiplicative schema is the comparison schema, in which a set is multiplied a number of times for a product. Comparison problems are introduced in the elementary grades after the equal groups schema and are regularly seen in late elementary school and into middle school. Most comparison problems require

Donuts are sold in boxes of 12. If Mr. Towler bought 72 donuts, how many <u>boxes</u> did he buy?

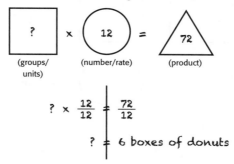

Figure 6.7. Sample equal groups problem.

Miguel made 9 baked goods. Nathan made twice as many. How many baked goods did Nathan make?

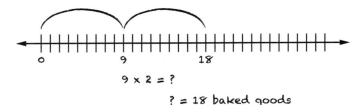

Figure 6.8. Sample comparison problem.

students to determine the product. Students can use a graphic organizer similar to the organizer used for equal groups problems or visualize the comparison of the original set on a number line. In Figure 6.8, the student used an open number line to focus on the set that is multiplied two times (i.e., twice).

Ratios or Proportions   In middle school, one of the most widely used schemas is for ratios or proportions. With word problems involving ratios or proportions, students identify the relationships among quantities. This schema can be used to solve word problems about ratios, proportions, percentages, or unit rate, and the unknown may be any part of the relationship.

In Figure 6.9, we present a typical ratios or proportions word problem using a graphic organizer from Jitendra and Star (2011). To solve this problem, the student uses an attack strategy to read the problem and make a plan, which is based on the schema (i.e., proportion) of the word problem. After the student draws the graphic organizer and fills in the important information, he or she may solve the problem using several methods. The student may identify the relationship between 15 and 45 (i.e., times 3) and apply this relationship to 4. Alternatively, the student could use cross multiplication and division.

A bus made 4 stops in 15 minutes. If the bus continues at this rate, how many stops will the bus make in 45 minutes?

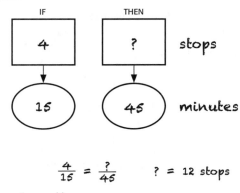

Figure 6.9. Sample proportions problem.

Dale Middle School has 440 students. The ratio of boys to girls is 3:5. How many <u>boys</u> are in the school?

$$\frac{3}{8} = \frac{?}{440} \qquad ? = 165 \text{ boys}$$

Figure 6.10.   Sample ratios problem.

In Figure 6.10, we show how the ratios or proportions schema is used in another way in middle school. In this problem, the student is presented with a ratio of 3 boys to 5 girls. The student learns to interpret this ratio as a fraction (i.e., 3 of every 8 students are boys). By translating the ratio to a fraction, the student can use a similar setup to the proportions problem solved in Figure 6.9. In this way, the ratios or proportions schema has a lot of flexibility that helps students solve complex word problems in middle school.

Combinations   A schema that is not as prevalent in middle school is the combinations schema. In a combinations problem, students are asked to determine the total number of combinations. For example, *Audrey has four skirts and five sweaters. How many combinations of outfits can she make with one skirt and one sweater?* Because the combinations schema is not used very often, we suggest that teachers focus more instructional time on the schemas that appear more often.

Multi-Step Problems

In middle school, students are often tasked with solving multi-step problems. These can be overwhelming for students with learning difficulties, but a strong understanding of word-problem schemas can alleviate frustration. To demonstrate how schema knowledge can aid in solving multi-step problems, look at Figure 6.11. To solve this problem, the student first uses an equal groups schema (shown with an equal groups equation of G [groups] × N [number in each group] = P [product]). This schema is used twice to calculate the price of the streamers and the price of the birthday hats. Then, the student uses the change schema to understand the change in Holly's amount of money. This is a change problem with multiple changes represented with the change equation of ST – C – C = E.

COMMON BUT INEFFECTIVE STRATEGIES

We conclude this chapter with a brief mention of two ineffective strategies that are often used to help students set up and solve word problems. Neither has an evidence base to support its use. The first ineffective strategy is the use of key words tied to operations. We often see key words posters hung in classrooms. These posters feature mathematics related key words (e.g., more, altogether, in all) connected to an operation (e.g., addition). The problem with this strategy is that students then play a seek-and-find game with word problems. Students look for a key word and then do the operation signaled by the key word without understanding the problem.

In some situations, key words will help a student solve a problem correctly. Consider the key word "altogether." *Maria raised $45 for her school's fundraiser. Colin raised $38. How much money did Maria and Colin raise altogether?* In this example,

Item	Cost
Streamers	$1.99
Hats	$2.49
Confetti	$0.99

Holly is having a birthday party. She buys 2 packages of streamers and 4 packages of hats. She pays with a $20.00 bill. How much money will Holly receive back?

$$G \times N = P \qquad\qquad G \times N = P$$

$$2 \times \$1.99 = ? \qquad\qquad 4 \times \$2.49 = ?$$

$$? = \$3.98 \text{ streamers} \qquad ? = \$9.96 \text{ hats}$$

$$ST - C - C = E$$

$$\$20.00 - \$3.98 - \$9.96 = ?$$

$$? = \$6.06$$

Figure 6.11. Sample multi-step problem.

the key word "altogether" signals the student to add the addends, which will result in the correct response. In other situations, however, the key word tied to an operation leads to an incorrect response. For example: *Maria and Colin raised $83 altogether for their school's fundraiser. If Maria raised $45, how much money did Colin raise?* With this example, adding 83 and 45 does not produce the correct answer. Also, key words related to one operation are often used in word problems with a different operation. For example, *Maria had 108 markers altogether. If she placed the markers in containers with 12 markers each, how many containers does Maria need?* A student relying on the key word strategy might see the word *altogether* and try to use addition to solve this problem, rather than using the appropriate operation, division. From a teaching perspective, it does not make sense to teach students a strategy that leads to incorrect responses.

The second ineffective strategy is defining word problems by the operation. Teachers often do this by telling students, "Today, we're solving division word problems." If this is the case, students do not need to read the word problem. All students need to do is divide the number that is greater by the number that is less. No reasoning is involved. We have also seen teachers present students with worksheets that are labeled with an operation at the top of the page. In the same way, no reasoning about the word problem is necessary. It is especially problematic to define word problems by operation because different students may solve problems using different solution strategies. For example, consider this problem: *Candace had 55 books and then she got a few more books for her birthday. Now, Candace has 62 books. How many books did Candace get for her birthday?* In this problem, some students may add (e.g., 55 plus what equals 62?) whereas other students may subtract (e.g., 62 minus 55 equals what?).

Neither approach is wrong. Teachers cannot describe this problem as an addition problem or subtraction problem. Instead, this is a change problem. There is a change in the number of Candace's books.

Instead of using key words tied to operations or defining word problems by operation, teachers should teach students to use an attack strategy and focus on schemas. By focusing on schemas, students learn how to understand the meaning of a word problem instead of having superficial methods (e.g., key words) for solving a word problem.

Ineffective problem-solving strategies not based on evidence:

- Using key words to indicate which operation to use
- Defining word problems by the operation used

SUMMARY: TEACHING PROBLEM SOLVING

In this chapter, we described effective evidence-based Tier 2 and Tier 3 instructional strategies focused on problem solving. Because students are expected to set up and solve word problems to demonstrate their mathematics competency, it is important to teach effective practices for solving problems in the middle school. In this chapter, we first described different types of word problems that students may be asked to solve. The two most common types of word problems on standardized summative assessments are directive and routine. Directive problems require students to do or find something, whereas routine problems require students to interpret and manipulate numbers within a word-problem scenario. For both types of word problems, students should have an attack strategy that helps them walk through the problem-solving process. For routine problems, students should be taught to recognize the schema of a word problem to help them understand the underlying structure of the word problem. Avoid strategies that are not based in evidence, such as using key words and defining word problems by operations.

CHAPTER 7

Designing Interventions

In the previous two chapters, we discussed the use of evidence-based practices within Tier 2 or 3 intervention. It is clear what evidence-based practices should be used when teaching students with learning difficulties. In this chapter, we focus on the design of interventions for use at Tier 2 or Tier 3. We describe considerations for the design of the entire intervention, resources for identification of interventions and strategies to address mathematical content, and design of a single lesson within an intervention. This chapter and the following chapter should be used in combination for designing and implementing effective intensive intervention. We answer the following questions in this chapter:

- What is essential mathematics content for middle school mathematics intervention?

- How do you design the scope and sequence of a Tier 2 or Tier 3 intervention?

- What are the differences among the terms *evidence-based practices, evidence-based interventions,* and *evidence-based strategies*?

- Where can you locate evidence-based practices?

- How do you incorporate evidence-based practices within the outline of a daily intervention lesson?

ESSENTIAL MATHEMATICS CONTENT FOR MIDDLE SCHOOL

Tier 2 and Tier 3 instruction should focus on the essential content for middle school mathematics. Important considerations for teachers designing a scope and sequence of intervention include the domains of mathematics that students must learn in each grade as well as with the continuum of learning across grade levels in middle school. These considerations and the process of designing a scope and sequence are described in the next subsections.

Domains of Mathematics Learning

Before designing a scope and sequence for Tier 2 or 3 intervention, it is necessary to understand the domains in which students are expected to demonstrate mathematics competency in the middle school grades. In this chapter, we talk about domains as outlined by the *Curriculum Focal Points* of the NCTM (2006).

In sixth grade, the domains include number and operations, algebra, geometry, and measurement. Primary areas of focus are related to number and operations as well as geometry. Students should develop an understanding of multiplication and division with both fractions and decimals, learn to connect ratio and rate to multiplication and division, and understand how to interpret and use both expressions and equations.

In seventh grade, the same four domains should be the focus of intervention. Within the targeted domains of number and operations and algebra, teachers should help students understand proportions and proportional relationships and help students use all four operations with rational numbers and for solving linear equations. With respect to geometry and measurement, students should learn how to use formulas to find the surface area and volume of different three-dimensional shapes.

In eighth grade, students should establish mathematical competency within five domains (number and operations, algebra, geometry, measurement, and data analysis). Competency involves representing linear functions and learning to solve linear equations and systems of equations. Students should analyze two- and three-dimensional space and figures with respect to both distance and angle. Also, students should work on analyzing and summarizing data to answer questions.

So across middle school, there are four domain areas in which students should develop mathematical proficiency: number and operations, algebra, geometry, and measurement. Why is this information important? Well, if these domains are foundational to understanding mathematics, then all mathematical content taught during Tier 2 or 3 intervention should focus on one or more of these domains. Prior to the development of the CCSS-M (National Governors Association Center for Best Practices & Council of Chief State School Officers, 2010) and the release of the Curriculum Focal Points (NCTM, 2006), the mathematical standards within the United States were described as encompassing a lot of breadth but little depth (Porter, McMaken, Hwang, & Yang, 2011).

Revised sets of content standards provide a stronger focus for intervention, but you need to provide an even more detailed focus within Tier 2 and Tier 3. Why is that important? Primarily because students with learning difficulties require not only instruction on middle school content standards but also remediation on elementary school content standards. You will probably need to go back and reteach mathematical concepts and procedures from the elementary grades in order for students to demonstrate success with middle grades mathematics content. Because Tier 2 and Tier 3 intervention often require a focus on content from previous grades and a student's current grade, teachers must be judicious and focus on essential mathematics content (e.g., content from the curriculum focal points).

Continuum of Mathematics Learning

Before developing a scope and sequence, first focus on the continuum of mathematics learning across grade levels. Some may call these progressions (https:// achievethecore.org/page/254/progressions-documents-for-the-common-core -state-standards-for-mathematics). A continuum of learning helps you understand what mathematical content, if any, may need to be reviewed or retaught before moving onto the mathematical content at a subsequent grade level. In the following subsections, we focus on the continuums of learning related to number and operations, algebra, geometry, and measurement in order to emphasize the importance of mathematics instruction within these domains.

Number and Operations   Foundational to all other domains of mathematics is number and operations. Students first develop an understanding of operations with whole numbers and then move to rational numbers (i.e., fractions, decimals, and percentages). In middle school, one important area related to number and operations is knowledge about computation of fractions, decimals, and percentages. Remember from Chapter 4, Gersten, Beckmann, and colleagues (2009) noted that intervention materials in the middle grades should focus intensely on rational numbers. In Figure 7.1, we provide a sample continuum related to computation with fractions going all the way back to third grade. We started with third grade because many middle school students with learning difficulties perform several grade levels below their current grade level.

To create Figure 7.1, we selected standards foundational to operations with rational numbers and how students develop knowledge in this area across the grade-level continuum (CCSS-M, 2010). Let's say that a seventh-grade teacher needs to ensure that her seventh-grade student meets the seventh-grade content standard of adding, subtracting, multiplying, and dividing rational numbers. In her class, it is possible that a student with a learning difficulty has misconceptions going all the way back to third or fourth grade. If this is true, Tier 2 or Tier 3 intervention must use this continuum and go back to fill in gaps at third, fourth, or fifth grade. A teacher may need to check that the student understands the fundamentals of a fraction (i.e., third-grade standard) and the basics of addition and subtraction of fractions (i.e., fourth-grade standards). Then, the teacher needs to help the student learn how to add and subtract fractions and multiply fractions (i.e., fifth-grade standards). Without these skills, it would be unlikely that the student will succeed with the seventh-grade content standard of performing all four operations with rational numbers. The continuum of learning informs the mathematics content that a teacher may need to teach within Tier 2 or Tier 3.

Please note that we show this continuum of learning for number and operations, but there are others. To put together necessary continuums within number and operations, consult the CCSS-M progressions or progressions related to your state content standards in mathematics. Also note that the continuums that some teachers use may be different from those of other teachers when the continuums are student-specific.

3rd	4th	5th	6th	7th	8th
Understand a fraction as the quantity formed by one part when a whole is partitioned into equal parts	Understand addition and subtraction of fractions; understand a fraction as a multiple of a unit fraction	Add and subtract fractions with unlike denominators; multiply a fraction and a whole number	Compute quotients of fractions	Apply properties of operations to add, subtract, multiply, and divide rational numbers	Solve linear equations with rational number coefficients

Figure 7.1. Sample continuum of number and operations.

3rd	4th	5th	6th	7th	8th
Identify arithmetic patterns and explain them using properties of operations	Generate a number pattern that follows a given rule	Use parentheses, brackets, or braces in numerical expressions and evaluate expressions	Use variables to represent numbers and write expressions	Apply properties of operations to add, subtract, factor, and expand linear expressions	Solve linear equations with one variable

Figure 7.2. Sample continuum of algebra.

Algebra

Figure 7.2 shows a continuum of learning related to algebra. When teaching students to solve linear equations in eighth grade, consider reviewing the content standards from previous grade levels and providing focused instruction related to such standards.

Geometry and Measurement

Figure 7.3 displays a continuum related to learning in the domains of geometry and measurement. In order to understand how the Pythagorean theorem applies to triangles, learning from previous grades about two-dimensional shapes, especially triangles, is necessary. It is essential that students understand the attributes of triangles (i.e., third- and fifth-grade content standards) and different types of angles (i.e., fourth-grade content standards). Students should also have knowledge about right triangles (i.e., sixth-grade content standards) and the angles within triangles (i.e., seventh-grade content standards).

Developing a Scope and Sequence

You are tasked with developing a scope and sequence for Tier 2 and Tier 3 instruction because every student has individual strengths and areas that require supplemental instruction. It would be nice if a scope and sequence could be as simple as the continuum shown in Figure 7.1, but a scope and sequence often combines multiple continuums. For example, for an eighth-grade student to be successful applying the Pythagorean theorem (see Figure 7.3), students need to be able to perform operations related to number and operations in Figure 7.1 and understand variables and how to solve equations as described in the algebra continuum in Figure 7.2. What's more, this is a simplified view of how different continua can be used to create a scope and sequence.

3rd	4th	5th	6th	7th	8th
Understand that shapes may share attributes	Draw points, lines, line segment, rays, angles (right, acute, obtuse), and perpendicular and parallel lines	Understand attributes belonging to a category of two-dimensional figures (e.g., triangles)	Find the area of right triangles and other triangles	Use facts about supplementary, complementary, vertical, and adjacent angles to solve for an unknown angle in a figure	Apply the Pythagorean theorem to determine unknown side lengths in right triangles

Figure 7.3. Sample continuum of geometry and measurement.

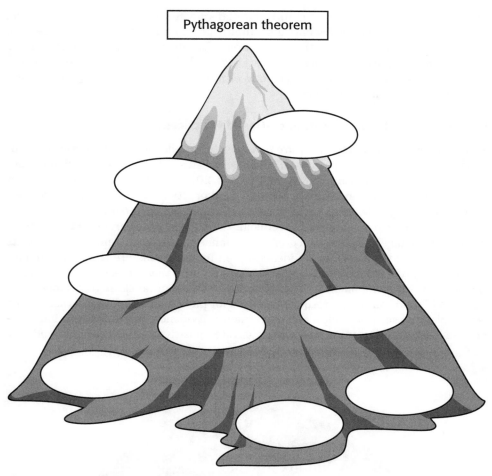

Figure 7.4. Visualization for design of scope and sequence.

It might be helpful to visualize this process in terms of a mountain (Powell, Fuchs, & Fuchs, 2013). The outcome from Tier 2 or Tier 3 intervention is placed at the top. In this example, students need to learn how to apply the Pythagorean theorem. However, a teacher examines a student's strengths and weaknesses to determine which skills are foundational to understanding and working with the Pythagorean theorem. As described in the previous paragraph, parts of the path to the top of the mountain might include instruction on operations or on setting up and solving equations. Most likely, no mountain will be the same for every student, so we provide a downloadable version of Figure 7.4 as a template to be filled in by you.

IDENTIFYING INTERVENTION CONTENT

Once you have developed a scope and sequence, you must determine how specific skill deficits will be targeted through intervention. Federal laws require that students receive interventions that are evidence-based (Every Student Succeeds Act of 2015 [PL 114-95]; IDEA of 2004 [PL 108-446]). That is, the intervention methods chosen must show consistent positive results for similar students based on scientific research. Most teachers, however, do not have unlimited access to current educational research. It can be difficult to determine the evidence base for intervention methods and harder still to compare the effectiveness of several available choices. Here we describe levels of evidence-based practices and resources for locating intervention practices and evaluating the available evidence.

Distinguishing Levels of Evidence-Based Practices

As introduced in Chapter 2, there are three levels of evidence-based practices to consider: evidence-based interventions, evidence-based strategies, and promising practices (Hughes, Powell, Lembke, & Riley-Tillman, 2016). The levels refer to the amount of supporting research evidence available for the practice; see Figure 7.5 for the hierarchy of these levels that fall under the umbrella term *evidence-based practices*.

The top, or most supported, level is an *evidence-based intervention*. This term refers to a packaged intervention program that has shown consistent positive results in scientific research studies. Evidence-based interventions are the gold standard for use with students with learning difficulties because these interventions typically include multiple components (i.e., they address the essential skills that support the target skill) and contain all resources needed for implementation, such as sequenced lesson plans or scripts, games, and assessments. Evidence-based intervention packages save planning time and have demonstrated positive results for most students.

Figure 7.5. Hierarchy under the umbrella term *evidence-based practices*.

Sometimes, however, it is not possible to locate an evidence-based intervention package that targets a specific student need, or budgetary constraints may prevent the purchase of a prepackaged system. In this case, you should examine the next level of evidence-based practice.

This second level to consider is an *evidence-based strategy*. This term refers to a framework or teaching method that shows consistent positive results for students in scientific research studies. Evidence-based strategies provide a method or framework for effective practice but do not provide sequenced or scripted lesson plans. However, many of these practices form the basis on which evidence-based interventions are built. For example, research shows that explicit instruction is an instructional framework that is effective for struggling learners across subjects (Archer & Hughes, 2011). Similarly, the Concrete-Representational-Abstract (CRA) strategy discussed in depth in Chapter 5 has a positive impact on student performance for a variety of mathematics concepts. Targeted strategies such as incremental rehearsal; taped problems; and cover, copy, compare effectively bolster fact fluency in students struggling with fluency. Evidence-based strategies provide how-to information to guide teachers in developing their own intervention materials and can be very helpful when Tier 2 intervention packages are unavailable or for meeting very specific student needs in Tier 3 interventions.

The lowest level of evidence-based practices is a *promising practice*. This term refers to a teaching strategy that currently has a limited evidence base (i.e., there are few completed research studies) but for which the available evidence is positive. Because documenting a strong research base for new methods and strategies requires both financing and time, there will always be interventions or strategies for which the evidence is not yet fully vetted. If a proven intervention or strategy is unavailable, promising practices that have some evidence of effectiveness are preferable to practices with no research basis or those with negative results from previous studies.

Locating Evidence-Based Practices

Next, we describe how teachers can locate evidence-based practices and evaluate the available evidence for themselves. Several web sites exist whose content is managed by universities and/or funded by the U.S. Department of Education, and these web sites organize and rate the growing body of research on evidence-based practices for struggling learners. The following are some of the most commonly used sites:

- What Works Clearinghouse (https://ies.ed.gov/ncee/wwc), managed by the Institute of Education Sciences' National Center for Education Evaluation and Regional Assistance.

- The IRIS Center (https://iris.peabody.vanderbilt.edu), managed by Peabody College at Vanderbilt University

- Evidence for ESSA (http://www.evidenceforessa.org), managed by the Center for Research and Reform in Education at Johns Hopkins University

- Evidence Based Intervention Network (http://ebi.missouri.edu), managed by the University of Missouri

- National Center on Intensive Intervention (https://intensiveintervention.org), managed by American Institutes for Research

Each of these online resources organizes information differently and has unique strengths and limitations; therefore, it may be helpful to become familiar with more than one of these platforms.

Locating Interventions for Specific Needs   Each of the web sites offers a way to search for methods of intervention in mathematics. The focus of each site is different and warrants independent exploration. A brief snapshot of each is provided next.

The What Works Clearinghouse site targets solid Tier 1 (i.e., whole class) intervention packages, and studies referenced on this site seldom disaggregate data specific to students with mathematics difficulties. However, practice guides are available for a range of topics, from working with students in an MTSS program to specific skill sets such as fractions, problem-solving, and algebra skills. These practice guides rate various evidence-based strategies that teachers may find useful to understand best practices and to refer to in designing instruction for intervention.

The IRIS Center site has an educator-training focus and provides online modules on various aspects of education (e.g., assessment, classroom management, school improvement), including training on providing intervention to struggling students. Also, the site provides information about various evidence-based practices and provides links to outside resources for detailed research information on each.

The Evidence for ESSA site lists evidence-based interventions (i.e., packaged curriculum materials) for mathematics and reading and rates the research base for each as strong, moderate, or promising. In addition to research findings, the site provides information about cost, as well as staffing and professional development requirements for implementation. The site does not list evidence-based strategies, which may be necessary at Tier 3.

The Evidence Based Intervention Network addresses evidence-based practices for mathematics, reading, and behavior and organizes these practices under four categories of student need: acquisition, proficiency, generalization, and motivation. The site provides a brief for each evidence-based practice that includes the standards addressed, a description of the intervention or strategy, procedures, and links to research supporting the practice.

The National Center on Intensive Intervention web site focuses on intensive interventions for students who do not respond adequately to typical intervention methods. Teachers can search for targeted interventions developed to work with students at Tiers 2 and 3 by both subject and grade-level band. The site provides detailed information on the studies used to validate each practice. For intervention packages, each site provides information on program specifications, training required, cost, and where to obtain materials; for strategies, the site provides a detailed description on how to use the strategy. The site also provides webinars and coursework for training teachers on how to intensify interventions at Tier 3.

Evaluating the Evidence Base   Each of these web sites has a system for rating the available evidence base of the interventions themselves. Strong evidence for an intervention includes three components:

1. Confirmation of measurable improvement in the performance of students receiving the intervention compared to either students who did not receive the intervention or to their own preintervention performance

2. Replicated results (i.e., more than one study was conducted and similar positive results were obtained)

3. Clear similarities between the participants in the research performed and the students in need of intervention (e.g., similar grade level, socioeconomic status, or disability category)

Generally, web sites rate the first two components, measurable improvement and replication, and will provide information regarding the participants of the study. It is up to you or MTSS Leadership Team at your school to determine which practices show the best evidence base for students who are similar to those in your class or school.

DESIGNING AN INTERVENTION LESSON

At times, a premade intervention package may be unavailable. For instance, budgetary concerns may prevent the purchase of an intervention, or there may be no intervention available for a specific skill. Or, perhaps a student is not responding to a packaged intervention in a satisfactory manner and intensive Tier 3 intervention is required. In these situations, you will be expected to use evidence-based strategies and promising practices to develop your own intervention lessons. To facilitate lesson design, we describe four core components of an effective mathematics intervention session rooted in the evidence-based strategies of explicit instruction and the CRA strategy: 1) a warm-up, 2) a conceptual learning activity, 3) practice with procedural and conceptual components, and 4) a lesson wrap-up. We extend the example of applying the Pythagorean theorem to provide some examples for these lesson components.

Warm-Up

Lesson warm-ups are brief activities (i.e., 2 to 3 minutes) intended to get the student ready for thinking mathematically and to prime the student for success. The goal of the warm-up is to remind the student of something he or she already knows about the focus topic and to connect that knowledge to the new target concept or skill. Some suggestions for warm-up activities are fluency drills, a review of previously learned concepts and vocabulary related to the day's lesson, or a think-aloud about a previously worked problem (Powell & Fuchs, 2015).

For the student who needs to apply the Pythagorean theorem to solve for unknown side lengths, teachers can choose from many related warm-up activities depending on the student's previously determined strengths and weaknesses and where the student is in the planned scope and sequence. For example, the student might need fluency practice with squaring numbers or determining square roots. Alternatively, it may be appropriate to review related terminology such as *perpendicular, right angle, right triangle, sides, hypotenuse,* or *squared numbers* and *square roots.* The student may require a quick reminder of the symbolic notation used to represent squaring and square roots or practice balancing simple equations to be successful using algebra to find solutions. As the student progresses to more complex understanding, using a think-aloud with a worked example of a word-problem scenario in which students apply the Pythagorean theorem might be an appropriate warm-up activity.

Conceptual Learning Activity

Students with mathematics learning difficulty often require targeted instruction to develop the conceptual understanding needed to apply learned strategies and to recognize procedural errors (Geary, 2004; Gersten & Chard, 1999). When teaching an intervention lesson, you may need to preface procedural instruction with conceptual exploration using manipulatives, models, or representations. This lesson component reinforces the meanings of unfamiliar terminology, allows for discussion about conceptual relationships, and sets a purpose for learning new procedures. As the student moves through the scope and sequence, basic concepts should be reviewed as more complex concepts are introduced.

Our student applying the Pythagorean theorem needs to understand several foundational concepts before applying procedures to solve complex problems such as the one shown in Figure 7.6. Early in the scope and sequence, the teacher may use models or drawings to focus the student's attention on the defining characteristics of right triangles and related terminology. The student might measure the side lengths of right triangles, beginning with ratios of 3:4:5 in early lessons, then move to triangles for which the length of the hypotenuse is difficult to determine precisely by measurement. The student will need to understand that $a^2 + b^2 = c^2$ is an unchanging relationship in all right triangles, regardless of what the triangles look like (i.e., the ratios of the side lengths and how the triangle is positioned on the page). Also, the student will need to recognize that the relationship remains the same even if the right triangle is only a portion of a larger figure.

Practice With Conceptual and Procedural Components

Just as conceptual understanding increases the accuracy and application of procedural skills, practice with procedures extends conceptual understanding (Rittle-Johnson, Schnieder, & Star, 2015). During this part of the lesson, the student will apply conceptual knowledge in an abstract way such as writing and solving equations, applying formulas, and making calculations. You should plan to use guided practice to teach procedural skills while emphasizing conceptual understanding. You will model

In $\triangle ABC$, $\overline{BD}$ is perpendicular to $\overline{AC}$. What is the length, in inches, of $\overline{AC}$?

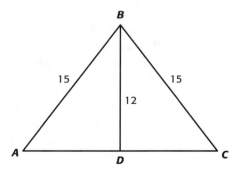

Figure 7.6. Problem scenario using the Pythagorean theorem. (*Source:* Partnership for Assessment of Readiness for College and Careers, 2015.)

the targeted procedure several times while slowly releasing supports until the student can be independently successful.

Our focus student will need to learn to use the equation $a^2 + b^2 = c^2$ in a flexible way. Procedural skills specific to applying the Pythagorean theorem include labeling the sides of the triangle correctly (i.e., determining which side is the hypotenuse), solving for the length of the hypotenuse, and solving for a side length. The student will also need to review or learn procedures related to balancing equations, squaring numbers, and finding square roots.

Wrap-Up

The wrap-up is a brief review of the day's lesson, with opportunities for independent practice of skills learned. This lesson component can be used to assess whether the student understood the lesson and can apply the concepts and procedures taught within the current and previous sessions independently. This information should tell you whether the student is ready for the next step in the scope and sequence or needs to review previously taught material.

The wrap-up for the student working with the Pythagorean theorem would be determined by the content of the day's lesson and previous lessons. The goal is to provide a spiral review of concepts and procedures previously covered, evaluate progress, and establish a starting point for the next lesson.

SUMMARY: INTERVENTION DESIGN

In this chapter, we discussed how to determine the scope and sequence of an intervention program, including considerations such as the domains and continua of mathematics learning as well as the process of planning a scope and sequence. We described the different levels of evidence-based practice and online resources available for locating and evaluating evidence-based practices to meet your students' needs. Last, we broadly outlined components of an intervention lesson: a warm-up, a conceptual learning activity, practice with both conceptual and procedural components, and a wrap-up, and applied them to an example.

CHAPTER 8

Implementing Interventions Within a Multitiered Framework

In the previous three chapters, we have discussed evidence-based practices for use within Tier 2 or Tier 3 intervention. In this chapter, we put all of this information together to provide examples of how middle school teachers provide Tier 2 and Tier 3 intervention. We also focus on fidelity of implementation that helps ensure that targeted instructional efforts are fruitful. We answer the following questions:

- Who are the students who require mathematics support through MTSS? What support system must a school have in place to support them?

- What does mathematics instruction look like within Tier 1?

- What does mathematics instruction look like at Tiers 2 and 3?

- Why is it important to implement evidence-based interventions and strategies with high levels of fidelity?

- How is response determined within MTSS?

THE SCHOOL SUPPORT SYSTEM

In this section, we discuss students with learning difficulties and the support system that schools must have in place to provide appropriate mathematics services for all students.

Students With Learning Difficulties

The focus of this book is mathematics support for students with learning difficulties. In some cases, your students may have a school-diagnosed disability (e.g., specific learning disability) and IEP goals related to mathematics. These students likely require supplemental support beyond the general education classroom, and that support can be provided with Tier 2 or Tier 3 intervention. In other cases, your students may not have a disability diagnosis but may have demonstrated low performance in mathematics that is persistent across grade levels (Nelson & Powell, 2018). In research, these students are often referred to as students with *mathematics difficulty*. In this book, we identify both students with mathematics disability and difficulty as *students with learning difficulties in mathematics*.

In our view, it does not matter whether a student has an identified disability related to mathematics or whether a student struggles with persistent low performance in mathematics. In both cases, these students require additional instructional support. This support may be provided through differentiation in the general education classroom. By middle school, however, most students with learning difficulties have substantial gaps in mathematics knowledge and require supplemental support outside of the general education classroom (Wei, Lenz, & Blackorby, 2013).

> It does not matter whether a student has an identified disability or struggles with persistent low performance in mathematics—these students require additional support.

Mathematics Support for These Students

Within an MTSS framework, Tier 2 and 3 intervention for students with mathematics learning difficulties needs to be individualized and adaptable. We will call this data-based individualization. In Figure 8.1, we revisit our outline of the entire MTSS framework with the perspective of data-based individualization. Much of this

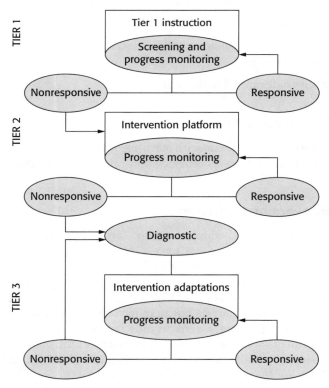

Figure 8.1. Multi-tiered system of support (MTSS) framework.

framework has been developed by the National Center on Intensive Intervention (https://intensiveintervention.org).

Let us start with Tier 1. Tier 1 instruction should be based on evidence-based practices that have been shown to benefit most students most of the time. In this model, Tier 1 is mathematics instruction provided in the general education classroom, and differentiated instruction is provided. All students are screened using some type of universal screener (see Chapter 10). Students with low scores on the universal screener are progress monitored (using a mathematics progress monitoring system; see Chapter 12) to determine whether these students are benefitting from the Tier 1 instruction. When students are responsive during the 6 to 10 weeks of progress monitoring, they remain in Tier 1. When students are nonresponsive, they begin Tier 2.

In Tier 2, teachers develop an intervention platform. This is the jumping off point for supplemental instruction. The intervention platform should be based on an appropriate scope and sequence (see Chapter 7) and evidence-based practices (see Chapters 5, 6, and 7). Tier 2 instruction should be provided to small groups (i.e., three to eight students) of students with similar mathematics needs. Because students who require Tier 2 are behind their peers in terms of mathematics performance, Tier 2 needs to be a focused and concentrated effort. That is, instruction needs to occur regularly during the school week, at least two to three times a week, for a concentrated amount of time (e.g., 30 to 45 minutes). Tier 2 also needs to last a substantial number of weeks (e.g., 10 to 15 weeks) during the school year. As soon as the intervention platform is put into place and small-group instruction begins, students' progress is continually monitored to understand whether the instructional platform is helping them reach their instructional goals. Every 4 to 8 weeks, you will analyze your students' progress monitoring data to determine whether they are responsive or nonresponsive. Responsive students remain in Tier 2 or move back to Tier 1. Nonresponsive students move to Tier 3.

In Tier 3, you understand that the Tier 2 intervention platform is not enough for students with persistent learning difficulties. So, first you conduct a diagnostic assessment to identify each student's strengths and weaknesses (see Chapter 11 for more information about diagnostic assessments). Then, adaptations to the instructional platform are made. Adaptations may be related to how much instruction students receive (i.e., more days per week, more minutes per day) and the evidence-based practices used within the platform (see Chapter 2 for more detailed information about adaptations for Tier 3). For example, a student may need more time to build fluency with mathematics facts, or you may need to incorporate more concrete models or manipulatives to help a student understand mathematics concepts. Many different adaptations can be made; however, you should be judicious with adaptations to the instructional platform and start with only a few. As the adaptations are made and instruction continues, progress monitoring also continues. As shown in Figure 8.1, instruction and intervention always occur with progress monitoring. The progress monitoring aspect is just as important as the instructional components so that teachers can use the data to understand the impact, if any, of the Tier 1, 2, or 3 instruction.

A diagnostic assessment is conducted to learn how to adapt the intervention platform.

SAMPLE TIER 1 INTERVENTIONS

Before describing effective Tier 2 and 3 interventions, it is important to describe effective Tier 1 practices. Tier 1 instruction should utilize evidence-based practices. In this section, we highlight two Tier 1 interventions designed with students with learning difficulties in mind.

Example 1: Seven-Step Attack Strategy

Krawec and colleagues (2012) worked with seventh- and eighth-grade students with and without learning disabilities. All students with learning disabilities were diagnosed by the school district. Across an entire school year, all students received focused instruction related to setting up and solving word problems. Teachers explicitly modeled how to use a seven-step attack strategy for working through a word problem (see Chapter 6 for more information about attack strategies). This attack strategy helped students read (for understanding), paraphrase (your own words), visualize (a picture or diagram), hypothesize (a plan to solve the problem), estimate (predict the answer), compute (do the arithmetic), and check (make sure everything is right). After students reached mastery with the seven-step attack strategy, teachers continued to model, using think-alouds, how to apply the strategy to different types of word problems. Students practiced word problems with scaffolded support (i.e., guided and independent practice with appropriate feedback) with the ultimate goal being that they internalized the attack strategy and applied it to novel word problems.

We can identify several evidence-based practices for students with learning difficulties from the word-problem intervention Krawec and colleagues (2012) implemented. First, teachers used explicit instruction to model and review the seven-step attack strategy. Second, teachers taught students an attack strategy (see Chapter 6 for a description of the evidence supporting this practice). Third, students had multiple practice opportunities across the school year to become proficient using the attack strategy. Fourth, students were encouraged to use multiple representations to represent the information within word problems. That is, students drew pictures or used graphic organizers to represent word problems. Fifth, teachers were consistent with mathematical language used with the seven-step attack strategy so that students learned to internalize the word-problem process. Sixth, teachers provided focused instruction on setting up and solving word problems. These efforts paid off as the students with learning difficulties demonstrated an increase in the number of word-problem strategies employed from pre- to posttest. Another important finding from this research is that students without learning difficulties also benefited from the intervention and outperformed students in the comparison group. The authors noted that the intervention is equally effective for students with learning difficulties and their peers without difficulties.

Example 2: Schemas for Word Problems

Also with a focus on problem solving—which demonstrates the need for effective word-problem instruction for students with and without learning difficulties—Jitendra, Star, Dupuis, and Rodriguez (2013) worked with seventh-grade students. The focus of instruction was explicitly teaching students about word-problem schemas related to ratio, proportion, and percentage (see Chapter 6). The schema strategy taught during intervention also introduced students to a four-step attack strategy for working through a word problem. The attack strategy (DISC) involved these steps:

1. Discover the problem type (i.e., schema).

2. Identify information in the problem to represent in a schematic diagram.

3. Solve the problem.

4. Check work.

Every lesson consisted of explicit instruction that started with modeling by the teacher. This explicit instruction introduced the attack strategy to help students work through word problems. During the modeling, teachers asked high-level questions to encourage student thinking about the different types of schemas. Teachers also taught students multiple ways to approach and solve the same problem so as to encourage students to realize that some solution strategies may be more or less efficient. During the course of instruction, teachers scaffolded to provide more practice opportunities for the students to become proficient problem solvers. Teachers used schematic diagrams (i.e., multiple representations) to help students represent the word-problem information in a visual way.

SAMPLE TIER 2 AND TIER 3 INTERVENTIONS

Now we turn our attention to effective Tier 2 and 3 interventions and describe the participants in such interventions and the evidence-based practices utilized therein. This information shows how to combine many of the evidence-based practices that we have highlighted in previous chapters. The first two examples are Tier 2 interventions; the third and fourth examples are Tier 3.

Example 1: Multi-Step Equations

In a study conducted by Cuenca-Carlino, Freeman-Green, Stephenson, and Hauth (2016), students were identified as needing Tier 2 intervention after they demonstrated low performance on school benchmark assessments and standardized assessments. All students were 13 years old, and Tier 2 intervention was conducted in pairs for 12 weeks during 45-minute sessions occurring four times each week. The focus of the intervention was solving multi-step equations such as $5(x + 6) = 5x + 30$.

Instruction occurred in several stages, and explicit instruction was utilized across stages. The teacher provided planned review of mathematical language necessary to understand how to solve multi-step equations. For example, the teacher reviewed vocabulary terms such as "distributive property, combining like terms, variables, and inverse operations" (Cuenca-Carlino et al., 2016, p. 80). After reviewing vocabulary, the teacher modeled a mnemonic designed to help students to solve multi-step equations. This mnemonic reminded students to focus on the distributive property, to combine like terms, to use inverse operations, to multiply or divide, and to check work. During modeling, the teacher used the complete mnemonic for several problems and used think-alouds to demonstrate his or her thought processes. The teacher kept students involved during modeling by asking high- and low-level questions to gauge student understanding. To practice the mnemonic, the teacher engaged students in both guided practice and independent practice. During guided practice, the teacher continued to ask questions for understanding and encouraged students to self-monitor their work.

Example 2: Fraction Computation Problems

With sixth-grade students, all of whom demonstrated difficulty with solving fraction computation problems, Watt and Therrien (2016) implemented a Tier 2 intervention in small groups. The intervention occurred during 30-minute sessions, with 10 total sessions. Students learned to compare two fractions, simplify fractions, and add and subtract fractions with like and unlike denominators.

The intervention focused on using multiple representations with the concrete-representational-abstract framework. Teachers modeled how to use different manipulatives and explicitly taught mathematical language. Examples of vocabulary terms included "equivalent, numerator, and denominator" (Watt & Therrien, 2016, p. 313). When the teacher modeled, the teacher used think-alouds to help the students understand each step of solving a problem. The teacher modeling was combined with student guided practice opportunities in which the teacher provided corrective feedback when necessary. In addition to working with concrete manipulatives, teachers modeled how to use pictorial or visual representations and how to understand the numbers and symbols of fractions (i.e., abstract notation). A cumulative review of subsequently learned material was conducted via independent practice.

Example 3: Equivalent Ratios

We highlight the work of Hunt and Vasquez (2014) as a Tier 3 intervention because this was a mathematics intervention individually delivered to middle school students. All students had a learning disability, as diagnosed by schools, along with IEP goals in mathematics. The intervention included 15 sessions each lasting 25 minutes. The instruction focused on helping the students understand equivalent ratios. For example, students worked to solve problems like "if 3 cups of batter make 4 pancakes, how many cups of batter for 20 pancakes?" (Hunt & Vasquez, 2014, p. 183).

The intervention of Hunt and Vasquez (2014) utilized many evidence-based practices. During each session, the teacher used explicit instruction to present each task. Teachers asked students to engage in verbalization about the mathematics concepts and skills. Teachers also provided both affirmative feedback and corrective feedback. Multiple representations were used to help students develop a strong understanding of ratios and proportions, with both concrete models and visual representations used during the intervention. Some of the visual representations included tables used to show unit rate. All representations were tied to the abstract numbers and symbols used to represent ratios. As described by the authors, students engaged in meaningful practice opportunities, with the teacher providing different levels of support based on student need.

Example 4: One- and Two-Step Word Problems

Working with eighth-grade students with a school-diagnosed learning disability, van Garderen (2007) provided individual instruction related to solving one- and two-step word problems. This Tier 3 instruction, which occurred across the school year, lasted 35 minutes per session, with two to four sessions occurring per week. Students learned to solve word problems such as "Joe rode his bike 2 miles to the bus station. He then boarded a bus that took him 12.5 miles. When he got off the bus, he then walked 1 more mile to get to his friend's house. How far did Joe travel in all?" (van Garderen, 2007, p. 544).

During all instruction for this Tier 3 intervention, the teacher used explicit instruction. Students learned to generate diagrams (i.e., multiple representations) and how to use symbols within such diagrams. Teachers modeled how to draw pictorial diagrams and schematic diagrams. The schematic diagrams represented the structure of the word problem, and students learned how to utilize line diagrams or part–whole diagrams to represent different word-problem schemas. Within the word-problem instruction, the teacher modeled and students practiced an attack strategy: read the problem for understanding, visualize the problem, plan for how to solve the problem, compute the answer, and check the answer. As part of explicit instruction, the teacher used a variety of questions and feedback. Students also engaged in many different guided practice and independent practice opportunities.

IMPLEMENTATION OF INTERVENTIONS AT TIERS 2 AND 3

For Tier 2 and 3 interventions to be effective, they need to be implemented with fidelity. This is true for Tier 1 interventions as well. *Fidelity* means that the intervention is implemented as designed. All the interventions described in this chapter and those interventions identified as having a strong evidence base have been designed with a specific procedure to be implemented to enhance student performance on a specific outcome. When implemented with a high level of fidelity (i.e., doing most of the important things in the intervention), it is likely that the intervention will positively affect most students' mathematics proficiency most of the time. When implemented with low fidelity, however, it is not likely to affect students' mathematics proficiency in a positive way. This would be a waste of the students' time and your time, so it is essential to implement interventions as intended to the greatest extent possible.

To gauge fidelity, you can determine how well an intervention was put into place and delivered. In order to claim that change in mathematics performance has been due to a particular evidence-based intervention, it is necessary to establish guidelines related to the fidelity of implementation. First, you should define the goal of the intervention and define what fidelity of implementation would look like. Second, you need to determine an appropriate method for measuring fidelity. As described in the next subsections, fidelity information may be gathered in quantitative ways or qualitative ways. Third, you should determine who will measure and monitor fidelity. Will fidelity be measured by the teacher implementing the intervention or by an outside observer (e.g., another teacher, mathematics specialist, special education coordinator)? If an outside observer will measure fidelity, how will that information be shared with the teacher? Fourth, you should plan for how frequently fidelity information will be gathered. Will fidelity of implementation data be collected every session, once a week, or once a month? Fifth, when gathering data, will the fidelity observer collect data during the entire session or part of a session?

Often, checklists are used to assess fidelity of implementation. Such fidelity checklists

> When an intervention is implemented with a high level of fidelity, it is likely to positively affect most students.

can help teachers examine whether the instruction and materials were implemented as designed. Such checklists can also help teachers reflect on strengths and weaknesses of the intervention, especially if the intervention does not yield the desired results. We suggest that fidelity checks be conducted periodically (i.e., every few sessions) as a way for teachers to reflect on the implementation of any intervention.

Quantitative Measurement of Fidelity

Fidelity information can be collected in a quantitative fashion. This refers to counting how many times the intervention procedures are followed according to the original design of the intervention. The actual task of assessing fidelity might include an observation in the Tier 2 or 3 setting with systematic notes about the intervention procedures and how well they were followed. The overall goal is to document the accuracy of both the process and outcomes of the intervention. The specific behaviors, interactions, or procedures to be counted should be chosen and described in advance as a way of identifying which factors could predict the outcome of successfully completing the intervention.

For example, in a study about a problem-solving intervention, Xin and colleagues (2005) developed a checklist that contained critical steps to assess the teacher's adherence to the intervention. A doctoral student observed and evaluated the accuracy of instruction. The adherence was judged based on the presence or absence of each critical component. Fidelity of implementation was assessed for about 30% of the lessons. Fidelity observations were followed by feedback to the teachers whenever procedural implementation was less than 85% accurate.

In another example from a peer-tutoring intervention, Fuchs et al. (1997) developed a quantitative checklist to determine adherence to the peer-tutoring components. As shown in Figure 8.2, the teacher is given one point for following the procedures of the intervention. This point is circled if the teacher follows the specific procedure. The point is left uncircled if the procedure is not followed. Fidelity of implementation is calculated as the number of observed procedures divided by the total number of procedures. If a teacher follows 17 of the 18 procedures on the fidelity checklist, the teacher's fidelity of implementation is 94%. Typically, if using this type of checklist, teachers should strive for fidelity above 80% or 90%.

Qualitative Measurement of Fidelity

The measurement of qualitative fidelity refers to assessing the quality of the work conducted during the course of the intervention. In other words, qualitative fidelity is an analysis of how well the intervention was implemented through a quality lens. It is possible that one teacher could implement all of the components of an intervention as listed on a quantitative checklist and do them all very well, whereas another teacher could do all the same component but not do them very well. Quality of implementation is just as important as quantity of implementation.

In the example shown in Figure 8.3, a teacher can monitor his or her own fidelity in both a quantitative manner (i.e., the checklist) and a qualitative manner (i.e., the 1 to 10 scale). When qualitative fidelity information is collected, it is often through a numerical scale like the one shown, or through a scale with ratings such as Excellent, Good, Fair, Poor.

Example of Math PALS Implementation Checklist

Teacher: _____   **School:** _____

# of Students: _____   **Start time:** _____ **End time:** _____

Observer: _____   **Lesson #:** _____

circle = behavior observed
blank = behavior not observed
crossed out = not applicable

Teacher Behaviors

1   Announces it's time for Coaching
1   Students move to PALS places _____ Start Time _____ End Time (1–2 min.)
1   Teacher Reviews Coach's Question Sheet (if necessary)
1   Teacher Reviews Correction Procedure (if necessary)
1   Teacher reminds students when to switch roles
1   Teacher reminds students when to quit using Coach's Question Sheet and begin Self Talk
1   Teacher instructs students on new procedure, if applicable

Classroom Set-up

1   Higher performing math students are paired with lower performing math students
1   Students are seated next to their partners with Question, Point, & Coaching Sheet
1   Students should know who their partner is for the day (pairs posted)

Teacher Materials

1   Training materials, if needed
1   Timer
1   PALS Tutoring Command Card

Student Materials

1   Coach's Question Sheet
1   Coaching Answer Sheet (Coach)
1   Coaching Sheet (Player)
1   Point Sheet (Coach)
1   Pencils

Figure 8.2. Quantitative fidelity checklist. (*Source:* Fuchs, L. S., Fuchs, D., Hamlett, C. L., Phillips, N. B., Karns, K., & Dutka, S. [1997]. Enhancing students' helping behavior during peer-mediated instruction with conceptual mathematical explanations. *The Elementary School Journal, 97,* 223–249.)

DETERMINING RESPONSE TO INTERVENTION

We use all the information provided in Section II of this book to put together a strong instructional program for use within MTSS. Instruction, however, should never be provided without proper assessments (see Section III, Chapters 9–13) to determine whether the instruction is adequate for each student (Fuchs et al., 2012).

As outlined in Figure 8.1, the MTSS framework begins with Tier 1 or core instruction. This instruction should be evidence-based. Screening of all students should occur to identify students who may have difficulty with mathematics, and progress monitoring for a set number of weeks during Tier 1 should confirm such risk. All evidence-based instruction should be implemented with high levels of fidelity (Johnson & Smith, 2011).

Example of a Fidelity Checklist for a Lesson in Mathematics

Treatment Fidelity Self-Monitoring (Circle One):

          Weekly   Bi-monthly   Monthly

The following mathematics topic is being implemented at this time:
_____ Place a check next to each step as you complete it for a given lesson.
_____ Provide an objective for the lesson in concrete and measureable terms.
_____ Provide students a rationale for the strategy that you will be teaching them.
_____ Introduce the strategy through modeling.
_____ Use the strategy with the students with several problems (guided practice).
_____ Have the students repeat back the steps in the strategy.
_____ Have students work independently or in pairs to implement the strategy as they work
        on some problems together.
_____ Teach for generalization.
_____ Teach for maintenance

On a scale from 1–10, I implemented the lesson with this degree of fidelity (defined as
implementing the lesson utilizing the given steps or sequence):

            1   2   3   4   5   6   7   8   9   10
           Low fidelity   High fidelity

Figure 8.3. Quantitative and qualitative fidelity checklist. (From van Garderen, D., Thomas C. N., Stormont, M., & Lembke, E. S. *Intervention in School and Clinic* 48[3], 131–141, copyright © 2013 by Sage Journals. Reprinted by Permission of SAGE Publications, Inc.)

For students who demonstrate inadequate progress with Tier 1, Tier 2 is warranted. Tier 2 starts with an instructional platform. This is the jumping off point for data-based individualization. Similar to Tier 1, the instruction should have an evidence base and be implemented with fidelity. Frequent progress monitoring (i.e., brief assessments administered weekly) should occur to understand whether the Tier 2 instructional platform is helping students to the greatest extent.

When Tier 2 is not meeting the needs of students, Tier 3 is warranted. Before adapting any instruction within Tier 3, a mathematics diagnostic assessment should be conducted to determine a given student's strengths and weaknesses so the instructional platform can be adapted in a meaningful way. Fidelity of the evidence-based instruction is essential within Tier 3, as is continual progress monitoring.

The progress monitoring data collected within Tier 3 is frequently revisited by teacher and MTSS Leadership Team to understand whether the current Tier 3 intervention is helpful for a student. If not, the instructional platform is adapted again and again (Powell & Stecker, 2014) until the student is responsive to instruction and does not require such intensive intervention.

SUMMARY: IMPLEMENTING INTERVENTIONS WITHIN MTSS

In this chapter, we focused on putting together the instructional components outlined in Chapters 4, 5, 6, and 7. We described how evidence-based instruction fits within a three-tier MTSS model. We provided examples of Tier 1, 2, and 3 mathematics interventions and how evidence-based components were used within each of the interventions. We also briefly discussed the importance of measuring fidelity of implementation. Finally, as a preview to Section III, we briefly described how assessment is used to determine the effectiveness of evidence-based instruction within Tiers 1, 2, and 3—that is, to determine students' response to intervention.

SECTION III

Using Data to Make Decisions

OVERVIEW: SYSTEMATIC ASSESSMENT TO SUPPORT TEACHING

In this book, we approach the topic of assessment from an MTSS framework. We reference the powerful role assessments can serve in improving student achievement by using data to guide instruction. Chapter 9 addresses the question, "Why should we assess?" In this chapter, we discuss the general purposes of assessment and the ways assessment results can be used to make decisions, and we introduce broad categories of assessment (formative and summative; criterion- and norm-referenced). In Chapters 10 through 13, we focus on the different instructional decisions that you need to make within an MTSS framework and the specific types of assessments you can use to guide these decisions:

1. *Who needs assistance and how much assistance do they need?* Universal screening assessments (discussed in Chapter 10) are useful tools to identify students who are on track for meeting the learning objectives and those who may be at risk for failing to meet them. Results from these assessments can also be used to determine the degree of intensity of the support students will need to reach their goals.

2. *Why are students struggling? What background knowledge, errors, and misconceptions do students have that influence their learning?* You can use several types of diagnostic formative assessments (discussed in Chapter 11) to better understand students' areas of strength and areas of confusion. We focus on how you can use information from this chapter with Section II of this book to implement interventions to support student learning.

3. *Are interventions helping students learn? Are students making progress toward their instructional goals?* As you implement interventions, you must keep a close eye on students' learning. You can monitor students' progress using multiple types of tools, discussed in Chapter 12. We discuss how to use progress monitoring information to determine whether your students are learning at an appropriate rate to reach their instructional goals.

4. *Did students reach their goals and learn the content to the level that you expected?*
    After you provide instruction, summative assessments (discussed in Chapter 13)
    provide an important evaluation of whether your instruction was effective at help-
    ing students reach the instructional goals. We describe how to use results from
    summative assessments to find out *if* and *how well* your students learned the
    concepts of instruction.

In this section, we begin with a clear description of common terms used when implementing assessments and when interpreting and communicating about assessment
results. We provide teachers with a road map for selecting assessments based on the
types of decisions they are making. Each chapter discusses one type of instructional
decision; the type of assessment that will be most valuable for making that decision;
how, when, and with whom to use this type of assessment; and its technical characteristics. Moreover, we describe and share sample assessment reports and discuss how to
interpret the information to make the desired decisions. Finally, we discuss methods
for communicating the results with other educators, administrators, parents, and students. We share sample scenarios of communicating in person and in writing to support appropriate interpretation and use of the results by different stakeholders. These
discussions are situated within a nonthreatening culture of using data to improve
achievement.

   Although each chapter presents data from a different type of assessment separately, the data discussed in this section can be viewed as part of a larger cycle for
making instructional decisions. The cycle depicted in the figure shown here can be
used to guide decisions about individual students, as well as decisions about groups
of students at the classroom or grade level or across a system, such as within a school
or district. Throughout this section, we will situate our discussion of the assessment
systems within the cycle of decision making.

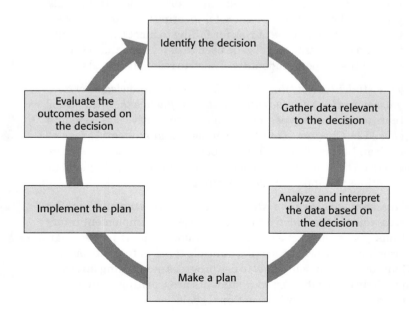

CHAPTER 9

Why Should We Assess?

Is it inevitable that teachers will have a love–hate relationship with assessment?

Many of us in the field of education seem to have a love–hate relationship with assessment systems. In many ways, we love to hate them. We complain about how state accountability tests narrow the curriculum by forcing teachers to teach to the test. We complain about district assessment efforts taking up too much instructional time and not providing feedback in a timely manner. We complain about a "testing culture" in which students focus on getting a good score or grade instead of a "learning culture" in which students want to learn. We are addicted to complaining about tests.

However, we are equally addicted to data. We actively seek out statistics that compare SAT scores of one high school's graduates with the scores of another high school's graduates to determine which is a "better" school. We drop everything the day the scores are released to examine closely how our students performed, and we are excited when our school's rating improves. We share students' classroom scores with our peers, celebrate our successes, and bemoan our failures.

In each of these instances, the assessment system has been the instrument of our decision-making. In some cases, the decisions we make might not align with the assessment system's intent. In these cases, we are basing our decisions on inappropriate data. For example, the purpose of the state accountability test

> We love to hate assessment systems, but we are equally addicted to data.

is not to narrow the curriculum. However, state accountability tests are designed to assess the topics that the state education agency finds to be the most important for students to know and be able to do. If only the assessed content is taught (as opposed to the topics specified in the content standards), an unintended outcome would be narrowing the curriculum. Similarly, SAT tests are not intended to be used to compare different high schools' relative quality; however, they do provide an indicator of the students' preparedness for college study.

We come from a balanced perspective of loving and hating assessments. Assessment results can be valuable in our decision making. We can use data from state accountability tests to identify students' level of proficiency with grade-level curriculum and how our schools perform compared to one another. Classroom assessment information can be used to gauge student progress and better understand why students struggle. On the other hand, administering assessments takes away from valuable instructional time, and interpreting results uses valuable teacher planning time. In addition, when assessment results are not used to improve student learning, that valuable time is just wasted.

We have seen many instances in which assessment systems have worked to improve student achievement in mathematics (see Gersten, Beckmann et al., 2009; you can download and review a summary of these studies at the Institution of Education Sciences web site at https://ies.ed.gov/ncee/wwc/PracticeGuides). Based on these experiences, we believe that assessments can be valuable tools and are essential for implementing MTSS, but you need considerable knowledge and skill to use assessment data to make decisions that support student learning. In this book, we share our experiences and insights into using mathematics assessment systems to improve student learning within an MTSS framework.

As educators, we can learn to love assessments. A not-so-new catchphrase in education is *data-based decision making*. Even though this phrase has been in the education lexicon since the early 2000s, teachers and administrators are left without much guidance as to how we should and should not use data to make decisions, especially as it relates to mathematics. In some cases, we may not know which data to use to make which decisions.

Which data? We are surrounded by data: attendance records, school referral data, in-class performance data, state accountability test data. We have so much data that we need a data warehousing system. Which data are important for making decisions to support mathematics achievement? In the exaggerated example depicted in Figure 9.1, we need to decide if a student needs supplemental mathematics instruction. However, the available data includes reading screener results, attendance records, behavior charts, and science quiz scores. Although useful for making some decisions, these data may not help us decide if a student needs supplemental mathematics instruction.

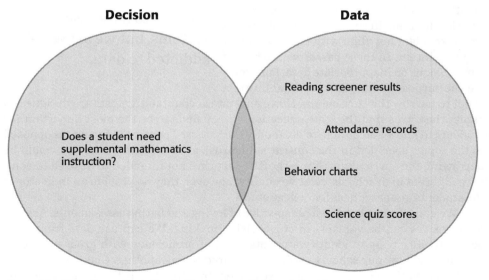

Figure 9.1. Venn diagram illustrating decision making with little relationship to data.

As you can see by the minimal overlap in these two circles in the Venn diagram, there is little relationship between our decision and our data.

Which decisions? On a daily basis, we are faced with hundreds of decisions: which students need extra help, is a student ready to go on to the next unit, which homework problems should I assign to which students. So which decisions require data and which data should a teacher use?

Given this landscape of data and decisions, it is no wonder we often suffer from "data paralysis."

Data paralysis is a serious issue that affects many teachers and administrators. We see "data paralysis" when schools have copious amounts of data but don't know how to ask the right questions or use the data to find the answers. We hope to turn this situation around by putting the decisions first. We assess to make decisions. Also, as we can see in the example shown in Figure 9.2, we want maximum overlap between our decision and the data that we collect. Just as we might miss the forest for the trees, we cannot lose sight of the decisions for (because of) the data.

In this section of the book, we hope to be your guide in breaking free from data paralysis so that you can make meaningful decisions within an MTSS framework. We help you by first identifying the questions you need to answer to support students' mathematics

> Q: Why do we assess?
> A: To make decisions.

achievement. Then we point you in the direction of the data that can be used to address these questions. We focus on various types of data that can be used to improve mathematics instruction to meet students' needs. We provide details about how and when to use formative assessment data and summative assessment data, and how to

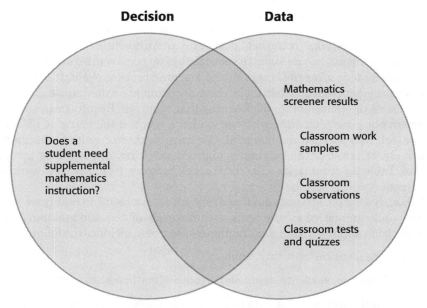

Decision　　　　**Data**

Does a student need supplemental mathematics instruction?

Mathematics screener results

Classroom work samples

Classroom observations

Classroom tests and quizzes

Figure 9.2.　Venn diagram illustrating decision making with a solid relationship to data.

communicate results and the decisions you make to parents and students. Our goal is to prevent "data paralysis" in your classrooms and school and, instead, to help you make meaningful use of student performance data to improve students' mathematics achievement.

To fulfill the "why" of assessment—making decisions—it is important for educators to be able to answer other questions related to assessment systems: when we assess, how we use the results, what we assess, and how we share the results.

WHEN SHOULD WE ASSESS?

Because the purpose of assessing students is to make decisions, you should assess only when you need to make a decision. As we said before, testing takes away from instructional time, so you should have a clear sense of how you will use the results from the test before you give it.

We know that you are swamped with decisions every minute of every day. In this section, we want to focus on the instructional decisions you make to support student learning in mathematics. Each type of decision may come at different points in the learning cycle, but they are generally divided into two categories:

> Q: When do we assess?
> A: It depends on the decision.

- Decisions made during the teaching and learning process

- Decisions made after the teaching and learning process

Typically, decisions made *during* the teaching and learning process guide instructional design and delivery while it is happening. Assessments that can help make these decisions are called formative assessments because they help inform instruction. Results from formative assessments provide valuable information we can use to make a variety of decisions, such as which students might benefit from being in the same instructional group, how instruction might need to be differentiated to meet the needs of all students, what is the best design for an intervention to support students with learning difficulties, and when to speed things up or slow things down.

Decisions made *after* the teaching and learning process evaluate learning outcomes. Assessments that can help make these decisions are called summative assessments because they summarize the learning that occurred. Results from summative assessments help us determine whether students reached the learning objective(s) and how well they learned the material. We may use these results to design future learning objectives, but the originally planned teaching and learning process is complete. Table 9.1 summarizes the differences between formative and summative assessments.

Although we often separate out these types of assessments, in reality we use both formative and summative assessments within a cycle of decision making. A typical cycle of decision making within a mathematics classroom includes the following steps:

1. Identify the decision we want to make.

2. Gather data about students' depth and breadth of mathematics content knowledge.

3. Analyze and interpret these data to understand students' current thinking.

4. Combine these data with our professional judgment to identify which instructional changes are needed to improve students' mathematics, as discussed in Section II of this book.

5. Implement these changes in our classroom instruction.

6. Observe student performance to evaluate our hypothesis.

These steps are illustrated in Figure 9.3.

Formative and summative assessments are used at different points within this cycle. Formative assessments provide meaningful information about students as we identify areas of instructional need and gather information about students' conceptual and procedural understanding of mathematics, conceptions and mis-conceptions, and level of background knowledge and skills. The specificity of data provided by different types of formative assessments provides insights into students' current thinking. We use this information to generate hypotheses about which instructional changes are needed. Throughout the teaching and learning process, we gather ongoing student performance data to evaluate whether students are making adequate progress. After we have implemented the changes, we use data from summative assessments to determine whether our hypotheses were accurate at meeting students' needs. Throughout Section III of this book, Using Data to Make Decisions, we will discuss different types of formative and summative assessments as they relate to specific decisions to be made within the instructional decision-making cycle.

You can read more about data use practices in a report written for the U.S. Department of Education by Hamilton et al. (2009), available for download at the Institution of Education Sciences web site at https://ies.ed.gov/ncee/wwc/PracticeGuides.

Table 9.1. Comparison of formative and summative assessment

	Formative assessment	Summative assessment
Purposes	• Monitors learning • Informs instruction • Gathers information about student misconceptions and background knowledge and skills	• Evaluates student learning • Informs future planning • Gathers information about student proficiency level with a concept
Timing	Occurs *during* the teaching and learning process	Occurs *after* the teaching and learning process
Frequency	Ongoing Depends on the decision	At the end of the learning Less frequent
Related decisions	• Which students need additional support? • Which students might benefit from being in the same instructional group? • How might instruction be differentiated to meet the needs of all students? • What is the best design for an intervention to support students who are struggling? • When can I speed my instruction up and when should I slow it down?	• Are students proficient with a given concept? • Which students receive passing grades? • How do classes perform compared to one another? • How effective is an instructional program?
Examples	• Universal screener • Diagnostic assessments • Systematic student questioning/ interviewing	• State standardized assessments • Unit tests • Semester exams

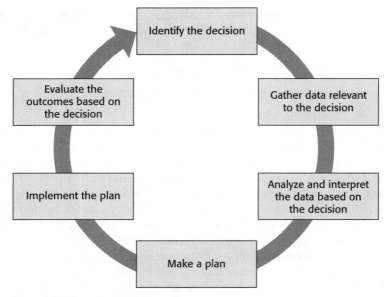

Figure 9.3.   The cycle of decision making.

HOW DO WE USE ASSESSMENT RESULTS TO MAKE DECISIONS?

The example of how a middle school mathematics teacher named Mr. Tran worked with a new student's assessment data will help to illustrate how to use assessment results to make decisions. Sebastian joined Mr. Tran's eighth-grade mathematics class from a school in a nearby district. On reviewing Sebastian's transfer paperwork, Mr. Tran found a copy of his math teacher's grade book (see Figure 9.4).

At first glance, because the scores appeared to be low, Mr. Tran suspected that Sebastian had struggled in mathematics. In talking with Sebastian, however, Mr. Tran got a different impression of his mathematics ability. As Mr. Tran probed Sebastian about his grades, he found out that Sebastian had scored near the top of his class on each assignment and consistently met or exceeded the criteria for demonstrating

Teacher: Mrs Smith					Period: 4th				
Student	Area HW	Area Quiz	Perimeter HW	Volume HW	Measurement Quiz	Surface Area HW	Surface Area Quiz	Review HW	Unit Test
Sebastian Fisher	83	73	68	58	65	75	69	78	71

Figure 9.4.   Math grades for Sebastian, provided by his previous teacher.

proficiency. Without knowing how to interpret Sebastian's scores, Mr. Tran could not make a decision about Sebastian's proficiency in mathematics.

As this scenario points out, just having scores from formative and summative assessments doesn't mean you are ready to make a decision. To make a decision, you need to interpret the results. Data interpretation sounds straightforward, but it is actually quite complex—and it is often the point at which we get stuck. *Interpretation* means to establish the meaning of something. In other words, data interpretation is "sense-making" or making sense out of the data.

To make sense out of formative and summative assessment data, you need to keep the decision you are trying to make in the forefront of your data interpretation. To guide this interpretation, ask yourself these questions for any formative or summative assessment:

1. Does the decision I want to make refer to a specific level of proficiency? For example, did each student meet the level of proficiency specified on my instructional objective? Does the student's current level of understanding demonstrate that he or she is on track for reaching proficiency at the end of the instructional unit?

    a. If you answered *yes,* you need to interpret data in reference to a criterion.

    b. If you answered *no,* ask yourself the next question.

2. Does the decision I want to make refer to comparisons across students? For example, when compared to other students, is this student struggling to understand the content? Which students in my class (or school) need the most help?

    c. If you answered *yes,* you need to interpret data in reference to a normative sample.

You may have answered yes to more than one of these questions. You can make multiple interpretations from the same data, but you need to be careful about which reference you use for which interpretations. In this section, we will talk about two types of referents you can use, criteria and norms, and how they will help you make decisions from formative and summative assessment results.

> Just having scores from assessments doesn't mean you are ready to make a decision. You need to interpret the results.

Criterion-Referenced Interpretations

If you want to interpret the data in reference to a specific level of proficiency, you are making a criterion-referenced interpretation. For example, Mr. Tran wants to know if Sebastian passed his last mathematics exam at his previous school. Mr. Tran needs to know the specific level of proficiency (or the criterion) for determining a passing score. Suppose Sebastian earned a score of 9 on his most recent exam. If the criterion for reaching proficiency (or passing) was set at 9, Mr. Tran would interpret this score as meeting the criterion (or passing). If the criterion for reaching proficiency (or passing) was set at 10, Mr. Tran would interpret this score as not meeting the criterion (or not passing).

In the example shown in Figure 9.5, the criterion for reaching proficiency was identified as a specific score on the test. Sebastian's score is then compared to this

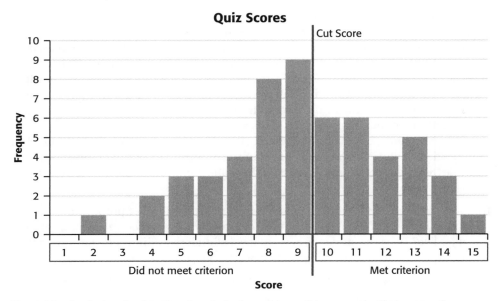

Figure 9.5. Graph of scoring data. Here, the criterion for reaching proficiency was identified as a specific score on the test (the cut score).

score to interpret the data. This score is called a cut score because it divides (or cuts) the data into groups based on the criterion. Knowing the cut score is essential for interpreting data in reference to a criterion.

To make a criterion-referenced interpretation, a student's score is compared to a specific standard (or criterion) of expected proficiency. If the student's score is above the standard (or criterion), we would say that he or she reached the specific level of proficiency; if below, we would say that he or she did not reach the specific level of proficiency. We typically associate criterion-referenced decisions with summative assessments (i.e., final exams, state accountability tests), but they are also useful for formative assessments (i.e., universal screeners).

The most widely known example of a criterion-referenced interpretation comes from state accountability tests. Most often, schools and districts use results from state accountability tests to determine the effectiveness of the overall instructional program at increasing students' knowledge and skill to the expected level of mastery. Under the requirements of the No Child Left Behind Act of 2001 (PL 107-110), students' proficiency in reading and mathematics is measured by state accountability assessments and compared to proficiency levels within the domain (i.e., the criterion). Results are typically reported in reference to the degree of mastery of the content expectations described in the state content standards. As such, students' results are reported as proficiency levels, such as "did not meet expectations," "met expectations," or "exceeds expectations." These proficiency levels are used to determine the adequacy of educational systems at making progress toward 100% proficiency on the state content standards (referenced as Adequate Yearly Progress in No Child Left Behind legislation).

In sum, when you need to "make sense" out of the data to make a decision that relates to a specific level of proficiency, you may be best served by interpreting the data in reference to a criterion. Later in this section, we describe how you can make criterion-referenced interpretations from data resulting from universal screening assessments, diagnostic assessments, and summative assessments.

Norm-Referenced Interpretations

If you want to interpret the data in reference to comparisons across students, you are making a norm-referenced interpretation. For example, Mr. Tran wants to know how Sebastian performed in comparison with the other students in his class. This information will tell Mr. Tran if Sebastian was performing above or below most of the students in his previous class. To compare Sebastian's scores with other students' scores, Mr. Tran could rank order all of Sebastian's classmates scores on a specific test or assignment and then identify where Sebastian's score fell within the ranking.

To make a norm-referenced interpretation, a student's score is compared to other students' scores on the same test. Sometimes the comparison is made to students from across the country, around the district, or within a classroom. Usually, these comparisons are reported as percentile ranks. A percentile rank is the ranking of the student's score in relation to other students' scores on the same test. (In the diagram in Figure 9.6, you can see that percentile rank is related to the normal distribution of scores.) For example, a percentile rank of 61 means that the student's score falls at or above 61% of the other students' scores. A common misunderstanding is that percentile ranks identify the number of items a student answered correctly; instead, percentile rank is related to the percentage of the population of test takers who scored at or below this score. In other words, a percentile ranking of 25 does not mean that the student responded correctly to 25% of the items, but rather that the student's score falls at or above 25% of the other students' scores.

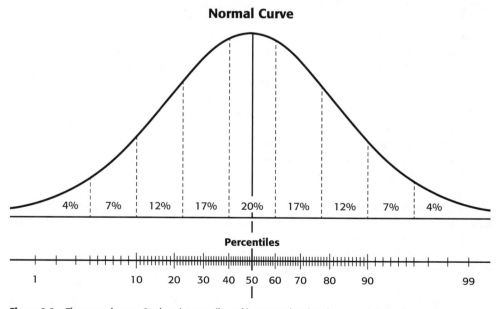

Figure 9.6. The normal curve. Students' percentile rankings are related to the normal distribution of scores.

A common example of a norm-referenced interpretation is the use of nationally standardized tests to evaluate a student's relative level of achievement. Often, schools and districts administer a nationally standardized test such as the Stanford Achievement Test (Pearson) to determine how their students are performing in reference to other students around the country. Sometimes this information is used to evaluate the effectiveness of specific educational programs at improving student achievement. Results from these tests display normative data such as percentile rank, normal curve equivalent score, and national grade percentile bands. As we have described before, the percentile rank identifies the percentage of students whom an individual scored as well as or better than. For example, in mathematics problem solving, a student might earn a percentile rank score of 54, which means that he or she scored as well as or better than 54% of other students around the country who took this test.

In sum, when you want to make a decision about a student's performance in comparison to other students, you need to interpret the data in relation to a normative sample. Unlike criterion-referenced interpretations, norm-referenced interpretations provide little or no information about whether a student reached a specific level of proficiency. In fact, all students could have reached the criterion for proficiency, but scores can always be ranked along the continuum from lowest to highest.

> Q: How do we use assessment results to make decisions?
> A: We evaluate the results against a referent (a criterion or norm).

WHAT DO WE ASSESS?

Deciding what to assess is an important topic. We would argue that, in a sense, it is the most important topic when using data to make instructional decisions because every other decision you make depends on how well you defined and assessed the content.

Even though deciding what to assess is one of the most important topics to cover, it is also relatively straightforward. Typically, you will have a good sense of what you want to assess based on the decision you intend to make. For example, if you want to make a decision about whether students in your class have mastered how to add, subtract, multiply, and divide rational numbers, you would select content that assesses students' ability to perform these tasks. Of course, you must make some nuanced decisions, such as determining if you will include items that assess the students' ability to model fraction operations using visual representations, apply properties of operations as strategies for executing the operations, solve real-world and mathematical problems, and justify or verify their responses. Conversely, if you were making a decision about fluency with fraction operations, you likely would not assess students' ability to draw, construct, and describe geometric figures (unless related to fraction operations).

However, one aspect of deciding what to assess is not so straightforward: determining the level of cognitive engagement to assess. *Cognitive engagement* refers to the thinking processes students use when learning or demonstrating their learning of the content. Examples of cognitive engagement include executing an operation, demonstrating understanding or applying reasoning, selecting and implementing a strategy, and justifying an answer. Even if you know what content you want to assess, it is important to think about what level of cognitive engagement you want to probe. In some cases, you might want to make a decision about students' conceptual understanding of fraction operations. In other cases, you may want to make a decision about students' procedural capability to execute fraction operations and their conceptual understanding. In still other cases, you might want to make a decision about students' flexibility with strategies when operating with fractions and verifying their answers. As you can see, selecting the level of cognitive engagement depends on the decision you want to make.

Levels of cognitive engagement can be described in many different ways. You might be most familiar with Bloom's Taxonomy as a way to describe levels of cognitive engagement with any subject matter. However, some levels of cognitive engagement are specific to mathematics. For example, the CCSS-M (2010) describes eight Standards for Mathematics Practice that they reference as "process and proficiency standards":

1. Make sense of problems and persevere in solving them

2. Reason abstractly and quantitatively

3. Construct viable arguments and critique the reasoning of others

4. Model with mathematics

5. Use appropriate tools strategically

6. Attend to precision

7. Look for and make use of structure

8. Look for and express regularity in repeated reasoning

As we introduced in Chapter 4, the National Research Council's report, *Adding It Up* (2001), identifies five strands of mathematical proficiency:

1. *Conceptual understanding* pertains to the functional grasp of mathematics that a student applies to concepts, operations, and relations. It involves being able to logically organize one's knowledge to integrate and understand concepts as part of a coherent whole.

2. *Procedural fluency* pertains to accurately and appropriately carrying out skills, including being able to select efficient and flexible approaches.

3. *Strategic competence* involves one's ability to formulate a problem in mathematical terms, to represent it strategically (verbally, symbolically, graphically, or numerically), and to solve it effectively. It is similar to problem solving and problem formation.

4. *Adaptive reasoning* involves the student's capacity to think logically about a problem, which requires reflecting on various approaches to solve a problem and deductively selecting an approach. Students who are able to do this are also able to rationalize and justify their strategy.

5. *Productive disposition* refers to a student's overall ability to perceive mathematics as worthwhile and to maintain a personal belief in one's own efficacy in solving problems.

You or your mathematics department might define the levels of cognitive engagement differently than these sources. Regardless of how you define them, it is important

Level of cognitive engagement	Item stem	Answer choices	Rationale for answer choice
Conceptual understanding	Which is equivalent to this ratio? 2 circles:3 squares	4 circles / 6 squares	Correct answer
		3 circles / 4 squares	$3 - 2 = 1$ and $4 - 3 = 1$
		4 circles / 5 squares	Added 2 to both sides
		2 circles / 1 square	2 circles out of 3 total
Procedural fluency	Which number makes these ratios equivalent? 4:12 ?:18	6	Correct answer
		10	$12 + 6 = 18$, so $4 + 6 = 10$
		54	$\frac{12}{4} = 3$, and $18 \times 3 = 54$
		3	$\frac{12}{4} = 3$
Strategic competence	Smith knows that the ratio of girls to boys in his school is 4:5. There are 180 boys. Which strategy could be used to find the number of girls?	$(180 \div 5) \times 4$	Correct answer
		$(180 \div 4) \times 5$	Used the wrong number in the ratio to find the unit rate.
		$(180 \div 9) \times 4$	Added $4 + 5$. Thought that 180 represented the total.
		$(180 \div 9) \times 5$	Added $4 + 5$. Thought that 180 represented the total.
Adaptive reasoning	Why are these ratios equivalent? 2:10 6:30	$2 \div 10$ is equal to $6 \div 30$.	Correct answer
		All of the numbers are divisible by 2.	Incorrect reasoning
		Both have the smaller number first in the ratio.	Superficial examination of problem
		$2 \div 6$ is equal to $30 \div 10$.	Procedural error

Figure 9.7. Examples of items that assess equivalent ratios at the different levels of cognitive engagement, using the National Research Council's classification.

to consider them in assessment and instruction. Not only should you use the levels of cognitive engagement when deciding what to assess, but you should also use them to guide instruction. Students need to have access to instruction across the levels of cognitive complexity to make sure they are developing a variety of mathematical proficiencies.

Figure 9.7 provides some examples of items that assess equivalent ratios at different levels of cognitive engagement, using the National Research Council's classification.

HOW DO WE SHARE ASSESSMENT RESULTS?

Because we assess to make decisions, we will act on assessment results. In nearly all examples, the actions we take will affect students, either directly or indirectly. As such, we need to communicate our decisions and actions to students and their families.

There are several steps you can take to prepare for this communication. Before communicating assessment results, it is important that you

1. Fully understand the score reports

2. Clearly articulate how you will use the results in conjunction with other data to make a decision

3. Have a plan for implementing the instructional changes

Once you have this information in place, results can be shared with parents and students.

Know the Score Reports

Before sharing any results, you should have a thorough understanding of results and what information is being communicated in the score reports. Although this sounds straightforward, some score reports are very difficult to understand, let alone communicate. If any aspect of the score report is confusing to your or your colleagues, it will likely be confusing to a parent or student. For example, grade-level equivalence is a reporting category found on many score reports, but is widely misunderstood and miscommunicated, leading to unnecessary confusion. (Grade-level equivalent scores do not indicate the grade in which the student is performing; i.e., a sixth-grade student with a grade-equivalent score of 8 is not performing at the eighth-grade level. Instead, the grade-equivalent score indicates the score point at which the median student in the grade would perform on the same test; i.e., the median student in grade 8 would perform on the sixth-grade test at this score point.)

Similarly, standard error of measurement is reported on most score reports, but it is a concept that many people have difficulty understanding and interpreting. Standard error of measurement is the error around the student's score that indicates the range of scores he or she would likely attain if administered the same test at another time. For example, a student might earn a scale score of 237 on a standardized test with a standard error of measurement of 25. Because of the error in this student's score (as indicated by the standard error of measurement), this student's score should be interpreted as ranging from 237 ± 25, for a range of 212–262.

As noted earlier, a score report may include a section titled National Grade Percentile Bands. These bands are designed to display the student's score visually when accounting for standard error of measurement. In the example described above, a student's percentile rank for mathematics problem solving was reported as 54, but in looking at the National Grade Percentile Bands, when accounting for the standard error of measurement, the student's score would fall roughly within the 40th to 60th percentile rank. As you can see, standard error of measurement is often confusing because it changes the interpretation of a single score into an interpretation of a range of scores.

Gather Additional Data

Multiple sources of data should be gathered that verify the results from any assessment system. Results from almost any test can be influenced by random errors. These random errors are not mistakes made by the student because he or she does not know the content, but instead are errors that are caused by random events that affect the way a student responds to the items. For example, the following circumstances could introduce random errors: a distraction such as a fire drill that affects your student's ability to concentrate; missing breakfast, which may cause sleepiness; or ambiguously worded items, which students might interpret in multiple ways. To make sure your instructional decisions are not based on flawed data, you should evaluate more than one data point to verify the results of any assessment system. Some sources of error may be systematic and should be addressed with accommodations or modifications (see Chapter 3 for a description of these changes and how IEP teams can help determine which changes might be needed).

Document Instructional Decisions and Changes

Remember that the goal of administering any assessment system is to make a decision. Regardless of which decision you will use the data to make, when communicating results, it is important to have clear documentation as to how the results help you make this decision.

Share Results

When sharing information with parents and students, human nature causes most people to scan the report quickly for important information (i.e., the test score). Remember the last energy bill you got in the mail; most likely you skipped over all of the introductory information and went right to the amount you owe. In that case, you know what the amount means to you and your budget, but when interpreting test results, most parents do not know what this information means to them and their child. To help with the interpretation, create a plan for how the reports will be presented and described. Here is a sample plan.

Step 1: Share general information about the test, such as

- The purpose of the test

- How the test will inform instructional decisions

- The content that was assessed

It is important that parents and students understand the reasons why you administered the selected assessment. Once they understand why the test was administered and how the information will be used, the score will have more meaning.

Step 2: Describe the scores on the report. Knowing what to expect from the score reports will help parents and students get an overall impression of the results. When you read your energy bill, you have a general sense of what to look for. You know that you will see a figure reported in dollars and cents. You have an idea of the range you might encounter, depending upon the season. You also know how the information will be conveyed. This basic understanding is built over years of reading and reviewing your energy bill. However, most parents and students have limited exposure to score reports from tests. Spending time helping them understand the scores will pay off in the future.

Step 3: Share the student's score. Once parents and students understand the purpose of the assessment and have a sense of scores they will encounter, they should have enough context for interpreting scores. Now you are ready to share information at a pace that is understandable for parents and students.

Step 4: Share the instructional decisions. Once parents and students understand the meaning of the score, they will likely be anxious to hear about what comes next. Share the instructional decisions you made prior to convening the parents. Emphasize that the decisions are intended to support the student's achievement. Lay out a plan for supporting the student within the school day as well as outside of the school day. Involve the parents as much as possible in designing the next steps. For example, brainstorm ways the parents can be supportive of mathematics at home (i.e., have the child estimate or add up the total cost of groceries while shopping, schedule time for use of the home or library computer to play math games or puzzles, or monitor completion of homework). Remember to be sensitive about the family's home life and not assume that they will have resources (financial or time) for providing additional support. If appropriate, set performance goals and develop a plan for monitoring progress toward reaching the goals.

Step 5: Answer questions. Parents and students will likely have many questions. Allow ample time for questions and discussion. Have access to information about additional resources available from the school or in the community to support the parents and students. Such information could include tutoring programs or organizations, web sites with grade-appropriate mathematics games and programs, or summer or afterschool mathematics or STEM enrichment programs.

SUMMARY: YOUR QUESTIONS ABOUT ASSESSMENT, ANSWERED

In this chapter, we provided an overview of why educators need to assess performance. We then focused on four questions surrounding assessment:

1. When do we assess?

2. How do we use the results?

3. What do we assess?

4. How do we share the results

Central to all of these questions is the decision you are trying to make. We also discussed the differences between formative and summative assessments and how both types of assessment are used in the decision-making cycle. Finally, to help review your school or district's data-use practices, you may want to collect information on your team's perception about the successful implementation of specific data use practices. The appendix to this chapter provides a reflection survey you may use for this purpose. (A downloadable, photocopiable version is available online with the other downloadable materials for this book.)

CHAPTER 9 APPENDIX

Team-Building Activity

To help review the data-use practices that are already in place in your school or district, you may want to collect information on your team's perception about the successful implementation of specific data use practices. The reflection survey shown in Figure 9.8 uses recommendations from the Institute on Education Sciences Practice Guide titled *Using Student Achievement Data to Support Instructional Decision Making* (NCEE 2009-4067) to organize your reflections. (This survey is also available online with the downloadable materials for this book at http://downloads.brookespublishing.com). By completing this reflection survey, you can identify areas of data use that are particularly successful in your school or classroom. You can also identify areas that you might want to improve. Taking inventory of what is going well and what you might want to work on is the first step in taking action to improve your practices.

REFLECTION SURVEY Using Data to Make Instructional Decisions

Directions: Reflect on the current practices in your classroom and at your school. Select the response that best aligns with your perceptions of the successfulness of the implementation of these recommendations. Also, identify who is primarily responsible for implementing the recommendation.

	How successfully are these recommendations implemented in your school?				How successful are you at implementing these recommendations?			
	Very successful	Successful	Somewhat successful	Not successful	Very successful	Successful	Somewhat successful	Not successful
Recommendation 1. Make data part of an ongoing cycle of instructional improvement.								
Collect and prepare a variety of data about student learning.	4	3	2	1	4	3	2	1
Interpret data and develop hypotheses about how to improve student learning.	4	3	2	1	4	3	2	1
Modify instruction to test hypotheses and increase student learning.	4	3	2	1	4	3	2	1
Recommendation 2. Teach students to examine their own data and set learning goals.								
Explain expectations and assessment criteria.	4	3	2	1	4	3	2	1
Provide feedback to students that is timely, specific, well formatted, and constructive.	4	3	2	1	4	3	2	1
Provide tools that help students learn from feedback.	4	3	2	1	4	3	2	1
Use students' data analyses to guide instructional changes.	4	3	2	1	4	3	2	1

(continued)

Teaching Math in Middle School: Using MTSS to Meet All Students' Needs by Leanne R. Ketterlin-Geller, Sarah R. Powell, David L. Chard, & Lindsey Perry.

REFLECTION SURVEY (continued)

	How successfully are these recommendations implemented in your school?				How successful are you at implementing these recommendations?			
	Very successful	Successful	Somewhat successful	Not successful	Very successful	Successful	Somewhat successful	Not successful
Recommendation 3. Establish a clear vision for schoolwide data use.								
Establish a schoolwide data team that sets the tone for ongoing data use.	4	3	2	1	4	3	2	1
Define critical teaching and learning concepts.	4	3	2	1	4	3	2	1
Develop a written plan that articulates activities, roles, and responsibilities.	4	3	2	1	4	3	2	1
Provide ongoing data leadership.	4	3	2	1	4	3	2	1
Recommendation 4. Provide supports that foster a data-driven culture within the school.								
Designate a school-based facilitator who meets with teacher teams to discuss data.	4	3	2	1	4	3	2	1
Dedicate structured time for staff collaboration.	4	3	2	1	4	3	2	1
Provide targeted professional development regularly.	4	3	2	1	4	3	2	1
Recommendation 5. Develop and maintain a districtwide data system.								
Involve a variety of stakeholders in selecting a data system.	4	3	2	1	4	3	2	1
Clearly articulate system requirements relative to user needs.	4	3	2	1	4	3	2	1
Determine whether to build or buy the data system.	4	3	2	1	4	3	2	1
Plan and stage the implementation of the data system.	4	3	2	1	4	3	2	1

Figure 9.8. Reflection survey: Using data to make instructional decisions. (*Source:* Recommendations from Hamilton, L., Halverson, R., Jackson, S, Mandinach, E., Supovitz, J., & Wayman, J. (2009). Using student achievement data to support instructional decision making (NCEE 2009-4067). Washington, DC: National Center for Education Evaluation and Regional Assistance, Institute of Education Sciences, U.S. Department of Education. Retrieved from https://ies.ed.gov/ncee/wwc/Docs/PracticeGuide/dddm_pg_092909.pdf)

CHAPTER 10

Who Needs Extra Assistance, and How Much? Universal Screeners

When we are using data to make instructional decisions, we need to first consider the types of decisions we are trying to make. As we discussed in the previous chapter, we follow a decision-making cycle to determine which data we need to make a specific decision. (To review this cycle, see the introduction to Section II of this book and the explanation of steps in Chapter 9.)

In this chapter, we discuss the first decision teachers and administrators need to make when implementing MTSS: Which students need extra help to reach their goals? Also, how much extra help do they need?

WHAT ARE WE AIMING FOR?

Every year when school starts, you are faced with many opportunities and challenges. You have the opportunity to work with new and perhaps continuing colleagues, meet new parents or guardians, and decide how best to help the students in your classes reach their goals. In some cases, these opportunities become exciting and welcome parts of your job. However, other times, these opportunities become challenges. For many teachers, the opportunity of helping students reach their goals can be a formidable challenge.

One of the biggest challenges many teachers like you face is getting to know your students—not only their names, but also knowing about them as learners:

- With which topics in the previous year's curriculum were they successful? With which topics did they struggle?

- Which types of learning activities are most successful in helping them learn? Least successful? Of these learning activities, which do they like? Which do they dislike?

- What special learning characteristics do they have?

Answers to each of these questions help you plan your instruction. Unfortunately, it can often take days, weeks, or even months to really know your students as learners. Until you understand your students' needs, you may not be providing them with the appropriate instructional opportunities to reach their learning goals. Consider this common scenario.

MS. WALKER'S GRADE 6 MATH CLASS

Ms. Walker is in her fourth year teaching math to students in grade 6 at Uptown Middle School. Before the end of the last school year, she spoke with the grade 5 teachers at the two elementary schools that send students to Uptown Middle School. She knows that the elementary school teachers worked hard to cover the math content standards, and the students' scores on the grade 5 state accountability test in math are generally good.

Because the grade 6 mathematics content standards are rigorous, Ms. Walker begins the year with a quick review of some of the critical topics from fifth grade, such as adding and subtracting fractions using equivalent fractions (CCSS-M 5.NF.1), and then starts instruction on the grade 6 material. However, by the end of the first grading period, Ms. Walker is disappointed that about 40% of her students are already showing signs of falling behind. She worries that they will continue to struggle as the year goes on and the content gets more difficult. She decides to adjust her instruction for the whole class; she slows down the pace and assigns more group work. Unfortunately, as the end of the semester comes around, Ms. Walker's students are far behind the other grade 6 classes.

This is a common scenario that plagues many teachers. Ms. Walker did not know her students as individuals. She assumed they all had the same background knowledge in mathematics and were equally prepared to begin learning the sixth-grade mathematics content. As a result, she provided the same Tier 1 instruction for all students. Without differentiating instruction, she compromised the learning opportunities for the range of students in her class. In the end, most students were behind in their learning of the mathematics content.

As this example illustrates, some students are on track for being successful in the current year's mathematics content, but others might need extra instructional help beyond the Tier 1 mathematics instruction. For those students who are on track, instruction should continue to support their learning of the content standards. (For specifics about how to tailor instruction to meet all students' needs, see Section II of this book.)

In some cases, as with the 40% of students in Ms. Walker's class, students may not be ready to learn the current year's mathematics content without extra instructional support. These students may have failed to learn the previous year's content, or perhaps they learned it in the previous grade but were unable to retain everything they learned over the course of the year. In other cases, these students have difficulty acquiring and applying new knowledge and skills to reach grade-level expectations, setting them back as their grade-level peers move on. For any number of reasons, these students are at risk of not reaching the expectations by the end of the year. Frequently, if students have not reached proficiency on the grade-level content standards, their performance on state accountability tests will not be adequate to demonstrate proficiency (i.e., earning a "does not meet" or equivalent rating). However, some students may pass the state accountability test but still not be proficient in the mathematics skills and knowledge needed to be successful in the next mathematics course. To be successful in the next grade, these students will need additional instructional support in Tier 2 or Tier 3.

As a teacher, you need a way to identify students who need extra help early in the school year—typically, those students identified as needing Tier 2 or Tier 3 intervention. Only by identifying these students early in the teaching and learning process can you effectively plan your instruction to provide them with the extra support they need to reach their goals. So, to plan instruction effectively from the very beginning of the school year, it can be helpful to have an assessment tool to help you make two key decisions:

> Only by identifying students who need extra help early in the teaching and learning process can you effectively plan instruction to provide the extra support they need.

1. Which students are on track for meeting these curricular expectations? Which students are at risk for not meeting these curricular expectations?

2. What is each student's relative risk of being off track?

WHAT TOOLS WILL HELP US MAKE THESE DECISIONS?

As we discussed earlier, formative assessments are used to inform instruction. Results from these tests should be used to make instructional decisions that we believe will improve students' learning. The first instructional decision answers a big question: Which students are and are not on track for meeting curriculum expectations? In order to answer this question, we need to administer a formative assessment tool. Within an MTSS framework, we administer a universal screener.

What Is a Universal Screener?

Universal screeners are formative assessments used to identify students who are and are not on track for reaching proficiency in the curricular expectations. Universal screeners are a cornerstone of MTSS and are also common in many fields. In medicine, for example, a typical universal screener for evaluating the health of major body systems is a blood panel, such as the basic metabolic panel. This blood panel provides indicators to determine kidney function, blood sugar levels, and levels of electrolytes. Doctors use the results from the test to determine whether patients are at risk for certain illnesses and whether they need additional testing. In another example, at many schools, all students are required to have their hearing screened once a year. These screenings provide information to the school nurse about which students may have hearing loss. If a student performs poorly on the hearing screening, they will be referred to an audiologist for a more thorough diagnosis. Other fields also use universal screeners.

Common to these examples of universal screening is the overall decision about risk status:

*   Are the body systems in a person generally functioning well, or are there indicators that something may not be working properly? How far outside of the normal range are the data?

*   Is a student able to hear all frequencies at a certain decibel level? Does a student need follow-up testing by an audiologist?

*   Is a country showing signs of economic growth or are there indicators that might point to risks of economic instability? How significant is the instability of the indicators?

In mathematics education, universal screeners function the same way:

- Do indicators suggest a student is progressing as expected toward meeting the curricular expectations, or is there evidence that the student is at risk for not reaching proficiency?

- How significant is the risk?

How Do I Use Universal Screeners to Make an Instructional Decision?

This subsection explains how universal screeners can help you make each of the instructional decisions noted previously.

Key Decisions from Universal Screener Data

1. Which students are on track for meeting curricular expectations? Which students are at risk for not meeting these curricular expectations?

2. What is each student's relative risk of being off track?

Which Students Are and Are Not on Track?   Determining which students are and are not on track for meeting the instructional goals (i.e., curricular expectations) can help teachers and administrators make several key decisions. As a teacher, you can use this information to identify students who need extra instructional support (e.g., students needing Tier 2 and Tier 3 support) to reach proficiency in the curricular expectations. This support might come in any of several forms:

- Differentiated instruction that provides additional scaffolding when new information is introduced

- A Tier 2 or Tier 3 intervention that targets previously taught (but not learned) concepts that will be integrated with new information

- Supplemental resources that provide extra practice in applying a skill, such as fact fluency

- Any number of instructional decisions that might generally help students get on track for reaching proficiency in the curricular expectations

For a more detailed discussion of possible intervention decisions, please refer to Chapters 7 and 8.

You can make instructional decisions such as those noted here by comparing students' scores on the universal screener to a predetermined criterion (see criterion-referenced interpretations). As we discussed earlier, interpreting data in reference to a criterion allows you to compare students' scores against a specific standard of performance to make a decision. In this case of a universal screener, the standard of performance is a cut score—that is, a specific point within the range of scores that is used to place students' scores into categories. This cut score divides the students' scores into at least two performance levels, or categories, for making decisions:

1. Students who are identified as being on track

2. Students who are identified as being at risk for not meeting the curricular expectations and needing Tier 2 or Tier 3 instructional support

In some instances, scores from universal screeners are evaluated against a criterion with more than two performance levels. As previously noted, within an MTSS framework, students' scores are frequently divided into three performance levels, or categories:

Tier 1: Students on track for reaching curricular expectations

Tier 2: Students at risk for not reaching curricular expectations who need strategic and targeted intervention

Tier 3: Students at risk for not reaching curricular expectations who need immediate and intensive intervention

The cut scores used to place students into performance levels likely will be already set for you by the publisher of the universal screener. They are typically set using one of two methods: normative student performance or predicted performance.

When Do I Set Cut Scores Using Normative Student Performance? Setting cut scores using normative student performance is most useful when your school or district is able to provide additional instructional support to a specific percentage of the student population. This is often the case when your school or district has limited resources for providing intervention and needs to manage those resources in a way that provides intervention for a specific number or proportion of students, such as 30%.

When setting cut scores using normative student performance, data are gathered from a specific sample of students taking the universal screener. This sample is called the normative sample, and it can be drawn from within your district or state or from across the country. These data are ranked in order of performance, and a cut score is set based on the percentage of students who reached that score. For example, a common cut score for identifying students who are at risk for not reaching curricular expectations is the 40th percentile. In other words, students scoring at or below the score at the 40th percentile are identified as being at risk for not reaching expectations; students scoring above the 40th percentile are identified as being on track for reaching expectations. An example is shown in Figure 10.1.

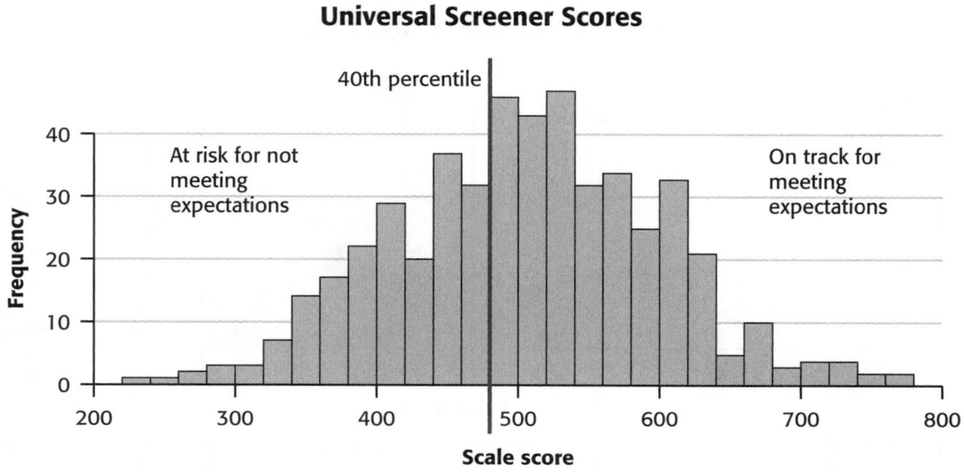

Universal Screener Scores

Figure 10.1. On universal screeners, the 40th percentile is commonly used as a cut score to identify which students are at risk of not meeting expectations.

The cut score in Figure 10.1 indicates the score on the universal screener at which 40% of the data from the normative sample are found. Based on your school or district's resources, you may set this normative cut score at different percentiles to optimize your resource expenses.

When Do I Set Cut Scores Using Predicted Performance?   Setting cut scores using predicted performance is most useful when your school or district is able to provide supplemental instructional support to any student who is predicted to be at risk for not reaching curricular expectations. In other words, if you have unlimited resources to apply to intervention in mathematics, we recommend using predicted performance for setting your cut scores. When setting cut scores using predicted performance, data are gathered from a prior year's administration of the universal screener as well as from a summative assessment (i.e., state accountability tests). These data are used to determine which score on the universal screener predicted failure on the previous year's summative assessment. This is similar to the way a

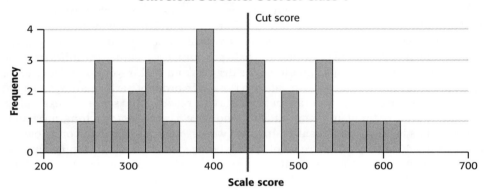

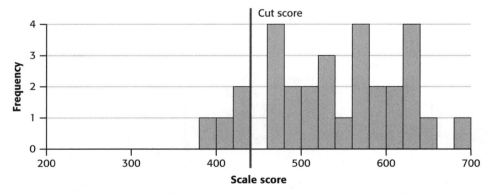

Figure 10.2. Bar graphs showing two classes' assessment results. Because many more students in Class 1 scored below the cut score, we can determine that this class as a whole is at greater risk of not meeting expectations and will need more resources.

doctor might explain to you the relationship between body weight and likelihood of heart attack. In other words, performance on the universal screener is statistically modeled to determine the cut score at which a student's odds change from being likely to fail the summative assessment to being likely to pass the summative assessment. Because this cut score is not related to normative student performance, it may include as few or as many students' scores as fall on either side of the score. For example, see Figure 10.2, which shows screener scores for two classes. Many more students in Class 1 are identified as "likely to fail" than in Class 2. Class 1 would require many more resources to assist these students, compared to Class 2. Again, this is why this approach is most appropriately used where there are few limitations on resources.

What Is Each Student's Relative Risk of Being Off Track?   As a teacher, knowing which students are and are not on track only gives you part of the picture for making instructional decisions. Some students might be well on their way to meeting the curricular expectations, but others may have just barely scored beyond the cut score. Conversely, some students might be off track but only by a small margin; however, some students might be significantly off track.

You can make these judgments by evaluating students' scores in relation to the cut score. If we think about students' scores on the universal screener as existing in a continuum from the lowest to the highest, we intuitively know that students with the highest scores have greater content knowledge and students with the lowest scores either have less content knowledge or are not able to demonstrate it on the assessment. This same continuum exists within the performance levels created after imposing a cut score.

For the students identified as on track, their scores exist along a continuum from the lowest to the highest. The lowest score is the score that is closest to the cut score. These students have less content knowledge than students whose scores are the farthest from the cut score (i.e., are the highest). Even though all of these students are identified as being on track for reaching the curricular expectations, students with scores closest to the cut score will need more instructional support to reach the curriculum expectations than students whose scores are farthest from the cut score. Using the graph in Figure 10.3, think about where Maria and Logan are on the curricular expectation and support spectrum. Both Maria and Logan are on track for meeting curricular expectations; however, because Maria scored close to the cut score, she may need strategic support to ensure that she remains on track.

For students identified as being at risk for not meeting the curricular expectation, their scores also exist along a continuum from lowest to highest. The lowest score is closest to the minimum score on the test; the highest score is closest to the cut score. Consider the students Nadia and Will from the graph shown in Figure 10.3. Even though both are identified as being at risk for not reaching the curricular expectations, the significance of the risk varies depending upon the placement of their score along this continuum. A student such as Nadia, whose score is close to the minimum score on the test, is at significant risk for not reaching the curricular expectations. This student will need immediate and intensive instructional support to reach proficiency. Although a student such as Will, who scores near the cut score, is still at risk for not reaching proficiency, this student may need less intensive support to meet the curricular expectations.

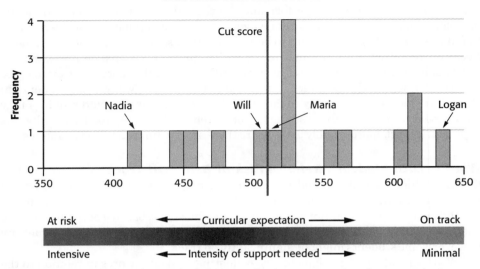

Figure 10.3. By analyzing and comparing individual students' scores on a universal screener, educators can deteramine which students have a greater or lesser risk of not meeting expectations and, consequently, which students need more intensive or less intensive support.

Knowing a student's relative risk of being off track will change the instructional decisions you make for the student. For example, a student who is off track by a small margin may benefit from differentiated instructional strategies and corrective feedback to address a few persistent misconceptions or errors. As shown in the graph above, Will would be considered one of these students because he is at risk for not meeting curricular expectations but scored very close to the cut score for being on track. With frequent monitoring, this student is likely to be on track for reaching proficiency on the grade-level content standards. In contrast, Nadia, who is off track by a significant margin, may have many persistent and fundamental misconceptions that can only be successfully addressed with a systematic instructional intervention.

You will need to carefully evaluate the students whose scores fall around the cut score. For example, Will scored just below the cut score and Maria scored just above. Although these students are placed into different performance levels, they are probably more alike than different. What separates them may very well be the response to one item. It is essential that additional information about their skills and knowledge from other sources (i.e., classroom tests, homework, summative assessments) be combined with the universal screener results to determine students' risk status.

As we described in Chapter 2, we recommend that you use a progress monitoring system (see Chapter 12). In Tier 1, you can administer progress monitoring measures for 6 to 10 weeks to confirm your findings from the universal screener. Data from progress monitoring measures help you determine whether Tier 1 instruction is providing the best level of support for your students. If a student's progress monitoring scores indicate adequate growth (i.e., acceptable and increasing slope) or meets a satisfactory benchmark, then the student should continue to receive Tier 1 mathematics instruction. If a student does not demonstrate adequate growth or meet a suitable benchmark, this student requires supplemental support.

When and to Whom Are Universal Screeners Administered?

Typically, a universal screener is administered in the beginning, middle, and near the end of the year to all students. Universal screeners should be administered in the beginning of the year to provide teachers and administrators with information early on that identifies students who are on track for meeting curricular expectations and students who are at risk for not reaching proficiency. Remember from Chapter 2 that we talked about Tier 1 as the primary prevention because we want to prevent further mathematics difficulty. To optimize the instructional time, you will have to support student achievement, you need this information as soon as possible after school starts.

Universal screeners are administered in the middle of the academic year to evaluate the change in students' knowledge and understanding over time. Systematically evaluating their mathematical knowledge and skills mid-year will allow you to make timely decisions to change instruction, if needed. If instruction is meeting students' needs, students will demonstrate growth from the beginning to the middle of the year, as shown in the graph in Figure 10.4.

Box-and-whisker plots are often used to display growth over time. The bold line in the middle of each box represents the median score, and the bottom and top lines on the box represent the lower and upper quartiles, corresponding to the 25th and 75th percentiles, respectively. This means that 50% of the scores are contained within the "box." The maximum and minimum scores are also included on these graphs and make the "whiskers."

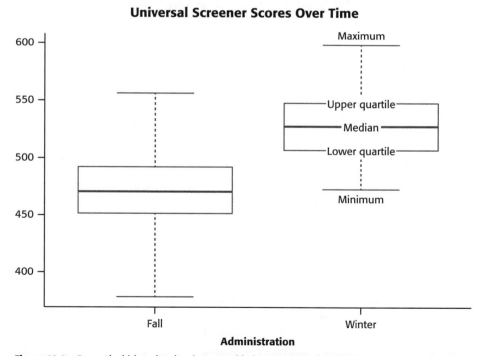

Figure 10.4. Box-and-whisker plot showing a notable increase in students' scores on a universal screener from fall to winter, indicating improved proficiency.

In the example shown in Figure 10.4, the median student score increased considerably from fall to winter, and the maximum and minimum scores also increased. This graph helps us conclude that overall, students' scores on the universal screener and their proficiency in mathematics increased from the beginning to the middle of the year.

If instruction is not meeting students' needs, their mid-year scores on the universal screener will indicate little to no growth. In contrast to the graph in Figure 10.4, the graph in Figure 10.5 shows that the median student score on the fall and winter universal screeners was approximately the same. Although the minimum score was higher than in the fall, the maximum score actually decreased from fall to winter. In addition, the upper and lower quartiles increased slightly, but considering all of these factors together, it appears that little to no growth occurred from fall to winter for this group of students.

Finally, universal screeners should be administered near the end of the school year when there is still enough instructional time to provide meaningful information for decision making. Because universal screeners are formative assessments, it is important that your school or district schedule the last administration so that the results are back in your hands in time for you to make instructional changes that will support students in meeting curricular expectations during the current school year. Administering the spring universal screener during the last week or two of school when there is little time to implement instructional changes is not useful.

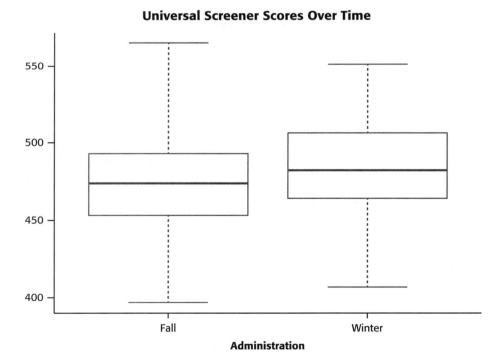

Figure 10.5. Box-and-whisker plot showing little increase in students' scores on a universal screener from fall to winter, indicating minimal growth in proficiency.

Universal screeners are administered to all students to evaluate everyone's potential risk status. Just as blood panels are routinely collected from all people during annual physical exams and indicators of national economic growth are regularly tracked for all countries, universal screening data in mathematics should be gathered for all children. For students who are on track for reaching curricular expectations in the fall, gathering data from universal screeners at the middle and near the end of the year helps teachers evaluate whether students are continuing to make adequate progress toward their goals. Some students who were identified in the fall as being on track for reaching expectations may fall behind as the content gets more complex across the school year. If information is not gathered from these students until the end of the year, valuable instructional time will be lost. Conversely, some students who were identified in the fall as being at risk for not meeting expectations may show enough growth by the middle of the year to be on track for reaching curricular expectations. For these students, the instructional decisions the teacher made after the fall administration of the universal screener were successful in helping the student reach their goals.

By gathering data in the beginning, middle, and near the end of the year from all students, you can also use universal screener results to determine whether all students are making progress. Consider Micah, a student who is expected to reach proficiency on the curricular expectations. On the fall administration of the universal screener, Micah's score showed that he was performing near the top of the class. At the middle of the year, his score on the universal screener identified that he was still on track for reaching curricular expectations, but there was not much growth from the beginning to the middle of the year, as indicated in Figure 10.6. For this student, instruction was not helping him reach his goals.

> By gathering universal screening data throughout the year for all students, you can also use the results to determine whether they are making progress.

What Are the Characteristics of a Universal Screener?

As we discussed earlier, to be useful for making instructional decisions, all assessment systems must produce reliable results that lead to valid interpretations. With universal screeners, important considerations for reliability include being sure that different forms administered throughout the year have the same difficulty level, because comparisons will be made about growth over time. If the assessments vary in difficulty, then the increases or decreases in scores over time may be due to the differences in the tests, not necessarily students' growth in mathematics. If items are open-ended and need to be read and scored by individual raters, it is also important that the raters arrive at the same outcome for each item. If one rater grades harder than another, then the scores will not be reliable.

When evaluating validity for universal screeners, key considerations include the accuracy of the cut scores for predicting student performance on the outcome measure (usually the end of year assessment), content alignment with curricular expectations (the national, state, and district standards), and efficiency of administration and scoring, which are described in more detail in the following subsections.

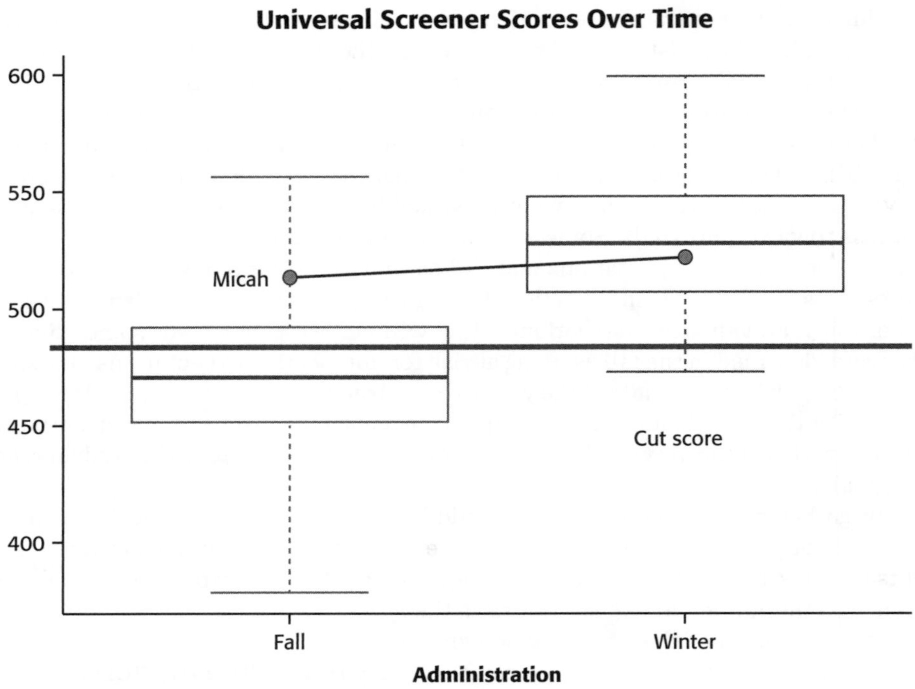

Universal Screener Scores Over Time

Figure 10.6. Graph illustrating how, although Micah's test scores show he is on track to meet grade-level expectations, these scores demonstrate minimal growth over time.

Classification Accuracy As noted earlier, establishing a cut score is an important process for implementing universal screeners. The cut score is used to place students into at least two categories: 1) on track for reaching curricular expectations, and 2) at risk for not reaching curricular expectations. Because the primary purpose of administering a universal screener is placement into these categories, statistical techniques should verify the accuracy of the cut score to make these placements. This information about the predictive ability of the test is typically described in a technical report, or you can ask the test provider to share this information. Before adopting or implementing a universal screener, the classification accuracy should be carefully evaluated.

If cut scores were set using normative student performance, you should evaluate the demographic characteristics of the normative sample in relation to your district's demographics. By comparing these two populations, the district can ensure that classification decisions are applicable in reference to the district's student population. In some instances, the normative sample may be very different from the students in your classroom or your district, which would call into question the cut scores' value. For example, the normative sample might include a small number of students from a specific state or region of the country, who might be systematically different from other student groups based on their exposure to different curricular expectations, instructional approaches, and/or policy decisions. In these cases, your district might want to create local norms for setting cut scores.

Content Alignment for Making Universal Screening Decisions   The content of universal screeners should align with the curricular expectations about which you and your colleagues are making decisions. For example, if you want to determine whether students are or are not on track for reaching proficiency in algebra readiness, the content of the universal screener should align with algebra readiness expectations.

In some cases, specific content statements might be more important than others for various reasons (i.e., one content statement might have particular importance for subsequent grades). For example, consider the content statement from grade 7 CCSS-M (National Governors Association Center for Best Practices & Council of Chief State School Officers, 2010, 7.EE.4): "Use variables to represent quantities in a real-world or mathematical problem, and construct simple equations and inequalities to solve problems by reasoning about the quantities."

Students' proficiency in these skills and knowledge is particularly important as students analyze and solve linear equations and pairs of simultaneous linear equations in grade 8 and in algebra. As such, when evaluating an existing universal screener or designing your own for grade 7, you might want to emphasize the skill and knowledge in 7.EE.4, compared to those in other statements such as the following (National Governors Association Center for Best Practices & Council of Chief State School Officers, 2010, 7.SP.3): "Informally assess the degree of visual overlap of two numerical data distributions with similar variabilities, measuring the difference between the centers by expressing it as a multiple of a measure of variability." Whereas this standard should be taught in seventh grade, this standard compared to 7.EE.4 might not receive as much emphasis on an algebra readiness universal screener, because understanding data distributions is not a foundational skill for algebra.

To make appropriate placement decisions, alignment of the universal screener needs to be evaluated for both the mathematical content of the items and the level of cognitive engagement (discussed in Chapter 9) in which students interact with the content. Both factors should be evaluated to determine if the screener results will provide valuable information regarding students being or not being on track for meeting the curricular expectations. For example, if the content statements of a universal screener align with the curricular expectations, but the items assess only procedural fluency as opposed to a breadth of mathematical thinking, decisions about students' possible risk status may not be valid.

Efficiency of Administration and Scoring   The administration of universal screeners should be efficient for both you and your students. In other words, it should use as little instructional time as is necessary to get reliable information and should be straightforward to give and interpret.

Universal screeners in mathematics should take about 20 minutes of instructional time to administer (Gersten, Dimino, & Haymond, 2011). However, enough information about students' skills and knowledge must be gathered to get reliable data. If your district is creating a universal screener, it is important to design the test carefully to be efficient in assessing key skills and knowledge. If your school or district is purchasing a test, questions about efficiency of administration and scoring should be asked of the test provider or considered carefully during piloting.

Some commercially available universal screeners are designed as computerized adaptive tests (CATs). CATs are designed to provide reliable data in the fewest number of items possible. To get a reliable score, the test delivers items that are targeted to the student's ability level by adjusting the difficulty of the items based on the items the student gets correct and incorrect. Typically, these types of tests get reliable results more quickly than tests that are a fixed number of items. Also, for any test that is administered on the computer, students' responses can be scored and reported quickly. Because universal screeners should be used to inform decision making, teachers and administrators need the results as soon as possible after administration, making the CAT type of universal screener very useful.

Districts can create their own universal screeners or use commercially available tests that align with these characteristics. The MTSS Leadership Team works together to evaluate the evidence for reliability and validity to determine if the universal screeners being used meet these criteria. Some organizations, such as the National Center on Intensive Intervention, provide resources for evaluating commercially available universal screeners (see the Academic Screening Tools Chart at https://charts.intensiveintervention.org/chart/academic-screening).

How Do I Communicate Screener Results to Parents and Students?

Sharing assessment results with parents and students is an important part of administering a universal screener. Considering that formative assessment results should be used to guide your instruction, sharing results from the universal screener can help parents and students understand the reasons why you made specific instructional decisions, such as providing Tier 2 instruction. As we noted previously, when preparing to communicate results, it is important that you fully understand the reports, understand how results from the universal screener are used in conjunction with other data to make decisions, and have a plan for implementing instructional changes. Once you have this information in place, results can be shared with parents and students.

Know Universal Screener Assessment Reports   Most commercially available universal screeners have resources for interpreting reports. These documents may be available online, or they may be included as hard-copy resources that are supplied by the test publisher. You should plan on thoroughly reviewing these materials before discussing the results with parents and students.

Gather Additional Data   Multiple sources of data to verify results from the universal screener can come from a variety of sources. Progress monitoring data are an important part of this process. You can also gather data such as student work samples from in-class projects or homework assignments, performance on other assessments such as weekly quizzes or the state summative assessment, and observational data to verify the student's score on the universal screener. A student's score on a universal screener is just one piece of data and should not be used in isolation to make major instructional decisions.

Document Instructional Decisions and Changes   Remember that the goal of administering the universal screener is to make decisions about these questions: Are there indicators that suggest a student is progressing as expected toward meeting the curricular expectations, or is there evidence that the student is at risk for not reaching proficiency? How significant is the risk?

Once these questions are addressed with results from the universal screener and verified with additional data, you can make instructional decisions. For students who are on track for reaching curricular expectations, you might decide that the student will benefit from receiving high-quality evidence-based Tier 1 instruction in the general education classroom without additional support. You may continue to monitor the student's progress to verify that the student is making adequate progress.

For students who are not on track for reaching curricular expectations and are "nonresponsive" to Tier 1 instruction, they will likely need Tier 2 instructional support to meet the grade-level expectations (see Chapter 2 for information about designing an intervention platform).

Share Results   You may want to consider augmenting the sample plan discussed in Chapter 9 with these details for sharing results from a universal screener.

Step 1: Share general information about the universal screener, such as

- The purpose of the test

- How the test will inform instructional decisions

- The content that was assessed

It is important that parents and students understand that the universal screener is intended to help you plan instruction; it is not a high-stakes summative assessment used to evaluate the student. Once parents and students understand why the test was administered and how the information will be used, the score will have more meaning.

Step 2: Describe the distribution of the scores from the universal screener. Knowing the range of scores provides parents and students with an overall picture of the possible score value the child could have scored. This type of information can be shared as a histogram, as shown in Figure 10.7.

A histogram displays scores from the universal screener on the x-axis and the number of students in the class or grade level earning each score on the y-axis. Showing parents and students the histogram provides a visual representation of the distribution of scores.

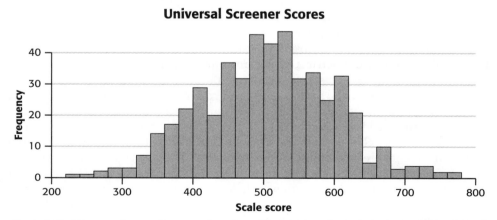

Figure 10.7. Histogram (bar graph) representing universal screener data. The *x*-axis displays possible scores and the *y*-axis displays the number of students who earned each score, providing a visual representation of the score distribution for a class or grade.

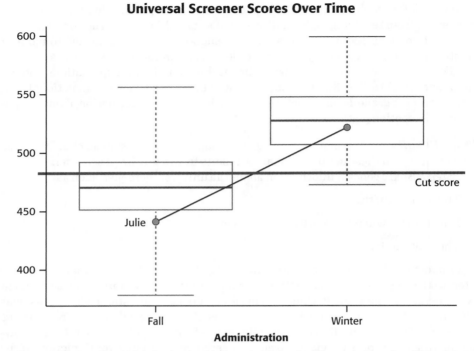

Figure 10.8. Box-and-whisker plot showing the change in Julie's universal screener scores from fall to winter.

For the middle- and end-of-year administrations of the universal screener, it is helpful to share performance trends over time. This information can be shared as a box-and-whisker plot, as shown in Figure 10.8.

A box-and-whisker plot shows the time of administration (early, middle, end of year) on the x-axis and the distribution of the scores on the y-axis. Line graphs, either alone or superimposed on a box-and-whisker plot, can also be used to show performance trends over time, as in Figure 10.9.

Step 3: Describe the cut scores. Identify the cut scores on the histogram and describe their meaning. If the parents or student are having difficulty understanding the meaning of a cut score, you might consider making an analogy to something familiar, such as speed zones. The "cut score" for speeding or not speeding is the MPH (miles per hour) listed on the speed zone sign. If you are driving slower than the MPH, you are not speeding; if you are driving faster than the MPH, you are speeding.

Just as the speed zone can be used to predict (but not determine) whether you will get a speeding ticket, parents and students should know that the cut scores on the universal screener are predictors of future performance, but not dictators of it. Appropriately designed instruction, consistent effort on the student's part, and support from home can render the prediction wrong. The reason for administering the universal screener is to change the outcome of students who are at risk for not reaching the curricular expectations, in order to prevent failure.

Step 4: Share the student's score. Once parents and students understand the purpose of the universal screener and have a sense of the distribution of scores, they

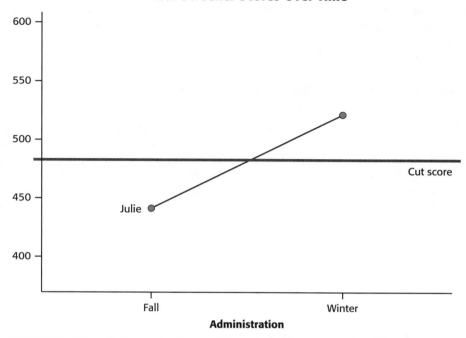

Figure 10.9. Line graph showing the change in Julie's universal screener scores from fall to winter.

should have enough context for interpreting the student's score. Now you are ready to share information at a pace that is understandable for parents and students. To do so, use the following process:

1. First, show where the student's score is located on the histogram, box-and-whisker plot, or other graphic display provided on the score report. Provide as much description as possible. For example, state whether the score is above or below the cut score for risk status. Identify how far above or below the student's score is from the cut score. Describe the growth rate over time by looking at the student's score on the box-and-whisker plots. Providing this information will set the foundation for understanding the instructional decisions you made that will be introduced later in the discussion.

2. Second, share the score report generated from the test publisher. It is likely that additional information is provided on this report. For example, if the standard error of measurement is provided, it would be helpful to interpret this information in light of the student's score and risk status.

3. Third, share the additional information that was gathered to verify the results from the universal screener. It is important to emphasize that the universal screener represents the student's performance on one test that was administered on one day, but given the evidence that has been gathered, these results indicate a trend in the student's performance or understanding.

Step 5: Share the instructional decisions. Once parents and students understand the meaning of the score, they will likely be anxious to hear about what comes next. Share the instructional decisions you made prior to convening the parents.

Step 6: Answer questions. Parents and students will likely have many questions. Allow ample time for questions and discussion.

SUMMARY: USING UNIVERSAL SCREENERS

The first decision teachers need to make is often, "Which students need extra support and how much support do they need to be successful?" In this chapter, we explained how universal screeners, a type of formative assessment, can help teachers answer these questions. Universal screeners are administered to all students and can be given multiple times a year to monitor which students are on track or are at risk for not meeting curricular expectations, as well as the level of support students need in order to be successful. We also provided guidance on how to interpret scores and make valid interpretations from universal screener reports, including how to share results with parents and students.

CHAPTER 11

Why Are Students Struggling? Diagnostic Assessments

In the previous chapter, we identified a universal screener as a useful tool for determining if students are on track for reaching their goals or at risk for not being successful with mathematics content expectations. Although this is often the first decision you will make when examining student performance data, it is far from the last. As we discussed, results from the universal screener can be used to make some important instructional decisions, such as determining whether students need extra instructional support, such as from Tier 2 or Tier 3 interventions. However, these results do not provide all of the information needed to support student learning.

Throughout Section III of this book, we reference a decision-making cycle, described in Chapter 9, to determine which data we need to make a specific decision. In this chapter, we discuss the decision you need to make as soon as a student is identified as struggling in the content: Why is this student struggling?

WHAT ARE WE AIMING FOR?

Suppose that Martha is a student identified as being at risk for not reaching the mathematics content expectations in grade 7, based on the results on the fall administration of the universal screener and progress monitoring measures. To gather more information, Mr. Chang, Martha's mathematics teacher, reviews Martha's performance on the grade 7 accountability assessment. Out of the nine questions on measurement, Martha missed five. Moreover, she missed four out of eight questions on geometry and two on algebra. Mr. Chang decides that Martha needs extra instructional support in measurement followed by additional work in geometry. Mr. Chang uses best practices in instructional design and delivery (such as those described in Section II) to create a Tier 2 intervention platform for Martha, but Martha's progress monitoring data and performance on the winter universal screener indicates that she has not made significant improvements. Why did Martha's scores not improve?

What Mr. Chang did not understand about the errors Martha was making on the measurement and geometry items was the underlying cause of these mistakes. Just knowing the domain in which a student is having difficulty may not be enough information to understand why the student is making mistakes.

> The decision you need to make as soon as a student is identified as struggling in the content: Why is this student struggling?

In Martha's case, each of the items she missed involved operations with rational numbers. More specifically, these items required Martha to take information from a given context to determine the necessary operation, set up the equation, and execute the operation in order to arrive at the solution. Here is a sample of such a test item (based on a released item from the 2011 State of Texas Assessments of Academic Readiness in mathematics, from the Texas Education Agency):

> A jewelry box is in the shape of a rectangular prism. It has a height of 4.25 inches, a width of 5 inches, and a length of 6 inches. What is the volume of the jewelry box in cubic inches?

This item is identified as assessing measurement concepts; however, additional skills and knowledge are needed that extend beyond students' understanding of the formula for volume. Martha did not have the skills to use the contextual information in this problem to set up and solve the equation to find the jewelry box's volume. Without understanding the reasons for Martha's errors, Mr. Chang was not able to provide the necessary instructional support to help Martha reach her goals.

As this scenario points out, once a student is identified as being at risk for not reaching the curricular goals, teachers need to decide what types of instructional support the student needs in Tiers 2 or 3 in order to be successful in the mathematics content expectations. In the instructional chapters in Section II, we discuss in depth the types of instructional design and delivery features that can be used to support student learning. However, a critical component to implementing these instructional design and delivery features is selecting appropriate content for the struggling student. This content selection is based on the underlying content-related reasons why the student is struggling.

In summary, to design the best Tier 2 or Tier 3 intervention platform, you need to make decisions related to the following questions:

1. In which areas of the curriculum is the student struggling? In which areas is the student being successful?

2. What are the persistent errors the student makes when solving problems?

3. What are the student's underlying misconceptions about the content?

WHAT TOOLS WILL HELP US MAKE THESE DECISIONS?

Because information on students' background knowledge and skills, errors, and misconceptions will be used to inform the intervention platform, you need to administer a formative assessment tool to gather this information. Specifically, you can administer diagnostic formative assessments, which can support your understanding of students' areas of strength and weakness as well as students' errors and the sources of their misconceptions. This information supports your design and delivery of instruction, including content to teach or reteach, pacing, and review strategies.

What Is a Diagnostic Formative Assessment?

Diagnostic assessments are formative assessments that are administered to students who are nonresponsive to Tier 1 or Tier 2 instruction and are used to identify the underlying cause of their struggles. Diagnostic assessments are most often used when a system (e.g., a body system, mechanical system, or learning system) is suspected of having a problem. In medicine (see Figure 11.1), if initial screening of the patient's symptoms

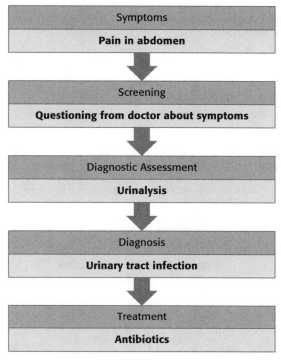

Figure 11.1. Screening and diagnostic assessment as steps in medical intervention for a health problem.

causes a doctor to suspect that a patient may have a urinary tract infection, a diagnostic test of the urine is ordered to detect signs of an infection. If signs of an infection are found (usually elevated levels of white blood cells), the urine sample is further analyzed to determine the type of bacteria causing the infection. Knowing the type of bacteria will allow the doctor to prescribe the best antibiotic for treating the infection. For mechanical systems, such as your car, if a mechanic hears you describe a pinging sound when driving uphill, the mechanic might conduct a diagnostic test of the cooling system to determine if the system is clogged. Once the results of this test are examined, the mechanic can determine the best solution to fix the pinging sound you hear.

In both of these examples, the diagnostic assessment is used after gathering initial information about the problem to determine why the symptoms are occurring. This information is subsequently used to determine the best treatment to resolve the issue.

In mathematics education, diagnostic assessments are used for the same purposes, as shown in Figure 11.2.

What Is *Not* a Diagnostic Formative Assessment?

In this chapter, we are discussing diagnostic assessments for making instructional decisions within an MTSS framework. In education, diagnostic assessments can have other purposes, such as a clinical diagnosis of the presence of a medical condition or disability. For example, in special education, a school psychologist or other licensed

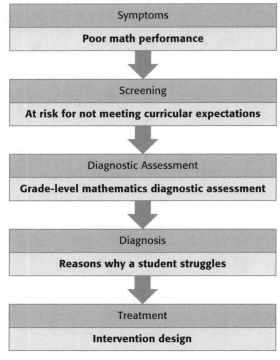

Figure 11.2. Screening and diagnostic assessment as steps in educational intervention for a problem with academic performance.

and qualified practitioner may administer diagnostic assessments to determine if a student has a specific learning disability. Although these diagnostic assessments are used in education, they may not directly inform instruction. As such, we will not classify them as "diagnostic formative assessments."

How Do I Use Diagnostic Formative Assessments to Make Instructional Decisions?

Depending on the instructional decisions you want to make, different types of diagnostic formative assessments can be used. Because testing takes time away from instruction, it is important to consider the decisions that will be made from the diagnostic formative assessment results before selecting a diagnostic test. Remember, there are three decisions you can make from diagnostic formative assessments.

Key Decisions From Diagnostic Formative Assessment Data

1. In which areas of the curriculum is the student struggling? In which areas of the curriculum is the student being successful?

2. What are the persistent errors the student makes when solving problems?

3. What are the student's underlying misconceptions about the content?

If the desired decisions cannot be made based on the data collected, instructional time will be wasted. Following are descriptions of these three types of decisions that you might want to make and the diagnostic formative assessments that can help make the decision. Different types of diagnostic formative assessments defined and discussed in this section include skills inventories, error analyses, dynamic assessments, and cognitively based diagnostic assessments.

Where Is the Student Struggling—and Where Is the Student Successful?

If a student has been identified as being nonresponsive to Tier 1 or Tier 2 instruction based on results from the universal screener and progress monitoring system, determining areas of the curriculum in which a student is struggling and/or has mastered the content can help teachers and administrators make several key decisions to support the student's success. Depending on the significance of the student's risk status, additional Tier 2 or Tier 3 instruction may be needed.

To differentiate Tier 1 instruction, teachers can use information about the student's strengths and areas of weakness to provide these supports:

- *Determine which prerequisite concepts and skills need to be reviewed prior to beginning instruction on new concepts.* For example, before introducing how to find the circumference of a circle, students who struggle with operations with rational numbers may need additional review focused on multiplying rational numbers.

- *Identify instructional grouping based on similar skills or different skills, depending on the goals of the instructional activity.* For example, students who struggle with solving equations might be placed together in a group so that the teacher can provide the small group with targeted intervention on this topic. Students can also be grouped based on different skills so that they can provide peer support to one another. For example, a student who struggles with adding fractions but understands perimeter might be paired with a student who struggles with measurement formulas but who is proficient with operations with rational numbers. This way, students can provide peer support.

To design the Tier 2 or Tier 3 intervention platform, teachers can use information about the student's strengths and areas of weakness to provide these supports:

- Prioritize the content of the intervention

- Determine preview/review topics

- Determine content of cumulative review

These decisions require detailed information about the student's level of mastery of specific concepts and skills. This type of information can be obtained by administering a diagnostic formative assessment referred to as a skill inventory. Skill inventories assess the student's level of mastery of specific skills and concepts taken from the curricular expectations or from a list of prerequisite concepts and skills. The student takes a series of items for each concept and/or skill. The student's responses are collected and reported by concept and/or skill.

The decision about the student's strengths and areas of weakness is made by evaluating the number of items for each concept and/or skill the student got correct out of the number attempted. This list of student's strengths and areas of weakness

Score Report for Zachary

Skill	Number of items	Score	Skill analysis
Represent a ratio with a model	4	4	●
Describe situation using a ratio	5	2	◉
Generate equivalent ratios	3	1	◉
Find unit rates	5	2	◉
Solve real-world problems involving ratios	5	0	○
Convert decimals to percentage	4	4	●
Convert fractions to percentage	4	2	◉
Find the percentage of a number	3	0	○

● = Mastered
◉ = Partial mastery
○ = Not mastered

Figure 11.3. Score report for Zachary with data from his skills assessment.

can be used to make the decisions noted previously. An example of the data from a skill inventory is shown in Figure 11.3.

One concern that should be noted when using skill inventories to make instructional decisions is the (un)reliability of the student's scores for each concept and/or skill. As we discussed in Chapter 9, reliability refers to the consistency of the test results. In many cases, students taking skill inventories complete only a few items per concept and/or skill. When results are obtained from just a few items, we do not know if the student's responses are consistent over the range of items within the concept or skill. For example, a student, Lily, might miss two out of three items assessing unit rate. However, because we only know the Lily's responses on three items, we cannot say for sure that she struggles with unit rate. We can suppose that because she missed two items, she struggles with unit rate, but there is so little data to make this determination with confidence. It is possible (even conceivable) that Lily could have missed one item due to chance. If she missed one out of three, we might make a different instructional decision for this student. As such, information obtained from administering a skill inventory should be used in conjunction with other information to provide more evidence that supports your instructional decisions.

What Are the Persistent Errors the Student Makes When Solving Problems?
To design the Tier 2 or Tier 3 intervention platform, teachers often want to know what errors or mistakes the student is consistently making as he or she is responding to mathematics items. These errors or mistakes indicate the skills or knowledge with which the student is currently struggling. For example, when a student is struggling to add fractions with unlike denominators, the teacher might want to know if the student is 1) simply adding the denominators without finding a common denominator, or 2) executing the strategy to find a common denominator incorrectly, or 3) finding the common denominator, then adding the denominators. Understanding the types of errors or mistakes the student is making can help you determine which skills or knowledge needs to be remediated to correct the mistakes.

Knowing students' errors or mistakes can be used to provide these supports:

- Design targeted instruction to remediate the mistakes

- Design judicious and cumulative review activities to build and sustain new knowledge and skills

- Create fact practice activities to reinforce problematic procedural skills

This type of information is most useful for students who are making a few mistakes consistently. Students who are making many mistakes may have significant gaps in their background knowledge or persistent misconceptions that need more intensive and targeted interventions. Other types of diagnostic assessments would be most useful for these students, such as the cognitively based diagnostic assessment described later in this section.

To identify a student's errors or mistakes, you need to conduct an error analysis. Error analysis is the process of reviewing student's responses to mathematics items to diagnose a pattern of mistakes. Errors can be classified into two categories: slips and bugs (Ginsburg, 1987). *Slips* are random errors or mistakes that students make as they complete mathematics items. These errors or mistakes do not follow a pattern and likely occur by chance (i.e., the student was momentarily distracted by something happening in the classroom, the student misunderstood the task or misread the problem). Because no pattern of errors is evident, these are random errors. (Note: As noted earlier, if a student is making a lot of random mistakes, it is likely that he or she may have a more significant misunderstanding and should take a different type of diagnostic assessment).

Bugs are persistent errors or mistakes that indicate a pattern of misunderstandings. The goal of error analysis is to diagnose the bugs in student's responses. Ashlock (1994) classified computational bugs into three basic categories:

1. *Wrong operation:* The student consistently uses the wrong operation when solving a math problem

2. *Computational or fact error:* The student uses the appropriate operation but makes an error involving basic number facts

3. *Defective algorithm:* The student uses the appropriate operation but makes a non-number fact error in one or more steps of applying the strategy or selects an incorrect strategy.

Figure 11.4 shows an example of a fraction division problem and possible bugs, which can be classified into these three categories.

Students may have other types of persistent errors or mistakes. In some instances, these errors may be associated with solving word problems, and they may

Original problem	Correct solution	Wrong operation	Computational/ factual error	Defective algorithm
Solve. $\frac{7}{9} \div \frac{1}{2}$	$\frac{7}{9} \times \frac{2}{1} = \frac{14}{9} = 1\frac{5}{9}$	$\frac{7}{9} \times \frac{1}{2} = \frac{7}{18}$	$\frac{7}{9} \times \frac{2}{1} = \frac{16}{9} = 1\frac{7}{9}$	$\frac{9}{7} \times \frac{1}{2} = \frac{9}{14}$

Figure 11.4. Example of a division problem and possible bugs in three categories: wrong operation, computational/ fact error, and defective algorithm.

include errors made when interpreting and applying the mathematical language, such as decoding, vocabulary, and translation of the text to number sentences (see Chapter 6 for a description of the skills students use to solve word problems).

You can analyze a struggling student's responses to mathematics items on any number of assignments, including homework, tests or quizzes, or classroom activities. The first step is to determine whether the student's mistakes are slips or bugs. If the student is making a lot of slips, the student may have a persistent misconception that can only be diagnosed with a different type of diagnostic assessment, such as the cognitively based diagnostic described later in this chapter. If you suspect the student has one or more bugs in his or her thinking, you need to carefully analyze the responses to determine which types of errors or mistakes are occurring. A bug can be diagnosed if a pattern of errors or mistakes appears from the analysis. You can track the number and types of bugs on the skill analysis report, as shown in Figure 11.5.

Although error analysis can provide timely information for adjusting instruction so as to avoid reinforcing incorrect procedures, this information may provide limited insights into the underlying cause of the student's errors or mistakes. A concern when implementing error analysis is that teachers may focus on correcting the procedural errors without recognizing the conceptual understanding that provides the foundation for the procedural skill (Russell & Masters, 2009). For some students, the error can be easily corrected with targeted instruction or review. However, other students may have persistent misconceptions that interfere with future learning. If this is the case, error analysis may only mask the underlying symptoms.

Score Report for Zachary

Skill	Number of items	Score	Skill analysis	Numbers and types of bugs		
				Wrong operation	Fact error	Defective algorithm
Represent a ratio with a model	4	4	●	–	–	–
Describe a situation using a ratio	5	2	◐	–	1	2
Generate equivalent ratios	3	1	◐	–	1	1
Find unit rates	5	2	◐	2	1	–
Solve real-world problems involving ratios	5	0	○	3	2	–
Convert decimals to percentage	4	4	●	–	–	–
Convert fractions to percentage	4	2	◐	–	1	1
Find the percentage of a number	3	0	○	–	–	3

● = Mastered
◐ = Partial mastery
○ = Not mastered

Figure 11.5. Score report for Zachary with data from his skills assessment and details about bugs affecting his performance.

If this is suspected, additional data should be collected about the student's conceptual understanding. Such data can come from conducting an interview with the student. When interviews are diagnostic in purpose and systematically linked to instruction, they are often referred to as dynamic assessment. Dynamic assessments follow a specific interview protocol that intersperses assessment tasks with feedback or instruction to help determine a student's responsiveness to the instruction. If the student responds quickly to the instruction and corrects his or her mistake, the error was likely a slip. However, if the student does not respond quickly to the feedback or struggles to understand his or her mistake, the error was likely a bug.

Similar to the concern raised when using skill inventories, reliable data are needed to make an accurate diagnosis of a student's errors. You may need to collect and analyze a large amount of student work to determine if the mistakes are random slips or persistent errors. This information can be collected over time.

What Are the Student's Underlying Misconceptions About the Content?

If a student is struggling to reach the curricular expectations, he or she might have underlying misconceptions about the content that are interfering with learning new material. These misconceptions typically relate to gaps in understanding knowledge that is foundational for the content. Thus, as students build off of their faulty foundational knowledge as they try to apply new information, misunderstandings compound and lead to persistent misconceptions. For example, if a student is struggling when working with rational numbers (i.e., applying operations to solve problems, discussing the solution with a peer, justifying the result), he or she may lack the foundational understanding of the concept of rational numbers, including the knowledge that fractions represent equal partitions of a whole or set, have magnitude, and can be represented on a number line. When trying to decompose (or compose) fractions as the precursor to understanding operations, this student's lack of foundational understanding of rational numbers may prevent him or her from grasping this new concept and skill.

Understanding a student's underlying misconceptions can help you understand why a student is struggling with the content. Knowing why the student is struggling may help you make key instructional decisions, including helping you to

- Determine where in the learning process the student's misconceptions emerge

- Design targeted intervention to provide foundational knowledge to support subsequent learning

- Determine the level of cognitive engagement in which the misconception manifests; for example, does the student understand the concept of the operation (e.g., addition as combining) but demonstrate confusion about the corresponding procedure (e.g., integrating knowledge of place value to add rational numbers represented as decimals)?

- Anticipate topics that the student might struggle with in the near future if the misconception is not remedied quickly

To make these decisions, you need an assessment tool that is based on theories of learning in the domain. We call these types of diagnostic assessments cognitively based diagnostic assessments. These types of diagnostic assessments should be based on an understanding of how students learn the domain-specific knowledge so that gaps in learning can be identified. In contrast to the skill analysis approach to diagnosis, cognitively based diagnostic assessments do not look to the content standards to identify areas in which the student has strength or is struggling, but instead look to theories about how students develop and integrate their knowledge to learn the content. Moreover, the skill analysis approach tests knowledge and skills in isolation of each other to determine which specific areas should be the target of instruction. In mathematics, however, we know that some skills and knowledge develop in combination with other skills and knowledge. Also, the development of proficiency may depend on multiple layers of cognitive engagement working together to develop a full sense of competence.

In contrast to error analysis, cognitively based diagnostic assessments look beyond the classification of mistakes that the student makes to identify the reasons for the mistakes. As such, their focus is not on cataloging the errors but instead understanding the student's misconception(s) that lead to the errors. Changing the focus of interpretation from listing errors to determining why the student made the error requires that the test be grounded in theories of learning the mathematical content.

When and to Whom Are Diagnostic Formative Assessments Administered?

Unlike universal screeners, which are administered to all students, diagnostic formative assessments are administered only to students who are nonresponsive to Tier 1 or Tier 2 instruction. Because these students often have persistent misconceptions or enduring difficulties learning the content, you need additional information from which to design supplemental instruction. Diagnostic formative assessments provide this information through the process of analyzing the student's skills, errors, or cognitive processes to design instructional interventions that are aligned with students' learning needs. Students who are responsive to Tier 1 or Tier 2 instruction may not have persistent misconceptions or enduring difficulties that would potentially prevent their subsequent learning. As such, diagnostic assessments are not necessary for these students and would take up valuable instructional time.

As discussed in the previous chapter, students' performance on the universal screener is evaluated in fall, winter, and early spring to determine whether they are on track for reaching curricular expectations or at risk for not reaching them. After determining which students are nonresponsive to your instructional efforts, you can administer a diagnostic formative assessment to make necessary instructional decisions. As such, the diagnostic assessment should be administered after the universal screener in fall, winter, and early spring.

What Are the Characteristics of a Diagnostic Formative Assessment?

As we discussed earlier, to be useful for making instructional decisions, all assessment systems must produce reliable results that lead to valid interpretations. In reference to diagnostic formative assessments, important considerations for reliability include the number of items administered for each skill and whether different scorers arrive at the same skill or error classification. When evaluating validity for diagnostic formative assessments, the key consideration for interpreting students' results to make decisions is the content that was sampled to create the test.

Reliability of Subscores   When analyzing the results from any diagnostic formative assessment, it is important to consider the reliability (or unreliability) of the students' scores. This is a particularly important issue with diagnostic formative assessments because the information we are seeking from the results is targeted to specific skills, errors, or misconceptions. As such, we expect multiple data points from the results of any one test. This is a very different approach from most tests: Most tests (including the universal screener and state accountability tests) provide one or very few scores for each student. A diagnostic formative assessment may provide multiple scores to account for the number of skills, errors, or misconceptions assessed on the test. For example, look at the score report from Zachary's skill analysis diagnostic formative assessment, shown in Figure 11.3. Eight skills are listed for which data on the student's proficiency are provided. Just as with an error analysis or cognitively based diagnostic assessment, score reports with multiple data points are expected and needed for making instructional decisions.

What is important to consider when using these data is the potential for measurement errors to arise that may compromise the accuracy of the results. Because results are based on the student's responses to a few items, we do not know if the student's responses are consistent over a larger range of items. For example, in looking at Zachary's score report, we see that he missed two out of three items assessing his ability to generate equivalent ratios. Because we only know his responses on three items, we cannot say for sure that he struggles with generating equivalent ratios. We assume that because he missed two items, he struggles with this concept, but we are basing our decision on so little data that it may compromise our confidence in this decision.

To increase our confidence, we can do two things. First, include additional items for each skill, error, or misconception so that any decision is based on as much performance from the student as possible. For example, if we had five items assessing Zachary's ability to generate equivalent ratios, we would have more confidence in the decision we made based on the results. Second, it is helpful to use other information about the student to verify results from diagnostic formative assessments. For example, we can review Zachary's homework or classwork for evidence of his ability to generate equivalent ratios. We could also ask him direct questions about implementing the procedure to verify the results.

Also, because the information from diagnostic formative assessments is being used to design Tier 2 or Tier 3 instruction and not to make classification decisions, it is important to remember that the results from diagnostic formative assessment are low stakes for the student. For example, if these results indicate that a student needs additional help learning how to generate equivalent ratios but the student really didn't need extra help, the error in the decision will be caught quickly when the teacher provides additional instruction. As such, measurement errors that occur when diagnosing students' skills, errors, or misconceptions should err on the side of underestimating students' proficiency so that any potential problems in students' learning are caught and addressed instructionally.

Content Alignment for Making Diagnostic Decisions   The content of the diagnostic formative assessment should align with the instructional decisions teachers are making. For each of the three decisions teachers can make from the diagnostic formative assessment results, the content of the items is important:

- If we are trying to identify areas of the curriculum in which the student is struggling, we need to precisely define which areas of the curriculum we want to target.

- If we are trying to classify specific errors a student is making, we need items that are designed to collect information about those errors.

- If we want to know a student's underlying content misconceptions, we need items that are aligned with theories of learning.

Because there are a limited number of high-quality mathematics diagnostic assessments available on the market, the MTSS Leadership Team at your school may decide to create your own diagnostic formative assessment. Perhaps the best place to start is with the score report. By beginning with the end in mind, the types of decisions you can make are at the center of the test development efforts. For example, if results from the winter administration of the universal screener indicate that a larger number of students were identified for Tier 2 instruction than were identified after the fall administration, you may want to administer a skills analysis diagnostic formative assessment on the skills and knowledge covered between the fall and winter administrations of the universal screener. Results from the universal screener may indicate that as the complexity of the content increased from fall to winter, many students did not gain the skills and knowledge they needed to continue to be successful in the core curriculum. Designing a skills analysis diagnostic formative assessment to cover specific content in which you suspect students are struggling may provide you with a road map for reteaching.

In contrast, if results from the fall administration of the universal screener identify a group of students as being at significant risk for not reaching expectations, you might decide to administer a cognitively based diagnostic formative assessment to identify the students' persistent misconceptions. This information may be used to design targeted interventions to provide the foundational knowledge the students need to be successful as they engage in the new year's curriculum. The content included in this diagnostic assessment would be grounded in theories of learning.

As these examples illustrate, the content of the diagnostic formative assessment should align with the instructional decisions you need to make. Because few diagnostic formative assessments are commercially available, you may need to design your own. A number of resources and books are available to help you write items.

How Do I Communicate Results to Parents and Students?

Sharing assessment results with parents and students is an important part of using diagnostic formative assessments and may help them understand the reasons you made specific instructional decisions. As we discussed in Chapter 9, when preparing to communicate results, it is important that you fully understand the reports, understand how results from the diagnostic formative assessment are used with other data to make decisions, and have a plan for implementing instructional changes. Once these steps have been followed, you are ready to share results with parents and students.

Know Diagnostic Formative Assessment Reports   When we talked about the reports for the universal screener in the previous chapter, we referenced typical features that might be presented on reports that are generated from commercially available universal screeners or district-created tests. In contrast, because not many diagnostic formative assessments are commercially available, you may be sharing your own reports with parents and students. Even though you have created these reports yourself, the information we discussed earlier still applies. Specifically, it is important to have a thorough understanding about what the results signify and what information is being communicated.

For commercially available diagnostic formative assessments, resources will likely be available that describe how to interpret the reports. You should be able to find these documents online or included as hard-copy resources supplied by the test publisher. These materials should be thoroughly reviewed before discussing the results with parents and students.

Gather Additional Data   Throughout this chapter, we have discussed the value of including multiple sources of data to help corroborate your findings from the diagnostic formative assessment. Because the diagnostic information provided from diagnostic formative assessments may be based on a small number of items, the scores are even more susceptible to the influence of errors. Just as you gathered additional information to help you make reliable instructional decisions for the student, sharing this information will help alleviate concerns from the parent and/or student about the persistence of the problem. Organize and present these additional data sources just as you would the other score reports, taking care to share relevant and useful information to justify the instructional decisions you made.

Document Instructional Decisions and Changes   As we have discussed, results from the diagnostic formative assessment can be used to inform the design and delivery of supplemental instruction for students who are nonresponsive to Tier 1 or Tier 2 instruction. You can make one of three specific decisions from these results:

1.   In which areas of the curriculum is the student struggling? In which areas of the curriculum is the student being successful?

2.   What are the persistent errors the student makes when solving problems?

3.   What are the student's underlying misconceptions about the content?

Because you selected the diagnostic formative assessment that would help you answer one of these specific questions, you should be able to proceed with making instructional decisions. Based on the results, you may decide to provide to implement specific instructional planning or delivery approaches as part of your Tier 2 or Tier 3 intervention platform.

Share Results   When sharing information, keep in mind that many parents and students have not seen diagnostic formative assessment results in the past. Parents and students will likely be anxious about the results because they are aware of a potential problem and are concerned about the student's progress. To help with the interpretation and potentially ease anxiety, create a plan for how the reports will be presented and described. Here is a sample plan that incorporates the steps described in Chapter 9.

Step 1: Share general information about the test, such as

•   The purpose of the test

•   How the test will inform instructional decisions

•   The content that was assessed

It is important that parents and students understand why the diagnostic formative assessment was given: to help design instruction to support the student's achievement. Once parents and students understand that you will use the results to make better decisions about how to support the student, anxiety may be reduced.

Step 2: Describe the types of scores on the report. Knowing the types of scores presented on the diagnostic score report provides parents and students with an overall picture of the possible score value the child could have scored. Some parents might be expecting to see a number or a graph, but some diagnostic formative assessment results might be a series of shaded circles or a list of error codes. Information presented in this manner may not be familiar to parents and the student. Describing the type of scores and their meaning (i.e., the meaning of open, partially shaded, and completely shaded circles) before sharing the student's specific scores may help everyone better understand the report.

Step 3: Share the student's score report. Once parents and students understand the purpose of the diagnostic formative assessment and have a sense of the types of scores, they should have enough context for interpreting the student's scores. Share information at a pace that is understandable for parents and students:

1. First, provide a general description of your evaluation of the strengths and areas in need of improvement based on the student's performance. It might help reduce everyone's anxiety if you begin with a review of the student's strengths.

2. Second, show the student's score report. Provide as much description as possible. For example, state the specific skills that were assessed and how many items the student took that measured the specific skills. Using the scores described in Step 2, identify how the student performed on the items assessing those skills.

3. Third, share the additional information that was gathered to verify the results from the diagnostic formative assessment. Discuss how this information verifies the results obtained from the diagnostic formative assessment.

Step 4: Share the instructional decisions. Once parents and students understand the meaning of the scores, they will likely be anxious to hear about what comes next. Share the instructional decisions you made prior to convening the parents.

Step 5: Answer questions. Allow ample time for both parents and students to ask questions and engage in a discussion.

SUMMARY: USING DIAGNOSTIC FORMATIVE ASSESSMENTS

Diagnostic formative assessments can help you determine why students are struggling. In this chapter, we discussed how diagnostic formative assessments can be administered to students who have been identified as struggling in order to determine the areas of the curriculum they are struggling with, the persistent errors they make, and the misconceptions they have about the content. Suggestions were also shared about how to communicate diagnostic formative assessment results to parents and students.

CHAPTER 12

Is the Intervention Helping? Progress Monitoring

Following from the assessment framework and cycle of decision making established in the previous chapters, we now talk about how to integrate ongoing data collection into your instructional decision making. In previous chapters, we identified the value of a universal screener for helping to identify students who are on track for reaching their goals or at risk for falling behind. We also emphasized the importance of using diagnostic assessment results to guide the design of your Tier 2 or Tier 3 intervention platform. In this chapter, we focus on evaluating the effectiveness of instruction at helping students reach their goals. We address the question, "Are my instructional strategies helping students learn?"

WHAT ARE WE AIMING FOR?

The following vignette illustrates how a teacher might use data obtained from a progress monitoring system to evaluate, and make decisions about, his or her instructional strategies.

MS. MARTINEZ'S GRADE 6 MATH CLASS

Ms. Martinez, a sixth-grade mathematics teacher, administered a universal screener to all students in her classes. She used the results to determine which students might be at risk for not reaching the grade 6 curricular expectations. In each of her classes, she identified a small group of students who might be struggling to learn the content. She administered a diagnostic assessment to better understand why each student is struggling. Then, she integrated the diagnostic assessment results with her understanding of evidence-based practices to create a small-group intervention for students with similar patterns of performance.

In essence, Ms. Martinez's decisions about what content to focus on in the intervention, the pace of instruction, the example sets, and other relevant decisions are built upon the hypotheses she generated about what will help her students learn the material to the depth and breadth that is expected. Now, just as if she were testing a hypothesis in science, Ms. Martinez needs to evaluate whether the intervention she designed is helping each student learn. The best way to test these hypotheses is to systematically gather and analyze ongoing data about student performance. Only by evaluating these data can Ms. Martinez determine if the interventions she designed appropriately met each student's individual learning needs.

This scenario highlights two points:

1. Your intervention platform is based on what you can determine about student learning—that is, your informed hypotheses as a teacher.

2. These hypotheses need to be carefully evaluated to determine whether they are plausible.

The chapters in Section II focus on how to plan instruction that supports student learning. When you analyze the academic performance and characteristics of students who are not meeting expectations in math, you form hypotheses about why these students are not meeting expectations and what interventions could help them to do so. In this chapter, we focus on testing these hypotheses to determine if the intervention platform you designed had the intended result of improving student learning. Specifically, we want to evaluate interventions using these questions:

1. Is student learning of mathematics content a result of the intervention platform I designed? Is growth observed after the intervention began?

2. What is the student's rate of learning? At the current rate, will the student reach his or her curricular goals within a specific time frame?

WHAT TOOLS WILL HELP US MAKE THESE DECISIONS?

To help make decisions about whether an intervention is helping a student learn the mathematics content at the appropriate rate, we want to gather ongoing student performance data. By collecting data over time, we can evaluate not only if the student is learning as a result of the intervention but also the rate at which he or she is learning. Understanding the rate of learning is important because we only have a finite amount of time within a school year to help all students reach the curricular expectations. We need to make sure that the Tier 2 or Tier 3 intervention we designed and are delivering is intense enough to help the student reach this goal. Because these decisions will be used to inform our instruction, we administer a formative assessment system. Typically, this system is referred to as progress monitoring system.

What Is Progress Monitoring?

Progress monitoring is a process of frequently collecting and evaluating student performance data in order to make decisions about the student's progress toward reaching his or her goal. Progress monitoring allows you to do exactly that: monitor progress. This assessment system includes multiple parallel tests that are administered over time to collect ongoing data about student learning. Data are used to determine if students are learning the content at an appropriate rate. Progress monitoring systems are used in many other fields besides education (although other fields might not call them *progress monitoring*). For example, after a child is born, the parents visit the doctor with him or her at regular intervals to check their child's weight, height, and a variety of other vital statistics. With each visit, the doctor plots the child's weight and height on a chart to show changes in growth over time. Parents can use this information to determine whether their child's diet is sufficient to help him or her grow at an appropriate rate. In essence, the doctor is monitoring the child's progress.

In mathematics education, the process of monitoring progress is much the same: we gather data at regular intervals, plot the changes over time, and determine if instruction is helping our students learn. The Center on Response to Intervention (https://rti4success.org) provides progress monitoring resources and a chart to compare and evaluate different progress monitoring tools. For more in-depth information, you may want to visit the Research Institute on Progress Monitoring (https://www.progressmonitoring.org).

How Do I Use Progress Monitoring Measures to Make an Instructional Decision?

Decisions about two questions can be made based on administration of progress monitoring measures:

1. Is the student learning as a result of the intervention?

2. What is the student's rate of learning?

Both decisions rely on administration of parallel forms of progress monitoring measures at regular time intervals that are displayed on a graph. Parallel forms will be discussed later in the chapter, but generally consist of forms of a test that are as similar as possible in the content, format, difficulty, administration, and scoring. Because results will be evaluated over time, regular time intervals are important for evaluating learning rates. Data are most typically displayed on a graph, such as the one shown in Figure 12.1, in which the x-axis is time and the y-axis is the student's score on the progress monitoring measures.

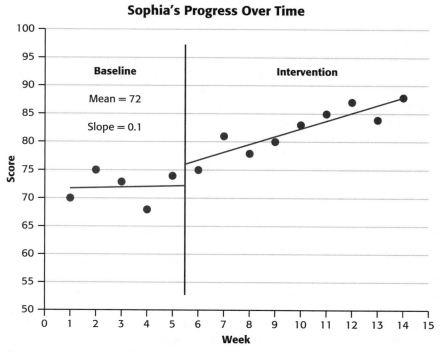

Figure 12.1. Sample graph of progress-monitoring data.

The information you gain from evaluating progress monitoring data can be used to determine if your hypotheses about what instructional supports the student needed were accurate. Depending on the observed performance, you might determine that 1) the intervention is helping the student learn the content, 2) the intervention is not helping the student learn the content, or 3) the intervention is sort of helping the student learn the content. You can use these outcomes to make further adjustments to your hypothesis about the student and therefore design a more targeted intervention.

As noted earlier, to make a decision based on progress monitoring data, you need to administer parallel forms of the assessment at regular time intervals and graph the results over time. This process requires a series of steps, outlined next and further explained afterward.

Progress Monitoring Steps

Step 1: Gather and plot baseline data.

Step 2: Set performance goals.

Step 3: Implement the intervention.

Step 4: Administer progress monitoring measures at regular intervals.

Step 5: Evaluate the student's progress.

Step 1: Gather baseline data. The first step is to gather baseline data. To do this, you can administer parallel forms of the progress monitoring measure before the intervention begins, in order to get a sense of the student's current performance. You need to gather enough data to observe a trend in the student's performance before you implement the intervention. You should gather enough baseline data so that you can see stable performance, which can typically be seen after three administrations of the progress monitoring measure.

To graph these data, first set up the student's graph by labeling the x-axis with time (typically in weeks) and the y-axis with scores appropriate to the progress monitoring system you are using. You can access a free resource from the National Center on Intensive Intervention to create progress monitoring graphs (https://intensive intervention.org/resource/student-progress-monitoring-tool-data-collection-and -graphing-excel). Plot the baseline data on the student's graph and label these data points as baseline, as shown in Figure 12.2.

It is also helpful to calculate descriptive statistics from the baseline data, such as the student's average score as well as the slope of the line of best fit. The student's average baseline score can be compared to the student's average score after the intervention has been implemented to determine how much (if any) learning has occurred. The slope of the student's baseline scores can also be used to determine any changes in the rate of learning after implementation of the intervention.

Step 2: Set performance goals. An important step in progress monitoring is setting performance goals. Performance goals provide a useful benchmark for determining if the student is learning at an appropriate rate to make adequate progress. A goal can also provide a tangible target for a student to work toward, and thereby can increase motivation.

Several factors should be included when setting goals. First, the goal should be ambitious but attainable. If the goal is too ambitious, the student might get discouraged

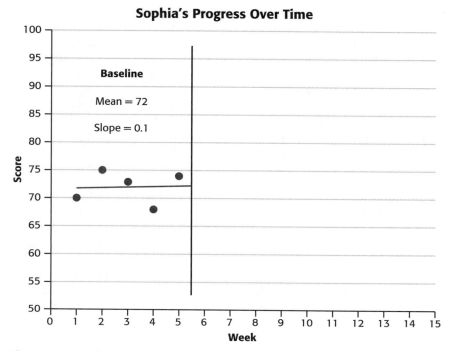

Figure 12.2. Sample graph of baseline data collected before implementing an intervention.

and lose motivation. However, if it is not ambitious enough, the student might not be motivated to work hard. Second, a performance goal can (and in most cases should) be raised to make it more ambitious. However, you should never lower a performance goal if the student isn't making adequate progress. Doing so may inadvertently demoralize the student and may send the inappropriate message that he or she is not capable of reaching an ambitious goal.

Some progress monitoring systems have a method by which you can set a goal. These systems often have benchmarks or growth rates that can be used to set a specific goal, including realistic and/or ambitious goals. A benchmark is often provided to help you understand when a student meets a minimum level of proficiency on the progress monitoring system. Benchmarks help you make criterion-referenced decisions and are typically set by the test developer. You can use the benchmark to set the student's goal.

If a benchmark is not provided by the publisher, or is not appropriate for setting goals, you can use growth rates to set goals. It is important to use the growth rate published in the progress monitoring system that you are using. Growth rates can be incorporated into the following formula developed by Fuchs and colleagues in 1993 to set a student's goal:

Goal = [Number of weeks of the intervention] × [Targeted growth rate] +
[Baseline score]

Some progress monitoring systems will not have benchmarks or well-established growth rates. In these instances, you can use intra-individual information to set a target goal. This method does not rely on extant data, but instead sets a goal for the student based on the individual student's baseline scores. Consider the following example: In January, a student was identified as being nonresponsive to Tier 2 intervention, so the teacher adapts the intervention to make it more intensive. The teacher administers a series of three progress monitoring measures to determine the student's baseline performance; the teacher will use the median score as the baseline. The teacher uses the formula above to determine the goal. Instead of using the published growth rate, the teacher uses the rate of 1.5, in order to set a goal that is 50% higher than the student's current performance. When setting the goal, it is important to remember that you can always raise a performance goal but should never lower it.

Before proceeding to the next step, plot the goal on the student's graph at the point in time in which you think it should be reached (e.g., at the end of the intervention). This will convey two pieces of information: 1) the target you are aiming for, and 2) when the intervention will be over. Draw a line from the baseline performance to the goal. This will serve as the aim line, as shown in Figure 12.3.

Step 3: Implement the intervention. Once you have gathered and plotted baseline data, calculated initial descriptive statistics, and set performance goals, you are ready to implement the intervention. It is helpful to mark the date of implementation directly

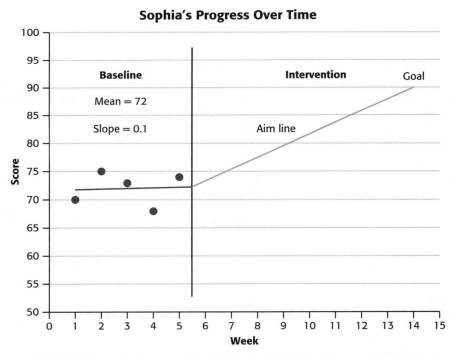

Figure 12.3.   Sample graph of progress-monitoring data that includes a performance goal and indication of when that goal should be reached after implementing an intervention.

on the student's graph for reference (as shown by the vertical line in Figure 12.3). During the implementation phase, it is often helpful to monitor whether you are actually implementing the intervention as intended (see Chapter 8 for information on fidelity of implementation). For example, have you made changes to the intervention platform from your original plans? Although these adjustments might be appropriate (e.g., based on systematic review of progress monitoring data), they should all be noted on the student's graph. Typically, these are noted by drawing a vertical line on the graph to indicate the date on which the intervention was systematically changed. This allows you to evaluate the student's performance before and after the intervention.

Step 4: Administer progress monitoring measures at regular intervals. To gather ongoing student performance data to evaluate the effect of the intervention on student learning, parallel forms of the progress monitoring assessment need to be administered on a regular basis. Typically, these measures are administered on the same day of each week during the intervention. However, if you are not able to administer these assessments on a weekly basis, you can administer them at an interval more suited to your schedule. However, you should try to administer them at least once per month.

Results should be carefully plotted on the student's graph. After you have at least three data points, draw a line that best fits the data. This will serve as the student's observed rate of growth, as shown in Figure 12.4.

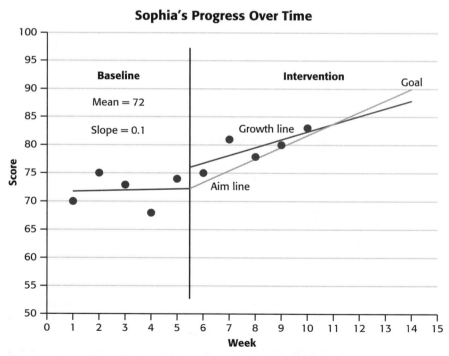

Figure 12.4. Sample graph of progress-monitoring data that includes information about the student's documented rate of growth after implementing an intervention.

Step 5: Evaluate the student's progress. After you have drawn a line to represent the student's observed rate of growth, you are now ready to make some decisions. Remember, we can use progress monitoring data to make two decisions:

1. Is the student learning the mathematics content as a result of the intervention design and delivery?

2. What is the student's rate of learning, and is it appropriate for reaching his or her goals?

We need to evaluate the student's progress with these two decisions in mind.
     In general, you will see one of the following patterns emerge:

1. The student's rate of growth line exceeds the aim line, as shown in Figure 12.5. This indicates that 1) the student is learning, and 2) if the student continues to learn at the same or similar rate, the student will exceed the performance goal. In other words, the intervention is supporting the student's learning needs and helping the student meet the expectations. Because the student has demonstrated success with the intervention, you may want to consider raising the goal.

2. The student's rate of growth line overlaps with the aim line, as shown in Figure 12.6. This indicates that 1) the student is learning, and 2) if the student continues to learn at the same or similar rate, the student will reach the performance goal. In other words, the intervention is supporting the student's learning needs.

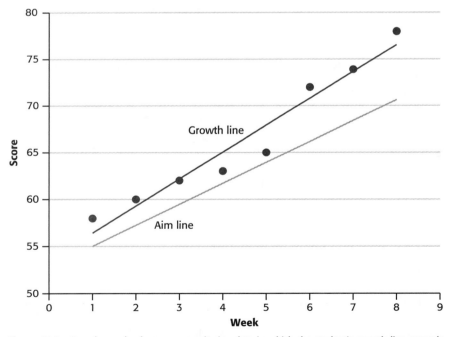

Figure 12.5. Sample graph of progress-monitoring data in which the student's growth line exceeds the aim line, indicating that if the student continues learning at the same rate, he or she will surpass the performance goal.

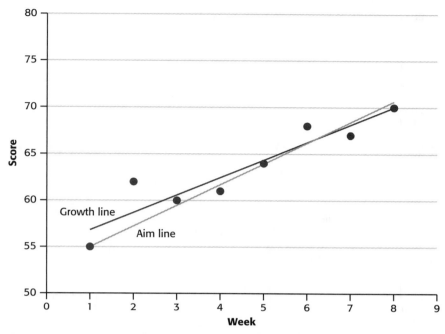

Figure 12.6. Sample graph of progress-monitoring data in which the student's growth line overlaps the aim line, indicating that if the student continues learning at the same rate, he or she will meet the performance goal.

You should continue to provide the intervention as planned and continue monitoring progress.

3. The student's rate of growth line is below the aim line, as shown in Figure 12.7. This indicates that 1) the student may or may not be learning, and 2) if the student continues to learn at the same or similar rate, the student will not reach the performance goal. In other words, the intervention is not supporting the student's learning needs and should be modified. See Chapter 2 for information on adapting the intervention.

Some progress monitoring systems will make this evaluation for you. However, you should know what to look for and when to make adjustments to the goal and/or the intervention design.

These same progress monitoring data and decision rules can be used to determine if a student is ready to make the transition from one level of instructional support to another. For example, consider a student who is currently receiving a Tier 2 intervention and whose progress is monitored frequently as part of the intervention approach. The teacher can use data from a universal screener as well as progress monitoring data to determine if the student is making sufficient progress to warrant reducing the intensity of the support services (i.e., returning to Tier 1 instruction). Just as we noted previously, the teacher may decide that the student is not making adequate progress toward his or her goal and might need more intensive Tier 3 intervention.

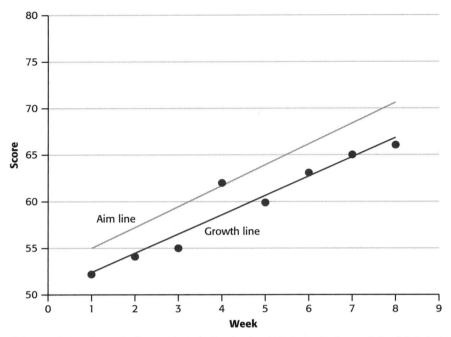

Figure 12.7. Sample graph of progress-monitoring data in which the student's growth line falls below the aim line, indicating that if the student continues learning at the same rate, he or she will not meet the performance goal.

Making instructional decisions based on systematic evaluation of progress monitoring data has been found to increase student achievement by providing teachers with detailed data for decision making.

When and to Whom Are Progress Monitoring Measures Administered?

Just like diagnostic formative assessments, progress monitoring measures are administered to students who are nonresponsive to Tier 1 or Tier 2 instruction. Because we want to know whether the instruction we designed is meeting the student's needs, we want to track changes in the student's performance over time. By evaluating these data over time, we can determine if the student is responding to the intervention as we had intended.

Typically, progress monitoring measures are administered at least monthly. The exact schedule depends on the student's goal and current level of performance. For example, a student with significant knowledge or skill gaps may have an ambitious goal and may be receiving intensive Tier 3 intervention. Progress toward this goal should be monitored weekly so that timely instructional decisions can be made to support adequate growth. However, a student with a less significant knowledge or skill gap may not be receiving such intense intervention. As such, changes in the student's performance might not be expected as quickly, so we might decide to monitor the student's progress by giving a progress monitoring test every other week.

What Are the Characteristics of a Progress Monitoring Assessment?

As with other assessments, to be useful for making instructional decisions, progress monitoring tests should produce reliable results that lead to valid interpretations. Several key features of progress monitoring measures distinguish this assessment system from others. Specifically, students' progress is monitored using a series of tests that are consistent in difficulty and sensitive to small changes in students' knowledge and skills. To maximize assessment efficiency, progress monitoring measures should be short in duration and easy to administer and score. Also, administration and scoring procedures should be standardized to ensure reliable data across administrations. As in other domains such as reading and writing, curriculum-based measures (CBMs) are frequently used to monitor progress in mathematics because they meet these requirements.

Mathematics CBMs are created by sampling from the year's curriculum or by identifying a test that would measure students' general knowledge of mathematics. The latter CBM is referred to as a general outcome measure and serves as a robust indicator of student knowledge and skills in the domain. The former, a curriculum sampling approach to CBMs, involves testing students on a representative sample of the knowledge and skills that will be taught during the year. CBMs created using the curriculum sampling approach include items that directly represent knowledge and skills students will learn in the curriculum. In contrast, the general outcome measure approach to CBMs is independent of the curriculum. That is, test items are not sampled from any particular set of content standards or textbooks but are thought to predict students' overall proficiency in mathematics. A common example of a general outcome measure in reading is oral reading fluency. Although oral reading fluency does not directly sample from the curriculum, student performance is highly correlated to other measures of reading.

Most of the currently available mathematics CBMs, such as the Monitoring Basic Skills Progress (MBSP; Fuchs, Hamlett, & Fuchs, n.d.) kit, are designed for students in elementary school and focus on monitoring students' computational skills. Some CBMs are designed to monitor students' conceptual understanding and application of procedures. When you are choosing a progress monitoring system, it is important to evaluate the content that is assessed.

There are a number of commercially available progress monitoring systems in mathematics from which you can chose. Because their cost can be significant, it is important to determine the best progress monitoring system for you and your school. To help navigate the myriad progress monitoring systems available, the National Center on Intensive Intervention, funded by the U.S. Department of Education, publishes an online rating system for progress monitoring tools (https://intensiveintervention.org). Tools are rated based on their psychometric properties (i.e., reliability of the results), alignment with progress monitoring standards (i.e., multiple parallel forms), and ability to support data-based decisions for individual students (i.e., decision rules). An independent panel of experts reviews each tool, so you can be confident that the reviews are not biased. An example of the Tools Chart from the National Center on Intensive Intervention is shown in Figure 12.8. These ratings as well as your professional judgment should inform your selection of a progress monitoring system.

When selecting a progress monitoring system, keep in mind the decisions you want to make. To determine if the student is learning at an appropriate rate as a result

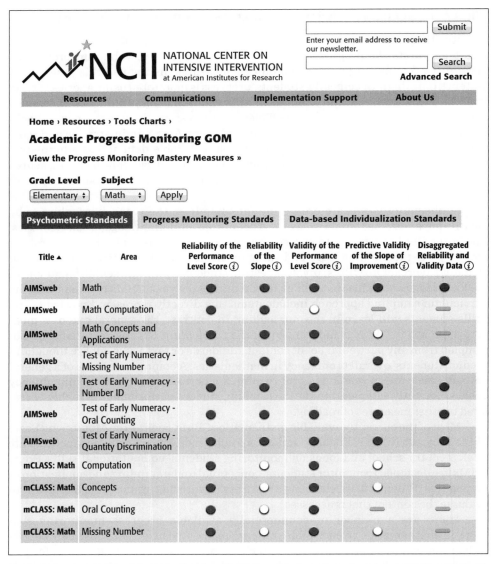

Figure 12.8. An example of the Tools Chart from the National Center on Intensive Intervention. (Reprinted with permission from National Center on Intensive Intervention. [2018]. Academic progress monitoring tools chart. Washington, DC: Office of Special Education Programs, U.S. Department of Education. Retrieved from https://charts .intensiveintervention.org/chart/progress-monitoring)

of the intervention, the progress monitoring system needs to include multiple parallel forms that are sensitive to small changes in the student's understanding. Also, because these tests will be given frequently, the tests need to be short in duration and easy to administer and score.

Parallel Forms for Administration Over Time   The term *parallel forms* means that there are many different test forms that are equal (or parallel) in difficulty. To monitor changes in a student's learning over time, you need the tests to stay the same over time. If the tests changed over time, it would be difficult to determine whether there was a change in the student's learning or whether the change in student performance was attributable to differing levels of difficulty on the tests. However, because we will be giving the tests frequently (at least once per month), we cannot give the student the same test. Therefore, we need to have different test forms that are equal (or parallel) in difficulty but do not have exactly the same items.

Test publishers of progress monitoring systems should provide evidence that the forms are parallel in difficulty. The National Center on Intensive Intervention (2017) suggests the use of item response theory modeling or strong alternate form reliability coefficients. However, you do not need to be an expert in either of these topics to evaluate a progress monitoring system. The Tools Chart provided by the National Center on Intensive Intervention can help you determine whether evidence is available that indicates the forms are parallel. You can also ask for this information directly from the test publishers. Most important, in order for you to make informed decisions about students' growth over time, evidence presented by the test publishers should convince you that 1) they created parallel forms, and 2) that the forms are comparable.

Test Forms Are Sensitive to Student Learning

Progress monitoring assessment systems should also be evaluated on their ability to represent small changes in student learning. Because we are using their results to determine if the intervention is helping the student learn at an appropriate rate, we need to monitor even small changes in the student's understanding. However, some tests are not able to detect these small changes. For example, consider a cumulative final exam administered at the end of the semester. This exam likely includes content taught throughout the semester; in many cases, multiple knowledge and skills are assessed in each item. A student's score on this exam represents a semester's worth of learning. For a student to change his or her score, significant learning may be required.

When monitoring progress, we want to recognize small changes in a student's knowledge and/or skills to determine if the intervention is supporting the student's learning at an appropriate rate. CBMs are designed to be sensitive to growth. The National Center on Intensive Intervention also evaluates this dimension and provides a rating for each progress monitoring system that is reviewed.

Administration and Scoring Considerations

As noted earlier, progress monitoring assessments are designed to be given on a regular basis (at least monthly). Because administering these tests takes instructional time, administration should be efficient for both you and the students. Most CBMs are timed and require 4–10 minutes to administer. We have worked with some teachers who find success in administering these tests at the very beginning of class on a regular basis (i.e., every Wednesday). The teacher places a stack of tests face down on the students' desks. When class begins, the teacher instructs the students to start the test. The students begin work and the teacher starts the timer. It is important that the exact same amount of time be given each week. If more (or less) time is given one week, the students' scores might improve (or go down), but not as a result of instruction. These results are inaccurate and might lead to inappropriate interpretations.

Because the goal of implementing a progress monitoring system is to make timely decisions to support student learning, you need to score and enter results from progress monitoring tests immediately. However, we know that there is nothing more frustrating than having stacks and stacks of papers to grade. Also, when you are implementing a progress monitoring system, you will have tests to score on a weekly basis. Some progress monitoring systems can be taken online with automatic data entry (i.e., Yearly Progress Pro). Others need to be printed and hand-scored (i.e., MBSP). As such, you need to select a progress monitoring system that will allow you to score the tests and enter the results quickly and efficiently.

Some teachers of older students (i.e., grade 7 or 8) have their students score the tests and graph the results themselves. Because these tests are "low stakes," meaning that the student is not receiving a grade based on the results, students often resist the temptation to cheat. More often than not, students are excited to see their results and plot their progress. However, keep in mind that because you are using these data to make instructional decisions, accuracy is of key importance. If students are not able to accurately score and plot the data, another plan is needed.

How Do I Communicate Results to Parents and Students?

Just as with any assessment system, it is important to consider how information from a progress monitoring system will be conveyed to parents and students. Because progress monitoring measures are administered to students who are nonresponsive to Tier 1 or Tier 2 instruction, you have likely had previous conversations with parents and students about assessment results. However, because parents and students may not be familiar with progress monitoring measures, it is important to plan for successful and meaningful communication. Again, when preparing to communicate results, it is important that you to fully understand the reports, understand how results are used to make decisions, and have a plan for the future. Once you have this information in place, results can be shared with parents and students.

Know Progress Monitoring Reports   Reports are a key feature of any progress monitoring system and typically include a graphical display as well as a table with the student's scores. Most commercially available progress monitoring systems have materials for generating reports by hand or electronically. Although you may be familiar with most parts of the report, plan on thoroughly reviewing these materials before discussing the results with parents and students.

Gather Additional Data   As with any assessment system, it is helpful to have additional data about the student's performance available to verify results from the progress monitoring system. You may find it most helpful to have data from the same time period in which the progress monitoring data were collected. For example, you could gather weekly quizzes that were given during the same time as the progress monitoring measures.

Document Instructional Decisions and Changes   Results from the progress monitoring system are used to determine 1) whether the student is learning as a result of the intervention, and 2) whether the rate of learning is adequate to reach the student's goal. Once these questions are addressed with results from the progress monitoring system, you can make instructional decisions. Refer to Step 5 (evaluate the student's progress) in the earlier discussion of the progress monitoring process to help interpret the student's scores.

Share Results   You may want to consider augmenting the sample plan previously discussed in Chapter 9 with these details for sharing results from a progress monitoring assessment.

Step 1: Share general information about the progress monitoring assessment, such as

- The purpose of the test

- How the test will inform instructional decisions

- The content that was assessed

It is important that parents and students understand that results from the progress monitoring system are intended to help you make adjustments to the intervention platform you designed. Once parents and students understand why the test was administered and how the information will be used, the score will have more meaning.

Step 2: Describe the type of scores. Typically, because CBMs are timed, scores are reported as a rate. The rate is usually displayed as the number correct per minute. Some CBMs report the number of correct digits the student earned per minute, whereas others report the number of items correct per minute. For some progress monitoring systems, results are reported as a scaled score. Helping parents and students understand the type of score is important for accurate communication.

Step 3: Describe the student's goal. Describe the process you used to calculate the student's goal and locate it on the graphical display (without showing the student's observed performance). The goal provides a reference point for subsequently interpreting the student's performance. You may also want to share the baseline data to indicate where the student began the learning process.

It may be helpful to reference prior discussions about the student's performance on the universal screener and/or diagnostic formative assessment. You likely already shared plans for the design of the intervention; however, if not, now would be a good time to describe the intervention you implemented.

Step 4: Share the student's scores. Once parents and students understand the purpose of the progress monitoring system, have a sense of the scores they will encounter, and know the goal, they should have enough context for interpreting scores. Now you are ready to share information at a pace that is understandable for parents and students:

1. First, show the student's observed performance on the graphical display (typically, a line plot). Provide as much description as possible. Providing this information will set the foundation for understanding the instructional decisions you made.

2. Second, describe the growth rate over time by looking at the line of best fit (refer to Step 4, Administer progress monitoring system at regular intervals, in the earlier section How Do I Use Progress Monitoring Measures to Make Instructional Decisions?).

3. Third, share the additional information that was gathered to verify the results. It is important to emphasize that the accumulated evidence indicates a trend in the student's performance and should be interpreted as corroborating evidence.

Step 5: Share the instructional decisions. Once parents and students understand the meaning of the score, they will likely be anxious to hear about what comes next.

Share the instructional decisions you made during Step 5, Evaluate the student's progress, in the earlier section How Do I Use Progress Monitoring Measures to Make Instructional Decisions?

Step 6: Answer questions. Parents and students will likely have many questions. Allow ample time for questions and discussion.

SUMMARY: PROGRESS MONITORING

Once teachers identify students who are nonresponsive to Tier 1 or Tier 2 instruction, students are provided with interventions and support based on their needs. In this chapter, we discussed how to monitor students' progress over time to determine if the instructional interventions being implemented are positively affecting student learning. Progress monitoring measures, typically administered at least monthly, can help you determine if students are improving and the rate at which they are improving. Suggestions were also provided about how to share progress monitoring data with parents and students.

ADDITIONAL RESOURCES

Center on Response to Intervention (https://rti4success.org)
National Center on Intensive Intervention (https://intensiveintervention.org)
National Center on Intensive Intervention. (2017). *Academic progress monitoring tools chart rating rubric.* Retrieved from https://intensiveintervention.org/sites/default/files/NCII _APM_RatingRubric_Oct2017.pdf
Research Institute on Progress Monitoring (https://www.progressmonitoring.org)

CHAPTER 13

Have Students Reached Their Goals? Summative Assessments

We all know that the goal of teaching is learning. We plan our lessons to provide students with important information, interesting activities, and meaningful problem solving to engage them in the learning process. Along the way, we evaluate whether students are gaining proficiency by asking them questions, reviewing their responses to homework or in-class problems, and observing their classroom discussions and work. However, to evaluate whether our instruction reached the ultimate goal of facilitating student learning, we need to administer a summative assessment. Results from summative assessments allow us to answer the question, "Did students learn?" This evaluation of outcomes is a key part of the cycle of decision making. Even though MTSS makes frequent use of formative assessments, summative assessments are still needed to support your instructional decision making. This chapter focuses on the summative assessments, such as unit tests and final exams, used in classroom settings.

WHAT ARE WE AIMING FOR?

The purpose and importance of summative assessments are illustrated by the example of Mr. Chande, a seventh-grade mathematics teacher.

MR. CHANDE'S SEVENTH-GRADE TIER 1 MATHEMATICS CLASS

At the end of the instructional unit on understanding and computing unit rates, Mr. Chande was certain he had done everything he could to design a high-quality learning experience for his grade 7 students. He carefully reviewed the prerequisite knowledge on equivalent fractions, and differentiated instruction based on students' prior knowledge. He systematically introduced the concept of a unit rate and demonstrated it with visual representations (e.g., a double number line). He incorporated guided and independent practice items that scaffolded students' application of unit rate to increasingly more complex problems, and he encouraged students' independence. He reviewed the students' work on these exercises and was happy with their performance. He was convinced that he provided an optimal experience that would ensure his students learned the concept of unit rate and could compute unit rates with independence.

However, as Mr. Chande began the next instructional unit on representing proportional relationships between two quantities and calculating equivalent ratios, many of his students started to struggle. They struggled to understand that a unit rate is a representation of a ratio. They could calculate that the unit rate for a 16-ounce cup of coffee that costs $4 is $0.25 per 1 ounce, but they struggled to extend this concept to understanding equivalent ratios. What Mr. Chande did not know was whether and how well his students had learned the concept of unit rate at the end of the previous instructional unit. Because Mr. Chande had been pleased with his students' performance on their independent practice work, he had decided not to administer a summative assessment upon completing that prior unit. As a result, he didn't really know whether or how well each student had learned the material. He was lacking crucial information needed to make an appropriate decision about when it was time to begin the next instructional unit.

As this scenario points out, even with the best-designed instructional unit that incorporates evidence-based practices, students will learn the material to varying degrees. The hope is that all students have reached or surpassed the minimum amount of learning needed to move on to the next instructional unit. To determine if students are ready to move on, the teacher needs to know if each student has reached a minimum threshold of learning so that he or she can be successful in future applications of the concepts, knowledge, or skills.

In summary, for Tier 1, Tier 2, or Tier 3 instruction, before moving on to the next instructional objective, you need to determine whether and how well each student has learned the instructional objective.

WHAT TOOLS WILL HELP US MAKE THIS DECISION?

To determine whether and how well each student has reached the instructional objective, you should administer a summative assessment that covers the objectives of the instructional unit. As we discussed at the beginning Section III, summative assessments are assessments of learning. These tests are given after the learning process has occurred to judge whether each student has reached the goals of instruction.

What Are the Benefits of Summative Assessments?

Although some people dread summative assessments, they can be positive for both teachers and students:

- For teachers, summative assessment results provide evidence that you met the goal of teaching: student learning. In some cases, student performance on the summative assessment will indicate that this goal was not reached. Knowing this outcome is also helpful for teachers because it gives you information you can use to plan your future instruction. Future instruction could include reteaching, providing supplemental review exercises, or implementing a number of instructional strategies discussed in Section II of this book.

- For students, summative assessments allow them to demonstrate their cumulative knowledge and skills. Sometimes we forget that students are working really hard to learn. Summative assessments provide students with evidence that their work and studying paid off. For some students, their performance might not be so positive. These students may react with frustration at themselves or at the teacher (or any number of scapegoats). Coaching should be provided to help students understand that teaching and learning are intertwined. The teacher's job is to help the student learn and the student's job is to engage and attend to the learning process.

Beginning and continuing this discussion throughout the student's academic career can help students understand their role in the learning process and develop healthy strategies for dealing with frustrations in their learning.

How Do I Use Summative Assessments to Make Instructional Decisions?

Because summative assessments are assessments of learning, results from summative assessments provide a measure of student proficiency in relation to the instructional objective. So, to determine whether each student has reached the instructional objective, you need to finalize your instructional objective. As discussed in Chapter 9, we use the criterion specified in the instructional objective to make a criterion-referenced interpretation.

What Do I Want Students to Learn?   Remembering back to your introductory teaching methods courses, you probably learned that instructional objectives should be observable and measurable. In fact, you probably had to write many objectives for multiple content standards and were judged on the components you included. Here is an example:

The learner will use a variable to represent an unknown quantity when solving 20 real-world problems to 80% accuracy.

Although simple, it has all of the required components: the content is specified (represent an unknown with a variable), the student's behavior or cognitive engagement is noted (use variable notation and solve problems), the condition for demonstrating proficiency is given (20 real-world problems), and the performance objective is documented (80% accuracy). Either by habit or mandated through policy, you probably still continue to write instructional objectives. However, over time, many of us lose the specificity by omitting one or more components of the objectives. In a quick review of lessons for middle school students on the Illuminations web site published by NCTM (https://illuminations.nctm.org), we noted that not one lesson identified the condition for demonstrating proficiency. Here is an example for a lesson designed to help students understand the relationship between recursive functions and exponential functions:

At the end of this lesson, students will

- Represent data using tables, graphs and rules
- Investigate patterns and make conjectures
- Explain their reasoning when making conjectures

Although this objective is carefully worded to specify the content and the behavior or cognitive engagement through which students will interact with the content, little information is shared about how to measure students' proficiency in reaching this objective. To revise this instructional objective to include all of the necessary components, we need to include a statement about the condition for demonstrating proficiency (such as the number and types of problems students will be able to independently complete after completing the lesson or unit) and the performance objective (such as the number or percentage of items students need to respond to correctly to demonstrate that they have mastered the content). Once these components are specified, you have a clear picture of how to design the summative assessment and what criterion you will use to determine if the students met the objective. In the next section, we talk about designing summative assessments and making criterion-referenced interpretations using the criterion you set in the instructional objective.

Did Each Student Learn the Required Content?
Your instructional objective specifies the criterion by which you will determine if each student learned the required content. The performance objective is the component that serves as this criterion. In our sample instructional objective in the previous subsection, we stated that the learner will use a variable to represent an unknown quantity when solving 20 real-world problems to 80% accuracy. The performance objective, or criterion, we specified is 80% accuracy, or 16 out of 20 problems. (Thus, 16 out of 20 will be the cut score on the summative assessment.) At the end of the instructional unit, we will give students a 20-item summative assessment. For students who answer 16 or more items correctly, we say that they met the instructional objective. They learned the required content to the degree of mastery required to move on to the next instructional unit. For students who answered fewer than 16 correct, we say that they did not meet the instructional objective. They did not learn the required content to the degree of mastery required to move on to the next instructional unit. For these students, additional instruction may be needed, either before moving on to the next instructional unit or simultaneously while receiving instruction on the next unit. (This additional instruction should be aligned with evidence-based practices; see specific recommendations in Section II.)

In this example, we compared students' scores on the summative assessment to the performance objective, or criterion, we specified in our instructional objective. Just as with any other test in which you are making a criterion-referenced interpretation (such as a universal screener), you compare students' scores to the specific performance objective to make a decision. In the case of a summative assessment, the performance objective is the criterion of mastery that you set in the instructional objective. This criterion of mastery divides the students' scores into at least two groups for making decisions:

1. Students who demonstrated mastery by scoring at or above the performance objective

2. Students who did not demonstrate mastery by scoring below the performance objective

Setting the performance objective, or criterion, is an important part of making a criterion-referenced interpretation. The criterion you set should be based on your hypothesis about the level of mastery of the required content that students need in order to be successful in future learning. In some cases, the content might be so important to future instructional units that you want all students to demonstrate 100% proficiency when working independently. In other cases, you might decide that it is okay if the student makes a few errors. You would set the criterion according to the amount of errors you would accept while still considering the student proficient.

This process provides you with information to determine whether each student has reached the instructional objective. In some cases, this is all the information you need to know. However, in many other cases (i.e., assigning grades, communicating with parents and students), you want to know *how well* the student learned the material. To make this type of decision, results are typically compared to other students in the class to make a norm-referenced interpretation.

How Well Did Each Student Learn the Material?   Although your instructional objective specifies the criterion by which you will determine if each student learned the required content, in many cases we want to evaluate students' scores on the summative assessment to determine how well they learned the material. For example, consider the summative assessment we would administer to assess whether students are able to use a variable to represent an unknown quantity when solving 20 real-world problems. When we evaluate the results, we can interpret each student's score in relation to the criterion to determine if each student reached the instructional objective. However, we might also want to recognize that some students may have learned the material with greater proficiency than others. This information may be useful for creating homogeneous groups of students for differentiated instruction, assigning targeted practice opportunities, or reporting grades.

Using summative assessment data to determine how well a student learned the material assumes that students with higher scores learned the material with greater depth and/or breadth than students with lower scores. For example, we would assume that a student with a score of 100% learned the material with greater depth and/or breadth than a student who earned a score of 80%. Depending on the performance objective, both of these students might have met the criterion for determining whether they reached the instructional objective. However, the added information of comparing their scores to each other tells us how well each learned the material in reference to the other.

To determine how well each student learned the material, we start by rank ordering the scores on the summative assessment. *Rank ordering* means that you sort the scores in descending order either electronically on a spreadsheet (such as Microsoft Excel) or manually by sorting papers from the highest score to the lowest score. By placing the scores in order, you can quickly determine how well each student learned the material in relation to other students. This type of sorting provides you with information about the relative depth and/or breadth of students' understanding compared to their peers.

To summarize how to make instructional decisions using summative assessments, let's come back to our example instructional objective. Say you gave all students in your class the 20-item summative assessment on using a variable to represent an unknown quantity in real-world problems to determine whether and how well each student reached the instructional objective. All of your students scored at or above 16. In response to the question about whether students reached the instructional objective, you could conclude that all of your students met the instructional objective of 80% mastery; your instruction was successful in helping students learn the material to the level needed to move on to the next instructional unit. However, you also want to determine how well each student learned the material so you can provide ongoing support as needed. By rank ordering the students' scores, you quickly identify those students who responded correctly to 16 out of 20 items and those who responded correctly to all 20 items. In response to the question about how well students learned the material, you could conclude that the students who scored at the cut score of 80% (16 out of 20 items) did not learn the material to the same depth and/or breadth as the students who scored 100%. Again, knowing whether and how well each student has reached the instructional objective allows you to make specific instructional decisions to support student learning.

When and to Whom Are Summative Assessments Administered?

Because summative assessments allow you to evaluate if your instruction reached the intended goal of facilitating student learning, all students who received instruction should take the summative assessment after the instructional unit. Each student's score is compared to the performance objective specified in the instructional objective to determine if the student reached the required level of mastery.

What Are the Characteristics of a Summative Assessment?

As we discussed earlier, to be useful for making instructional decisions, all assessment systems must produce reliable results that lead to valid interpretations. Summative assessments typically don't report subscores, so you don't have to worry about evaluating subscore reliability. Also, we aren't using summative assessments to make comparisons over time, so you don't need to worry about parallel forms. However, to make valid decisions about students' learning from summative assessments, important considerations include 1) alignment of the assessed content with the instructional objective, and 2) accuracy of the performance objective used as the criterion for making decisions.

Content Alignment for Making Summative Decisions   The content of a summative assessment should align with the objectives of the instructional unit. Depending upon the unit's scope, the content assessed on a summative assessment may be narrowly defined to cover a single objective or broadly defined to include multiple objectives. Most important, the content should be specific enough to help you answer the primary question: Did students learn?

Designing a summative assessment requires a list of steps, outlined next and further explained afterward.

Steps For Designing Summative Assessments

Step 1: Define the content to be assessed.

Step 2: Specify the number of items.

Step 3: Define what content will be assessed in each item.

Step 4: Write items.

Step 5: Evaluate items before and after giving the test.

Step 1: Define the content to be assessed. Include the knowledge or skills and the levels of cognitive engagement. Remember that the content includes both the knowledge and/or skills of the instructional objective and the behavior or cognitive engagement. Think back to the instructional objective we discussed earlier:

The learner will use a variable to represent an unknown quantity when solving 20 real-world problems to 80% accuracy.

The content is narrowly defined as "use a variable to represent an unknown quantity." The knowledge and/or skill is "variable" and the student's behavior or cognitive engagement is "use" and "solve." To determine if each student reached the required level of mastery of this instructional objective, the summative assessment should explicitly focus on using variables to solve problems.

Step 2: Specify the number of items. After you specify the content, you need to determine the number of items on the test. In some instances, you might specify the number of items in the instructional objective, such as in the example we have been discussing (i.e., 20 real-world problems). If you haven't done so, you can select a suitable number given the amount of time you have to administer the test and the depth of content you want to cover.

In general, there should be enough items on the test to get an accurate appraisal of each student's proficiency without the influence of too much random error. If tests are too short, random errors might dramatically change a student's score. For example, missing one item on a test that includes five items results in a score of 80%, but missing one item on a test that has 15 items results in a score of 93%. As we discussed in the chapter on diagnostic formative assessments (Chapter 11), a student can miss an item for any number of reasons including random slips. We hope that a student's responses relate directly to his or her level of proficiency in the assessed content; however, we know that sometimes random errors happen even when the student knows the material. For example, the student might make a computation error, misread the problem, misunderstand the directions, or make any number of other errors that are not related to the student's proficiency in the assessed content. Including a sufficient number of items can help prevent these random errors from making too big an impact on a student's score.

In contrast, we want to make sure that we don't have too many items. Too many items can negatively affect students, too: students become tired and begin making errors; students are overwhelmed by the number of items and lose motivation. Also, from a test design perspective, you may not gain any more information about a student's knowledge and skills when you add in more items. Unfortunately, there is no magic number of items. The key is to find the optimal number that will give you the best information about whether a student has sufficiently learned the material.

Step 3: Define what content will be assessed in each item. Once you know how many items you will include on the summative assessment, you can specify which knowledge and skills will be assessed by each item and at which levels of cognitive complexity. It is often helpful to put this information in a table (technically, this is called a test blueprint). Figure 13.1 is one possible way of defining the content for the instructional objective stated previously: The learner will use a variable to represent an unknown quantity when solving 20 real-world problems to 80% accuracy.

Content	Cognitive engagement			
	Procedural fluency	Conceptual understanding	Strategic competence	Adaptive reasoning
Understand the concept of a variable		2 items		
Represent a quantity with variable notation	4 items			
Construct a simple equation using variable notation from a real-world problem	3 items		2 items	
Solve for a variable	5 items			
Reason about the appropriateness of the solution				4 items

Figure 13.1. Sample test blueprint.

In Figure 13.1, you can see which content is being assessed at the different levels of cognitive engagement. Completing a blueprint like this will help you determine whether you are 1) including all of the knowledge and skills at the appropriate levels of cognitive engagement specified in your instructional objective and 2) putting an appropriate weight on each of these combinations based on the instruction you provided. The weighting of items in this sample may not be appropriate for another teacher's unit if the same content wasn't covered to the same depth of understanding.

A common mistake when designing summative assessments is to include items that assess prior instructional objectives. Although it makes great sense to include a cumulative review to evaluate whether students have maintained specific knowledge and/or skills, items that assess something other than the current instructional objective provide you with little or no information about each student's mastery of this objective. One way to include a cumulative review along with the summative assessment is to have two separate sections of the test: one for the summative assessment and one for the cumulative review. However, make sure you score them separately and evaluate only the items on the summative assessment section against the performance objective (or criterion).

Step 4: Write items. Once you have defined the content that will be assessed and the level of cognitive engagement, you can begin writing items. You have likely written many test items and know how much care needs to be taken to accurately and appropriately assess a student's knowledge and skills. We want to highlight a few key decisions to consider as you prepare to write items, including whether they will be situated within real-world contexts and the format of the items (i.e., constructed versus selected response).

Many times, the content standards or the level of cognitive engagement may dictate whether items are situated in real-world contexts or are context-free. Regardless of whether incorporating context into items is your choice or required by the content expectations, take care when writing items with real-world contexts to ensure that they are appropriate and accessible to all learners. For example, an item that requires knowledge of baseball innings or how to get a first down in football may positively or negatively affect students' performance depending on their familiarity with the context. The contexts you choose should be accessible to all learners. This ensures that the context does not distract students from the mathematics in the item and that the interpretations we make about the student are based on their knowledge of mathematics, not on their familiarity with unknown contexts. Also, when writing items with contexts, it is important to keep in mind the reading level of the text. The language should be grade-level appropriate and use common vocabulary words.

The item format choice is also an important consideration to keep in mind. The two most common formats are constructed response and selected response. Selected-response items include multiple choice, matching, true or false (even if the student writes in "true" or "false"), and any item in which a student selects an answer from a pool of possible answer choices. These types of items are used frequently in standardized testing and typically have four answer options. Although they are generally easier to score, it is important to write the items such that the three incorrect options (i.e., distractors) are plausible answers based on student misconceptions. In contrast, constructed-response items require the student to generate an answer on his or her own. These items may require students to write out how they solved a problem or to show all of their work and strategies. Constructed-response items generally take more time and effort to score than selected-response items. If this item type is chosen, you will need to determine how the items will be scored. They can be scored dichotomously (incorrect or correct), or partial credit may be given based on student work. As you write constructed-response items, you will also need to develop rubrics to ensure that the scoring criteria used are consistent among raters and across students. Regardless of the choice of item format, it is also important to make sure that the items are accessible for all students.

Step 5: Evaluate items (before and after giving the test). Often when we write a letter, paint a picture, or artfully decorate a cupcake, stepping back from it (both physically and metaphorically) allows us to gain perspective and objectivity. This same phenomenon applies to writing test items. Sometimes you need to step away from the items to be able to accurately evaluate whether they assess what you intend for them to assess. However, in some cases, it is nearly impossible to be objective about our own work; we might be our own worst critic or best cheerleader. However, when it comes to evaluating items, it is important to review each one thoroughly because you will be making decisions based on the outcomes.

One of the best resources you have for evaluating test items is your colleagues. A strategy we have used many times is to ask colleagues to read each item and tell us what knowledge or skill is being assessed and at what level of cognitive engagement. In essence, we are asking our colleagues to build the blueprint we created in Step 3. We then compare blueprints (the one we created and the one created by our colleagues) to determine the level of agreement. The outcome of this process is always eye opening and provides great insights into how someone else interprets the questions. If you have a trusted colleague or work within a professional learning community, this process can be helpful in getting an objective perspective on the quality of the items for making the decisions you intend to make.

Classification Accuracy

As we discussed in Chapter 10 on making universal screening decisions, when you compare a student's score to a criterion to make a decision, the accuracy of the resulting placement into categories must be considered. (See also Chapter 9 concerning how to "quantify" learning by reporting or interpreting along a continuum; e.g., scoring 80% indicates a student learned more than a peer who scored 70%, regardless of whether both students met the objective.) When interpreting results from a summative assessment, you are comparing the student's score to the performance objective and deciding whether the student

1.   Demonstrated mastery by scoring at or above the performance objective

2.   Did not demonstrate mastery by scoring below the performance objective

Because the consequences of this decision could be significant for the student (e.g., having to attend tutorials to review the material, receiving additional exercises), you want to be confident in placing the student in one of these two categories. Unlike test publishers, you likely won't be using advanced statistical techniques to verify the classification accuracy of the resulting placements. As such, you should verify the outcomes with additional sources of data. Other data such as homework or classwork can be used to corroborate the results from the summative assessment. If you see any patterns that don't make sense (i.e., a student aced the classwork but failed the summative assessment or vice versa), follow up with the student to make the most appropriate decision.

How Do I Communicate Results From
Summative Assessments to Parents and Students?

Summative assessments are designed to be evaluative: results help us determine whether and how well students each student learned the instructional objective. Because the ultimate goal of teaching is student learning, results from summative assessments provide you with an opportunity to reflect on your instruction and to determine if it accomplished the goal of facilitating student learning. Given summative assessments' evaluative nature, discussing the results can be an emotional process. In this subsection, we provide additional information about how to share summative assessment results in a way that should ease the emotional reactions from all people involved.

Most parents have experience interpreting summative assessment results from their own experiences in K–12 education. Keep in mind that parents' own personal experiences (whether positive or negative) will likely influence their reactions as you share their child's results. These same people were once in the child's place, listening to their teachers share results from summative assessments, and may also remember their own parents' reactions to these results. Being mindful that these conversations may be sensitive for some parents will help you in your planning and communication.

Consider this example: Jon has never had a cavity in his life. Each time he has gone to the dentist, he has received glowing results that indicate his teeth are "picture perfect." Then, to his surprise, one day he learns he has a cavity. How might Jon respond differently to each of these scenarios?

- Scenario 1: Upon finding the cavity, Jon's dental hygienist says, "Jon, you haven't been doing your job. I'm really disappointed. You have a cavity. I've told you how important it is to floss every day. You must not have been doing it right. We will need to make an appointment to get that drilled out. You've never had a cavity. Boy, it's going to hurt."

- Scenario 2: Upon finding the cavity, Jon's dental hygienist says, "Jon, I know that you have never had a cavity. I am seeing some decay in your tooth that looks like a cavity. We can fix this cavity. I know you are usually very careful about brushing and flossing your teeth. Is there anything we should talk about or review?"

Because the tone of the communication in Scenario 1 was blame, disappointment, and frustration, Jon likely responded with fear and possibly even some anger toward the dental hygienist. However, because the communication in Scenario 2 recognized that the cavity was a new occurrence, recognized Jon's efforts to take care of his teeth, and was generally supportive, Jon likely responded more positively. Although these scenarios are a bit exaggerated, we hope they illustrate the way in which sensitive information can sound and how that might influence the recipient's reactions.

Just as with any assessment system, when reporting results from a summative assessment, it is important that you fully understand the reports, understand how results are used to make decisions, and have a plan for the future. Once you have this information in place, you are ready to share the results of summative assessments with parents and students.

Know the Reports   Except in cases where you are administering a standardized summative assessment published by a test vendor, you will have created the reports yourself. To maximize the efficiency of the discussion, we recommend preparing a formal report to share each student's results (as opposed to showing parents the actual test with the student's responses, which might be distracting). This report does not need to be fancy but should include the instructional objective that was assessed as well as the method in which you will report the student's performance (i.e., raw score, percentage, grade).

Gather Additional Data   As noted earlier, it is especially important to gather additional samples of the student's work, such as homework or classwork, when you are evaluating if and how well each student learned the material. Your conclusions about the student's mastery should be verified with additional sources of data.

Document Instructional Decisions and Changes   As stated before, summative assessments are administered at the end of the instructional unit to determine if and how well each student has reached the instructional objective. Once these questions are addressed with results from the summative assessment, you can make instructional decisions. As discussed earlier, students who demonstrate mastery of the instructional objectives based on responses on the summative assessment are most likely ready to move on to the next instructional unit. However, students who do not demonstrate mastery of the instructional objectives (corroborated with other data sources) are most likely in need of additional instruction before progressing.

Remember that learning is a two-way process that requires collaborative and reciprocal actions: The teacher's job is to help each student learn, and the student's job is to engage and attend to the learning process. If you are able to communicate the dependent nature of teaching and learning in a supportive manner, you should be able to diffuse any tension that may arise.

Share Results   Again, keep in mind that most parents and students will have experience receiving results from summative assessments. These experiences likely range from really good to really bad. Your ability to communicate these results in a clear manner will set the stage for how parents and students will respond. Here is a sample plan that incorporates the steps described in Chapter 9.

Step 1: Share general information about the test such as

- The purpose of the test
- How the test will inform instructional decisions
- The content that was assessed

Sharing the instructional objective(s) will help parents and students understand the context of the assessment.

Step 2: Describe the type of scores on the report. Again, because you likely created the report, information might be displayed in a different format than parents and students have seen before. It is helpful to review the type of scores you will share and how the scores relate to the instructional objective. For example, if you are reporting raw scores but your instructional objective is stated as a percentage, provide the conversion to the parents and students to aid in interpretation.

Step 3: Share the student's score report. Once parents and students understand the purpose of the summative assessment and know what type of scores they will encounter, they should have enough information to understand the student's scores. Share information at a pace that is understandable for parents and students:

1. First, describe the student's scores in relation to the instructional objective. Provide a general statement to help the parents and student understand whether he or she met the instructional objective.

2. Second, describe the student's scores in relation to how well he or she learned the material. Provide as much detail about the student's depth and/or breadth of understanding as possible.

3. Third, share the additional data sources that were gathered to verify the results from the summative assessment. It is important to emphasize that the results on the summative assessment were corroborated with other data gathered over time. This information should provide evidence that these results indicate a trend in the student's performance or understanding.

Step 5: Share the instructional decisions. Once parents and students understand the meaning of the score, they will likely be anxious to hear about what comes next. Share the instructional decisions you made prior to convening the parents.

Step 6: Answer questions. Parents and students will likely have many questions. Allow ample time for questions and discussion.

SUMMARY: USING SUMMATIVE ASSESSMENTS

This chapter focused on the purpose and uses of summative assessments. Although not explicitly part of the MTSS process, summative assessments help determine if and how well students learned instructional objectives. Because summative decisions are tied to instructional objectives, it is critical to have carefully articulated instructional objectives that inform instruction within the classroom, and summative assessments should be constructed to align with these instructional objectives. This chapter provided suggestions on how to create summative assessments and how to share summative assessment data with parents and students.

SECTION IV

Implementing MTSS to Support Effective Teaching

OVERVIEW: PUTTING IT ALL TOGETHER

In this section, we put together all the ideas presented in previous sections of this book. In Chapter 14, we describe how instruction and assessment work together within an MTSS framework to provide appropriate supports for all students including those with learning difficulties. In Chapter 15, we provide readers with help in putting together school-level teams to design and implement MTSS. We also propose a multiyear timeline for implementation of MTSS. Because MTSS requires many different people working together, we explore successful collaboration among stakeholders in Chapter 16. Finally, in Chapter 17, we present the highlights and difficulties of MTSS implementation as described in interview responses from several stakeholders with experience in getting MTSS started in school settings.

In these final four chapters, we provide information to help you embark on effective design and implementation of MTSS for your school. We prompt you to think about the following:

1. How do all of the components of MTSS work together? In previous sections and chapters of this book, we described the MTSS framework, instructional considerations, and assessment considerations. Now it's time to put all of those components together into a working model for you and your school. In Chapter 14, we walk through the decision-making process for designing your MTSS model tier by tier.

2. Who are the players within a school-implemented MTSS framework? Multiple people work on the design of a school's MTSS framework, and even more people implement MTSS. Identifying the right people (Chapter 15) who can work collaboratively (Chapter 16) is essential for a successful and sustainable MTSS effort.

3. What's the typical timeline for MTSS implementation? A school should not try to get MTSS up and running in one school year. This could put too much pressure on stakeholders and lead to burnout with MTSS. A year-by-year approach typically leads to improved MTSS implementation. Therefore, we provide suggestions for developing and implementing MTSS over a 3-, 4-, or 5-year span (Chapter 15).

4. What are the greatest challenges in implementing MTSS? We interviewed several educators, administrators, and specialists who have implemented MTSS in their school or district. They describe their challenges and successes in Chapter 17. We hope that this information can guide you as you embark on implementation of MTSS.

CHAPTER 14

MTSS in Action

Many school leaders and teachers express an understanding of the very basics of MTSS but have difficulty with how to implement so many moving pieces (Regan, Berkeley, Hughes, & Brady, 2015). In this chapter and the ones that follow, we help you work through the process of designing an MTSS model and putting that model in place in middle school classrooms. In this chapter, we won't answer a lot of questions. Instead, we will guide you through thinking about the following:

- What is your overall model for MTSS?

- What does your Tier 1 look like in terms of assessment and instruction?

- What do assessment and instruction look like in your Tier 2 settings?

- How do your assessment and instruction work together in Tier 3?

DESIGNING YOUR MTSS MODEL

Figure 14.1 presents our framework for MTSS, introduced in Chapter 2. We use the common three-tier model.

Before your school begins implementing MTSS, you have to determine what MTSS will look like in your school. Some schools use this three-tier model. Other schools may have several iterations of Tier 2 or five different tiers. Currently, there is no research to support one MTSS model over another, so you and your colleagues must design the MTSS model that you want to employ.

One big hurdle in implementation of MTSS is communication among MTSS stakeholders (Thompson, 2013). Communication will be improved when all stakeholders have met and discussed the possible models for MTSS. Perhaps different teams of people present varied MTSS models, and the entire group has a vigorous and positive discussion about the direction of MTSS for your school. Drawing your final model as a diagram (as in Figure 14.1) or listing out its parts will help everyone on the MTSS Leadership Team and all implementers of MTSS understand the MTSS framework for your school. We talk more about the MTSS Leadership Team in Chapter 15.

To help you build your MTSS model, we'll walk through the three primary tiers of an MTSS framework.

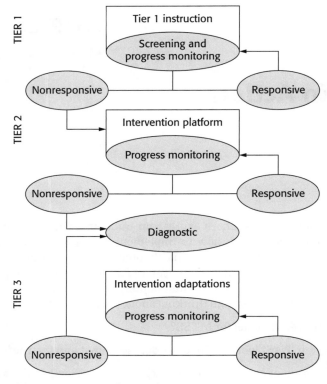

Figure 14.1.   Our MTSS framework.

Evaluating Tier 1 Instruction

Let's start with Tier 1, shown in Figure 14.2. (A full-size, downloadable, and photocopiable version of the Tier 1 evaluation form is available online with the other downloadable materials for this book; you may wish to download a copy to use for notetaking and planning as you read this section of the chapter.) First, you need to think about the instruction that is provided within Tier 1. In our experience, many schools have not evaluated their general education mathematics curriculum to determine whether the materials being used or the instruction being implemented is evidence-based.

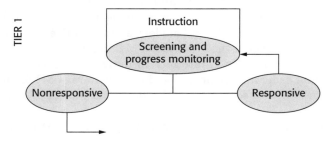

Figure 14.2.   Tier 1 of the MTSS framework.

Remember from Chapter 2 that *evidence-based* means that "multiple, high-quality studies that utilize research designs from which causality can be inferred" have demonstrated "meaningful effects on student outcomes" (Cook & Cook, 2013, p. 73).

Cook and colleagues (2015) provided a detailed list of qualities that should be assessed to determine whether a research study (about an intervention or specific curriculum) is high quality. This list includes evaluating each of the following aspects of the research:

> **Many schools have not evaluated the evidence backing their general education mathematics curriculum.**

1. Context and setting (i.e., where the research took place)

2. Participants (i.e., who were the students taking part in the research)

3. Intervention agent (i.e., who delivered the intervention)

4. Description of practice (i.e., the actual intervention or curriculum)

5. Fidelity of implementation (i.e., how well the intervention or curriculum was implemented)

6. Internal validity (i.e., the level of control of the intervention)

7. Outcome (i.e., the measures used as evidence for supporting the intervention or curriculum)

8. Data analysis (i.e., whether the data analysis was appropriate for the research questions)

Keep these aspects of the research in mind when you are evaluating research studies about instruction or intervention programs or practices.

Then, it's time to decide whether all, some, or none of the current Tier 1 instruction will remain in place in your MTSS model. Take a moment to write about what Tier 1 instruction will look like in your MTSS model. (If you like, use the full-size version of this form to take notes in the instruction rectangle of the model.) You may want to consider the following questions:

Basics about your Tier 1 instruction

- What mathematics instruction occurs in Tier 1? That is, what curriculum, textbook, intervention, or strategies do you or your teachers use?

- What is the evidence base for the materials used within Tier 1 instruction? Are the research studies high quality?

- Does the evidence show promise of transferring to the students in your school (e.g., were the participants similar to the students and teachers in your school, did the study take place in a similar school context)?

Logistics

- Who implements Tier 1 instruction?

- When does Tier 1 instruction occur (i.e., which days of the week and what time each day)?

- For how long (i.e., for how many minutes) does each session last?

- How, when, and how often will Tier 1 teachers receive professional learning experiences that can be used to improve Tier 1 instructional practices?

Fidelity

- How will fidelity of Tier 1 instruction to the intended delivery model be measured?

- Who will measure fidelity of implementation?

- What follow-up will be provided about fidelity of implementation (e.g., how will fidelity data be shared with teachers, what actions will be taken to improve fidelity)?

Planning Tier 1 Assessment

Second, you need to plan for two important assessment components in Tier 1: universal screening and progress monitoring. Your school may already have some type of mathematics screener in place. Perhaps you administer a test with fall, winter, and spring benchmarks. That could be used as your screener. We would rather you do not use data from a previous year's high-stakes assessment because those data are likely 6 months old or older. You want recent data on students' mathematics performance to help you determine which students are and are not on track to meet grade-level standards. For the students who are not on track (i.e., "at-risk students"), you will need to implement a progress monitoring system to examine how students respond to Tier 1 instruction. As we previously discussed in Chapters 2 and 12, we recommend that you monitor students' progress for about 6–10 weeks to determine if students are adequately responding to Tier 1 instruction or need additional support from Tier 2.

Figure 14.2 prompts you to decide whether your school's current assessment framework for Tier 1 is adequate (i.e., you have a reliable and valid universal screener and you have a reliable and valid progress monitoring system). Take a moment to write about the universal screener and progress monitoring measures you will use in your MTSS model. (Again, you may use the Tier 1 Evaluation, available online with the downloadable materials for this book, for this purpose, taking notes in the assessment oval.) You may want to consider the following:

Basics about your universal screener

- What universal screener do you use?

- Are the results from the universal screener reliable? What evidence do you have to support your conclusion?

- Do the results from the universal screener support valid decision making? What evidence do you have to support your conclusion?

Logistics about the universal screener

- Who will administer the universal screener in Tier 1?

- When will the universal screener be administered during classroom instruction?

- How and by whom is the universal screener scored?

- Who will make decisions about whether students require progress monitoring in Tier 1 (i.e., which students are at risk)?

Basics about your progress monitoring system for Tier 1

- What progress monitoring system will you use in Tier 1?

- Are the results from the progress monitoring system reliable? What evidence do you have to support your conclusion?

- Do the results from your progress monitoring system support valid decision making? What evidence do you have to support your conclusions?

- Does the progress monitoring system have alternate forms?

Logistics about the progress monitoring system in Tier 1

- Who will administer the progress monitoring measures in Tier 1?

- How often will the progress monitoring measures be administered?

- Is any technology necessary for administration and/or scoring of the progress monitoring measures?

- How and by whom will the progress monitoring measures be scored?

- Who will collect the ongoing data from the progress monitoring system?

Response decisions

- How and by whom will the results from the progress monitoring measures be graphed?

- Who will make decisions about response to Tier 1 instruction?

Finally, jot down notes about what happens when students demonstrate adequate response and inadequate response to Tier 1 instruction. What happens to students who demonstrate adequate response to Tier 1? What happens with students who do not?

Developing Tier 2 Intervention

Students who demonstrate inadequate response to Tier 1 require supplemental mathematics support provided through Tier 2 instruction.

As we discussed in Chapters 2 and 8, the first step in Tier 2 instruction is to develop an intervention platform. This intervention platform—the jumping-off point for Tier 2 instruction—should consist of an intervention or strategies that demonstrate an evidence base for effectiveness with students with learning difficulties in mathematics. In the world of reading intervention, many evidence-based interventions are commercially available on the market. In mathematics, however, considerably fewer options are available for teachers. That is, there are not many packaged evidence-based mathematics interventions for middle school students. As discussed in Chapter 7, the National Center on Intensive Intervention (https://intensive intervention.org) has a list of evidence-based interventions that might be helpful, as do Evidence for ESSA (https://www.evidence foressa.org) and the What Works Clearing-house (https://ies.ed.gov/ncee/wwc).

> Many evidence-based reading interventions exist, but there are fewer packaged mathematics interventions available for teachers of middle school students.

Based on our experience working with middle schools, you may have to collect your own materials and employ evidence-based strategies to deliver related instruction. For example, you'll use explicit instruction to teach solving ratio word problems and use two-color counters and colored clips to represent ratios. All three elements of this approach (i.e., explicit instruction, teaching word-problem schemas, and using multiple representations) have an evidence base (Gersten, Beckmann et al., 2009). If you feel uncomfortable creating your own materials, use mathematics problems from a textbook or workbook. Many times, it is appropriate to use mathematics problems from an earlier grade's textbook in your Tier 2 instruction. Collecting your own materials may take you more time than merely purchasing and using a packaged intervention, but often you will be putting together an intervention platform that is meaningful and appropriate for the students in your small-group instruction.

Look at the intervention platform rectangle in Figure 14.3. Take a moment to describe the intervention platform that you will put in place for your students. (Again, you may download and use the Tier 2 Evaluation form, available with the download-able materials for this book, for this purpose.) You may want to consider the following questions related to the intervention platform:

Basics about your Tier 2 instruction

- What Tier 2 intervention platform will you use?

- If you are using an evidence-based intervention, what is the evidence base? Are the research studies high quality?

- If you are using a collection of evidence-based strategies, what is the evidence base supporting each of those strategies? Are the research studies high quality?

- What extra materials (e.g., manipulatives, whiteboards, workbooks, flash cards) will you need to implement the Tier 2 intervention platform?

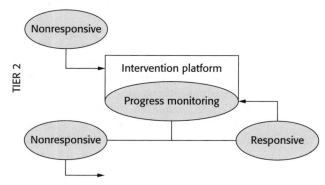

Figure 14.3. Tier 2 of the MTSS framework.

Logistics

- Who implements Tier 2 instruction?
- Where does Tier 2 instruction take place?
- What is the arrangement of the space for Tier 2 instruction?
- When does Tier 2 instruction take place (i.e., which days of the week and what time each day)?
- How many times per week does Tier 2 instruction occur?
- How many minutes per session is Tier 2 instruction?

Professional learning

- How will Tier 2 teachers receive professional learning experiences that can be used to improve the Tier 2 intervention platform?
- When will teachers receive these experiences?

Fidelity

- How will fidelity of the Tier 2 evidence-based intervention or strategies be measured?
- Who will measure fidelity of implementation?
- What follow-up will be provided about fidelity of implementation (e.g., how will fidelity data be shared with teachers, what actions will be taken to improve fidelity)?

Planning Tier 2 Assessment

After considering the intervention platform, you need to consider the progress monitoring that occurs during Tier 2 instruction. You may decide to continue using the same progress monitoring system you used in Tier 1. However, you may also determine that this system is not appropriate for Tier 2 (e.g., the mathematical content might be too difficult, or the measure may take too long to administer and score). If that is the case, you need to reevaluate the progress monitoring systems that are available and decide which is appropriate for the small group of students in your Tier 2 instruction.

The assessment oval in Figure 14.3 prompts you to think about your school's current assessment framework for Tier 2. Take a moment to describe the progress monitoring system you will use in your Tier 2 instruction. You may want to consider the following:

Basics about your progress monitoring system for Tier 2

- What progress monitoring system will you use in Tier 2?
- If you opted to use a different system than Tier 1, are the results from the progress monitoring system reliable? What evidence do you have to support your conclusion?
- Do the results from your progress monitoring system support valid decision making? What evidence do you have to support your conclusions?
- Does the progress monitoring system have alternate forms?

Logistics about the progress monitoring system in Tier 2

- Who will administer the progress monitoring measures in Tier 2?

- How often will the progress monitoring measures be administered?

- When, in the small-group instruction session, will the progress monitoring measures be administered?

- Is any technology necessary for administration and/or scoring of the progress monitoring measures?

- How and by whom will the progress monitoring measures be scored?

- Who will collect the ongoing data from the progress monitoring system?

Response decisions

- How and by whom will the results from the progress monitoring measures be graphed?

- How will goals be set for students receiving Tier 2 instruction (see Chapter 12)?

- Who will make decisions about response to Tier 2 instruction?

- How frequently will decisions about Tier 2 response be made?

- Which decision rules about response will be used to make decisions within Tier 2?

The final important components of Figure 14.3 are the ovals related to response. Consider these questions now. What's the pathway for students who demonstrate adequate response? What happens with students who do not demonstrate adequate response to Tier 2? Does your MTSS model keep them in Tier 2 for another iteration, or does the student move to Tier 3?

Tier 3: Diagnostic Assessment, Targeted Intervention, and Progress Monitoring

If a student requires Tier 3 intervention, that student has demonstrated (via progress monitoring data) that the current intervention platform is not meeting his or her needs. As described in Chapters 2 and 8, the first action in Tier 3 is to administer a diagnostic assessment. This diagnostic should be a mathematics assessment that covers a wide range of mathematics content. We have seen that schools often use the KeyMath-3 as a diagnostic (https://www.pearsonclinical.com/education/products/100000649 /keymath3-diagnostic-assessment.html), the Diagnostic Online Math Assessment (DOMA; https://www.letsgolearn.com/shop/store/product/doma-diagnostic-online -math-assessment-algebra/) or the Iowa Algebra Readiness Assessment (IARA; https://itp.education.uiowa.edu/iara/iara.aspx). You may want to refer to Chapter 11 for other approaches to gathering diagnostic information. The diagnostic assessment is meant to provide you, the teacher, with information about a student's strengths and weaknesses to better understand how to design your Tier 3 instruction.

Look at the diagnostic assessment oval in Figure 14.4. Let's first focus on the diagnostic assessment that you plan to use to inform Tier 3 instructional adaptations.

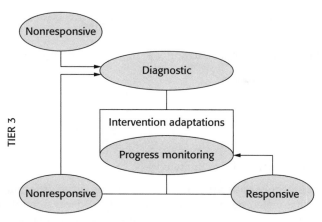

Figure 14.4. Tier 3 of the MTSS framework.

You may want to do a survey of different diagnostic assessments available within your school or talk to your school or district school psychologist and get recommendations from him or her. Then, write about your plan to gather diagnostic information. (You may download and use the Tier 3 Evaluation form, available with the downloadable materials for this book, for this purpose.) You may want to consider the following:

Basics about your diagnostic assessment

- What diagnostic assessment will you use within Tier 3?

- Are the results from the diagnostic assessment reliable? What evidence do you have to support your conclusion?

- Do the results from the diagnostic assessment support valid decision making? What evidence do you have to support your conclusion?

Logistics about the diagnostic assessment

- Who will administer the diagnostic assessment in Tier 3?

- When, between Tier 2 and Tier 3, will the diagnostic assessment be administered?

- Is any technology necessary for administration and/or scoring of the diagnostic assessment?

- How and by whom will the diagnostic assessment be scored?

Response decisions

- Who will interpret the results from the diagnostic assessment?

- Who will identify the student's strengths and weaknesses?

After administering the diagnostic assessment, it is time for you to make intervention adaptations based on the diagnostic information and your experiences working with the student. As we described in Chapter 2, there are typically six adaptations to consider:

1. Implement the intervention or strategy with greater fidelity.

2. Embed behavioral supports.

3. Increase your dosage of the intervention.

4. Adapt the mathematics content.

5. Utilize explicit instruction to the greatest extent.

6. Explicitly teach for transfer of knowledge.

In our experience, teachers usually implement two or three different adaptations at one time, but you are welcome to try more or fewer. The adaptations should be individualized to meet the needs of the student receiving Tier 3 instruction; there is no "one size fits all" approach. The idea is that you keep trying and fine-tuning adaptations until you find a successful mix for the Tier 3 intervention for your student. Just as before, you will continue administering the progress monitoring measures to determine if you have identified the most effective adaptations to support your students' needs.

> There is no "one size fits all" approach for adaptations.

Figure 14.4 includes a rectangle about intervention adaptations. Write about the adaptations that you will use in Tier 3. Consider the following:

Basics about your Tier 3 instruction

- What Tier 3 intervention adaptations will you consider?

- What extra materials (e.g., manipulatives, whiteboards, workbooks, flash cards) will you need to implement the Tier 3 intervention adaptations?

- What training do you require to implement different types of intervention adaptations?

- Who makes decisions about Tier 3 intervention adaptations?

Logistics

- Who implements Tier 3 instruction?

- Where does Tier 3 instruction take place?

- What is the arrangement of the space for Tier 3 instruction?

- When does Tier 3 instruction take place (i.e., which days of the week and what time each day)?

- How many times per week does Tier 3 instruction occur?

- How many minutes per session is Tier 3 instruction?

Professional learning

- How will Tier 3 teachers receive professional learning experiences that can be used to improve the Tier 3 intervention adaptations?

- When will teachers receive these experiences?

Fidelity

- How will fidelity of the Tier 3 intervention adaptations be measured?

- Who will measure fidelity of implementation?

- What follow-up will be provided about fidelity of implementation (e.g., how will fidelity data be shared with teachers, what actions will be taken to improve fidelity)?

Finally, you need to focus on the progress monitoring at Tier 3. More often than not, you can use the progress monitoring system used in Tier 2. You may, however, have to make adjustments to the grade level of the progress monitoring measures for students receiving Tier 3 adaptations, especially for those students with mathematics performance that is several grade levels below expectations. Importantly, progress monitoring in Tier 3 helps you understand whether newly introduced adaptations help the student (i.e., leading to increases in progress monitoring scores) or do not help the student (i.e., resulting in flat or decreasing progress monitoring scores).

Look at the assessment oval in Figure 14.4. Write notes about the progress monitoring system that you will use in Tier 3. It may be helpful to think about the following aspects of progress monitoring.

Basics about your progress monitoring system for Tier 3

- What progress monitoring system will you use in Tier 3?

- If you opted to use a different system than Tier 2, are the results from the progress monitoring system reliable? What evidence do you have to support your conclusion?

- Do the results from your progress monitoring system support valid decision making? What evidence do you have to support your conclusions?

- Does the progress monitoring system have alternate forms?

Logistics about the progress monitoring system in Tier 3

- Who will administer the progress monitoring measures in Tier 3?

- How often will the progress monitoring measures be administered?

- When, during Tier 3 instruction, will the progress monitoring measures be administered?

- Is any technology necessary for administration and/or scoring of the progress monitoring measures?

- How and by whom will the progress monitoring measures be scored?

- Who will collect the ongoing data from the progress monitoring system?

Response decisions

- How and by whom will the results from the progress monitoring measures be graphed?

- How will goals be set for students receiving Tier 3 instruction (see Chapter 12)?

- Who will make decisions about response to Tier 3 instruction?

- Who will make decisions about the adequacy of different adaptations?

- Who will be responsible for making changes to the adaptations?

- How frequently will decisions about Tier 3 response be made?

- Which decision rules about response will be used to make decisions within Tier 3?

After focusing on progress monitoring, turn your attention to the ovals related to response. What's the pathway for students who demonstrate adequate response? Do students move to Tier 1 or Tier 2? What happens with students who did not demonstrate adequate response to Tier 3? How are adaptations systematically handled within Tier 3?

SUMMARY: THINKING THROUGH THE TIERS

In this chapter, we reviewed a commonly used three-tier MTSS framework. The goal of this chapter was to help you think through important components of assessment and instruction within each of the three tiers. We hope that you found this exercise to be useful. In the next chapter, we will detail how to think about implementing your newly derived MTSS plan at your school.

CHAPTER 15

Assessing Your School's Readiness for MTSS Implementation

In this chapter, we will consider four key aspects of your school's readiness for implementing MTSS. First, we look at the critical role of your campus administration and their practices, actions, and beliefs that are needed to support implementation. Second, we talk about the role of an MTSS Leadership Team and how your campus can structure this decision-making group. Third, we help you think through the aspects of instruction and assessment practices that are already established in your school that can used within an MTSS framework, and practices that will need to be implemented. Finally, we talk about the role of professional learning and growth when implementing MTSS. Thus, in this chapter, we answer the following questions:

- Who are important school-related stakeholders for MTSS?

- How ready are you and your school colleagues to implement MTSS?

- What is your timeline for implementation of MTSS?

CAMPUS ADMINISTRATION

For many schools, the idea of implementing MTSS emerges as a possible solution to challenges teachers are facing in the classroom. Especially in middle and high school settings, teachers are often frustrated with limited time in the general education classroom to support the instructional needs of all students. For example, if a teacher's mathematics classes are 45 to 55 minutes (which is common in many middle schools), he or she might find it difficult to cover the core concepts in the grade level as well as provide additional support for the students who are underperforming and/or missing foundational content needed to understand the core concepts. As we have talked about in previous chapters, MTSS is a systems-level solution for meeting all students' needs within the school day. Even if the original idea emerged from the classroom, however, successfully implementing MTSS at the campus level requires strong support and actions from your campus administration. Because MTSS affects the whole school community, your campus administration should be involved in every step and help guide and shape how MTSS will be implemented on your campus.

Key Roles and Responsibilities

Several key actions are needed from your campus administration to support success-ful implementation. Figure 15.1 illustrates the process. First, your campus admin-istration should cast a long-term vision that ambitiously seeks to focus on success for all students—regardless of educational classification, demographic character-istics, family income or educational levels, or other variables that are often blamed for poor student outcomes. If you are considering implementing MTSS, then you have identified a problem at your school: not all students are succeeding or meeting high expectations. MTSS can be a catalyst for changing these outcomes, but only if all stakeholders are committed to full implementation (Blackburn & Witzel, 2018). Your campus administration needs to build consensus that all students can and will reach high expectations. All stakeholders need a deep personal commitment to this outcome.

Second, your campus administration needs to leverage current sources of excel-lence that support the goals of MTSS—by determining what practices, actions, and beliefs are already present that align with the vision of success for all students. Your administration needs to continue supporting the practices, actions, and beliefs that are working and, at the same time, identify ineffective practices or misaligned beliefs. Administrators must end practices or actions that are not effective at improving posi-tive student outcomes and work to change misaligned beliefs that not all students can succeed, which may undermine or poison the implementation of MTSS.

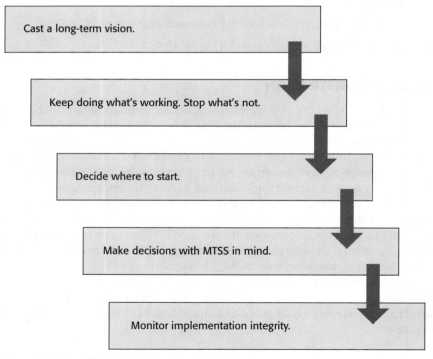

Figure 15.1. Key MTSS actions from campus administrators.

Third, your campus administration should establish short-term goals for implementation of MTSS. With the help of the MTSS Leadership Team (described in the next section), the administration needs to strategically plan the phases of implementation by considering the needs of your students and the practices that can be leveraged. For example, your campus administration might have the long-term goal that all students will meet high expectations in mathematics, but administrators may decide to implement MTSS in sixth grade first. In Chapter 17, Nicole, a district RTI coordinator, talks about the value of starting with a small pilot to identify campus needs and trouble-shoot problem areas.

Fourth, your campus administration needs to be courageously focused on the goals of MTSS throughout implementation. MTSS needs to be a schoolwide priority such that all decisions are filtered through its lens, including the distribution and allocation of financial resources, personnel resources, and time. When challenges or issues arise, your campus administration needs to make decisions that align with your school's long-term vision of success for all students.

Last, your campus administration needs to monitor the implementation of MTSS components to verify that they are being implemented with integrity. Implementation is the hardest part of enacting any initiative. All the planning in the world cannot account for the challenges and issues that come up once we start actually doing the work. That said, your campus administration needs to be keenly aware of how the components of MTSS are being implemented.

> Because MTSS affects the whole school community, your campus administration should be involved in every step.

Instruction at all tiers needs to align with what we know works—based on research evidence—to support student success. Assessments need to be administered following the appropriate protocols and timelines to allow for reliable results and valid decisions. Time for professional learning and collaboration must be protected and focused on key topics associated with supporting all students' success. By monitoring the fidelity of implementation of these components, your campus administrator can verify that stakeholders' good intentions are actually translated into good practices.

Evaluate Readiness: Your School's Administration

Now we take our first look at a school readiness checklist for MTSS. We will consider multiple aspects of school's readiness to implement MTSS, but first, consider the practices, actions, and beliefs present within your school. Remember, the intention of the activity is to identify aspects of your school that are, and are not, already in place to support implementation of MTSS. To implement it successfully, your school can build on existing aspects and determine the best options for establishing the aspects that are not yet in place.

Figure 15.2 shows a thumbnail of a form you can use to identify which practices, actions, and/or beliefs are already established. (A full-size downloadable and photocopiable version of the form is available with the downloadable materials for this book.) For these aspects, describe what is working well and what changes could be made to improve each one. For aspects that are not yet established, describe the current conditions that exist and what is needed to change them.

EVALUATE READINESS: Your School's Administration

	Is this practice, action, or belief already established?	If yes, what is working well? What changes could be made to improve this practice, action, or belief?	If no, what are the current conditions that exist? What is needed to change this practice, action, or belief?
There is campus-level support at the highest levels, including agreement to adopt an MTSS model and allocate required resources.			
There is an understanding of and commitment to a long-term change process (3 or more years).			
There is long-term commitment of resources for administering assessments and implementing tiered instructional support.			
The district leadership team has a basic level of knowledge of the research related to MTSS and the desire to learn more.			
There is expertise at the district and campus level with respect to research-based practices for academic success and positive behavioral outcomes.			

Figure 15.2.   School readiness checklist for campus administration.

MTSS LEADERSHIP TEAM

As we discussed, your campus administration is a vital part of the success of MTSS, but realizing the full benefits of MTSS requires a team effort. Although all members of the campus community will be involved in implementation, an MTSS Leadership Team is an important part of the success of this initiative. Its purpose is to establish a plan for implementing MTSS based on the long-term vision that was established by the campus administration. This team can help the campus administration enact the long-term vision and establish the short-term implementation goals. Working together, campus administration and the MTSS Leadership Team share leadership responsibilities and build valuable expertise needed to design, implement, and monitor MTSS (Lembke, Garman, Deno, & Stecker, 2010).

The MTSS Leadership Team works together to set ambitious but attainable short-term goals. To realize these goals, the MTSS Leadership Team needs to establish a detailed and coherent implementation plan with milestones and timelines for reaching these goals. The team's responsibilities include evaluating and selecting resources (e.g., instructional materials, assessment tools) needed for implementation, identifying the areas for professional learning and growth (e.g., evidence-based instructional practices, interpreting assessment data), evaluating the effectiveness of existing and emerging practices, and leading the school in making infrastructure decisions. These decisions include scheduling instructional time across the instructional tiers, establishing procedures for administering and interpreting assessments, and allocating time for collaboration (e.g., common planning time).

Key Stakeholders, Roles, and Responsibilities

The MTSS Leadership Team is led by the campus administration and includes other key stakeholders; in addition, several specific roles and responsibilities should be filled. The number of people may vary depending on your school's size and unique needs, but the team should be well balanced based on expertise. Key stakeholders may include school psychologists, behavioral specialists, special education and general education teachers as well as teachers of English learners and gifted and talented students, and parents and/or community members who have unique and valued perspectives. When selecting members of the MTSS Leadership Team, it is helpful to identify stakeholders who are able to communicate with people across the school community and who strive to make a positive impact on school and student success.

Key roles and responsibilities include that of the content specialist, the data specialist, and the MTSS coordinator, as described next.

Content specialist. To support content-related decisions about the curriculum, instruction, and assessment that will be implemented as part of MTSS, someone with content expertise should serve as the team's content specialist. This person may be the mathematics department chair or a lead teacher with deep knowledge about the mathematics curricular expectations, evidence-based practices in mathematics instruction, and technically adequate assessment practices. Responsibilities of the content specialist include evaluating and selecting instructional materials and assessment tools that will be used during implementation and supporting professional learning and growth opportunities for stakeholders involved in content implementation.

Data specialist. To support the use of assessment data within the MTSS framework, someone who is skilled in assessments should serve as the team's data specialist. This person may be an assistant principal, instructional coach, or teacher with expertise in collecting, analyzing, and interpreting assessment data. Responsibilities of the data specialist include establishing assessment administration guidelines and protocols, helping stakeholders analyze and interpret assessment results, and supporting the use of data to make instructional decisions. The data specialist should facilitate professional learning and growth opportunities related to making decisions based on assessment results, so that all stakeholders develop competence and confidence using data.

MTSS coordinator. To facilitate the implementation process, someone with organizational and communication skills should serve as the team's MTSS coordinator, a critical connection point for those involved in implementing MTSS. The coordinator not only needs to establish infrastructure procedures and routines associated with running meetings and documenting decisions but should also manage the communication systems between the MTSS Leadership Team and various stakeholders. The MTSS coordinator should maintain transparent communication throughout the implementation process.

Evaluate Readiness: Your School's Leadership Team

Now it is time to consider your school's readiness to implement MTSS based on the MTSS Leadership Team. Remember, the intention of the activity is to identify the aspects of an MTSS Leadership Team that are, and are not, already in place to support implementation. To successfully implement MTSS, your school can build on existing aspects and determine the best options for establishing the aspects that are not yet in place.

> The number of people on an MTSS leadership team may vary, but the team should be well balanced based on expertise.

Figure 15.3 presents a thumbnail version of a chart you can use to identify which practices, actions, and/or beliefs are already established. (You may obtain a full-size, photocopiable version of this form online with the other downloadable materials for this book.) Once again, for the aspects that are already established, describe what is working well and what changes could be made to improve each one. For aspects that

EVALUATE READINESS: Your School's Leadership Team

	Is this practice, action, or belief already established?	If yes, what is working well? What changes could be made to improve this practice, action, or belief?	If no, what are the current conditions that exist? What is needed to change this practice, action, or belief?
There is campus-wide commitment to distributed leadership.			
Key stakeholders* are willing to work together.			
There is a content specialist who is communicative and considered a leader on campus.			
There is a data specialist who is communicative and considered a leader on campus.			
There is someone who could serve as the MTSS coordinator who is communicative and considered a leader on campus.			
There is a common planning time for educators to make instructional plans and review assessment data.			

* For example, school psychologists; behavioral specialists; special education, English learner, gifted and talented, and general education teachers; and parents and/or community members.

Figure 15.3. School readiness checklist for the MTSS leadership team.

are not yet established, describe the current conditions that exist and what is needed to change them.

ASSESSMENT AND INSTRUCTION COMPONENTS

In this book, we have talked extensively about the assessment and instruction components needed to implement MTSS. In many cases, your school may already be engaged in some of the practices, actions, and beliefs discussed. Once again, it is important to take stock of what you are already doing so that you can build upon those components that are already in place and determine the best options for establishing those that are not in place.

Evaluate Readiness: Assessment at Your School

First, let's focus on assessment. Figure 15.4 shows a thumbnail of a form you may use to consider your school's readiness to implement MTSS based on assessment practices, actions, and/or beliefs that are already established. (You may obtain a full-size, photocopiable version of the form online with the other downloadable materials for this book.)

EVALUATE READINESS: Assessment at Your School

	Is this practice, action, or belief already established?	If yes, what is working well? What changes could be made to improve this practice, action, or belief?	If no, what are the current conditions that exist? What is needed to change this practice, action, or belief?
We administer a universal screener in mathematics to all students.			
We administer diagnostic assessments to students who are struggling, to document their strengths and areas of improvement.			
We monitor progress of students who are struggling or at risk for mathematics difficulties.			
We have structured conversations around assessment results to inform instructional decisions.			
We provide ongoing professional learning and growth opportunities for interpreting assessment results to guide instructional decisions.			
We have a data management system in place.			

Figure 15.4.   School readiness checklist for assessment.

EVALUATE READINESS: Instruction at Your School			
	Is this practice, action, or belief already established?	If yes, what is working well? What changes could be made to improve this practice, action, or belief?	If no, what are the current conditions that exist? What is needed to change this practice, action, or belief?
We use a research-validated Tier 1 instructional program in mathematics.			
We use (or are able to acquire) research-based supplemental intervention materials for Tier 2 support.			
We use (or are able to acquire) research-based supplemental intervention materials for Tier 3 support.			
We have highly trained educators to provide Tier 1 instruction with fidelity.			
We have highly trained educators to provide Tier 2 instruction with fidelity.			
We have highly trained educators to provide Tier 3 instruction with fidelity.			
We have systems in place to evaluate the fidelity of implementation of instruction in Tiers 1–3.			
We provide ongoing professional learning and growth opportunities for implementing evidence-based instructional practices.			
We provide ongoing professional learning and growth opportunities that focus on deepening teachers' content knowledge in mathematics.			

Figure 15.5.   School readiness checklist for instruction.

Evaluate Readiness: Instruction at Your School

Now, let's think about instruction. Figure 15.5 shows a thumbnail-size version of a form you can use to consider your school's readiness to implement MTSS based on instructional practices, actions, and/or beliefs that are already established. (You may obtain a full-size, photocopiable version of this form online with the other download-able materials for this book.) For these established aspects, describe what is working well and what changes could be made to improve each one. For aspects not yet established, describe the current conditions and what is needed to change them.

ONGOING PROFESSIONAL LEARNING AND GROWTH

Anyone who has spent time in a classroom knows that a teacher needs to be a master of not one, but many trades. To be effective teachers who create classrooms in which learning occurs, teachers need strong pedagogical skills to design effective and engaging lessons, analyze and interpret assessment results, build a culture of respect and nonjudgment, and support classroom management and effective classroom procedures and routines. Like Matthew (an eighth-grade mathematics teacher) said in Chapter 17, teachers also need deep content knowledge to sequence instruction to build expertise, deliver accurate information, link conceptual understanding with procedural knowledge, and more. In addition, teachers need to be able to effectively combine their pedagogical knowledge with their content knowledge to make meaningful decisions that guide instruction, respond to students' questions, identify and address misconceptions in students' thinking, and align a pedagogical approach with students' needs to meet specific content expectations.

The Importance of Ongoing Learning

Through their extensive work studying teacher learning, Ball, Thames, and Phelps (2008) categorized this specialized mathematical knowledge for teaching into three domains: specialized mathematical content knowledge, knowledge of content and students, and knowledge of content and teaching. The practices, actions, and beliefs needed for implementing MTSS seamlessly integrate with these sources of pedagogical knowledge, content knowledge, and pedagogical content knowledge.

Developing this rich body of knowledge and skills often takes years, through systematic study, feedback and reflection, and practical experimentation. Because most teacher preparation programs are not able to devote considerable time to developing expertise in these areas, most teachers will be faced with the task of acquiring this knowledge while they are on the job. It is important that teachers and administrators alike identify meaningful professional learning and growth opportunities that focus on supporting teachers' practices, actions, and beliefs and that will support implementation of MTSS.

Research on effective professional learning opportunities in mathematics points to the value of providing teachers with sustained and ongoing support that focuses directly on improving teaching practices within the classroom context to support student learning (Garet, Porter, Desimone, Birman, & Yoon, 2001). These opportunities should align with teachers' professional learning goals and the school's mission and allow teachers to collaborate with peers. To help realize the goals of MTSS, professional learning opportunities should be grounded in implementing research-based instructional practices, making instructional decisions based on assessment results, and designing learning environments that support all students' needs.

Evaluate Readiness: Professional Learning and Growth Opportunities

Now it is time to consider your school's readiness to implement MTSS based on the professional learning and growth opportunities your school provides. Figure 15.6 shows a thumbnail-size version of a form you can use to do this. (You may obtain a full-size, photocopiable version of this form online with the other downloadable materials for this book.)

TIMELINE FOR MTSS IMPLEMENTATION

You decided to read this book because you wanted to learn more about MTSS in the middle school as a systems-level solution for meeting all students' needs within the school day. At the beginning of this chapter, we talked through different school readiness checklists to help you understand how ready you and your colleagues are to

EVALUATE READINESS: Professional Learning and Growth Opportunities			
	Is this practice, action, or belief already established?	If yes, what is working well? What changes could be made to improve this practice, action, or belief?	If no, what are the current conditions that exist? What is needed to change this practice, action, or belief?
Professional learning and growth opportunities exist for all staff and across all roles within the school community.			
Professional learning and growth opportunities include ongoing support such as coaching, peer feedback, or professional learning communities.			
Professional learning and growth opportunities are aligned with the goals of MTSS.			
All stakeholders believe in the value of professional learning and growth.			
Opportunities to learn about MTSS exist for parents and other stakeholders within the school community.			
Professional learning and growth opportunities address relevant aspects of implementing MTSS.			
Professional learning and growth opportunities focus on improving learning by supporting the needs of all students.			

Figure 15.6.   School readiness checklist for professional learning.

implement (or continue implementing) MTSS. Now that you know your school's readiness for MTSS, it's time to think about creating a timeline for implementation.

Change in schools is difficult. It takes time. No school should try to implement its entire MTSS model in a year. Instead, we suggest a gentle rollout of MTSS across 3 to 5 years. In Figure 15.7, we present a 4-year implementation plan to help guide the actions of the MTSS Leadership Team. In this plan, investigating Tier 1 instruction and assessment using the guiding questions presented in Chapter 14 occurs in Year 1, with full implementation of Tier 1 changes in Year 2. During Year 2, determine the Tier 2 intervention platform and progress monitoring system, and plan for full implementation of Tier 2 changes in Year 3. Also in Year 3, Tier 3 instructional adaptations and diagnostic assessments can be reviewed and selected with full implementation of Tier 3 changes in Year 4.

Developing this timeline will likely generate lots of dialogue among members of the MTSS Leadership Team. In the following subsections, we give examples of some of the questions that should be discussed when developing your own MTSS timeline of implementation.

MTSS: The First Four Years

	YEAR 1	YEAR 2	YEAR 3	YEAR 4
		MTSS SET UP		
MTSS team	Select members for MTSS team; determine personnel for delivery for Tier 1	Determine personnel for delivery of Tier 2	Determine personnel for delivery of Tier 3	
MTSS plan	Determine MTSS plan for middle school	Implement plan at Tier 1	Continue implementation of Tier 1; implement plan at Tier 2	Continue implementation of Tiers 1 and 2; implement plan at Tier 3
Scheduling	Determine whether time is devoted to math instruction at Tier 1	Schedule Tier 2 intervention time within the school day	Schedule Tier 3 intervention time within the school day	
Training	Train all staff on MTSS structure with a focus on Tier 1	Train all staff on MTSS structure at Tier 2	Train all staff on MTSS structure at Tier 3	
		TIER 1		
Math screener	Choose screener	Implement screener		
Tier 1 math instruction	Review current evidence-based practices	Implement Tier 1 evidence-based practices with fidelity		
Math progress monitoring	Choose progress monitoring measure	Implement progress monitoring with "at-risk" students		
Decision making at Tier 1	Determine decision making process	Implement decision making at Tier 1		
		TIER 2		
Tier 2 math instruction		Review and select evidence-based Tier 2 interventions	Implement Tier 2 interventions with fidelity	
Math progress monitoring		Determine whether additional progress-monitoring measures are necessary for Tier 2	Implement progress monitoring with Tier 2 students	
Decision making at Tier 2		Determine decision-making process	Implement decision making at Tier 2	
		TIER 3		
Diagnostic assessments		Select appropriate math diagnostics	Pilot diagnostic assessments with select Tier 2 students	Implement diagnostic assessments with Tier 3 students
Tier 3 math instruction			Review and select evidence-based Tier 3 interventions	Implement Tier 3 interventions with fidelity; make adaptations based on diagnostic data
Math progress monitoring				Implement progress monitoring with Tier 3 students
Decision making at Tier 3				Implement decision making at Tier 3

Figure 15.7. Timeline for MTSS implementation.

Key Questions for Establishing an MTSS Model

Your timeline should consider the implementation of your MTSS model. That is, when is your MTSS Leadership Team going to be established and who is going to be on that team? How is MTSS going to be conceptualized in your school? That is, how many tiers of instruction will you provide? What decision-making process will be used to determine student movement between tiers? How will you alter the school master schedule to accommodate Tier 2 or 3 intervention? Some schools will provide a double class to students to implement block scheduling. Other schools may schedule an "intervention time" for 30 minutes within the school day that can be used for Tier 2 or 3 instruction (Bouck & Cosby, 2017). You may need to plan 2 years in advance for making a change to the school's master schedule, so reviewing the MTSS timeline helps put such changes on the radar of campus administrators and district staff. Also, how and when are all MTSS colleagues going to receive training about the MTSS model for your school and the "moving parts" of that model?

Key Questions for Investigating and Implementing Tiers

In Figure 15.7, the timeline includes a focus on Tier 1. What universal screeners will be used to identify students who may be at risk in mathematics? Which current evidence-based instructional practices are in place, and which practices need to be introduced into the Tier 1 setting? To determine response to Tier 1 instruction, which progress monitoring system will be implemented? Who will administer and score the measures? How will decisions be made about response to Tier 1?

For Tier 2, which evidence-based interventions or strategies will be employed to form an effective Tier 2 instructional program? What type of progress monitoring measures will be used in Tier 2? Are these measures the same as or different from the measures used in Tier 1? When and how frequently will progress monitoring data be collected at Tier 2? When and how will decisions be made about student response within Tier 2?

Finally, in Tier 3, which diagnostic assessments are available within the school for assessing students' strengths and weaknesses? If none are available, which diagnostic assessments will the school use or purchase? Who will administer these assessments and how will they be trained? How will diagnostic assessment data be used to adapt Tier 3 mathematics instruction? Will the same progress monitoring measures as Tier 2 be used to monitor student progress in Tier 3? How and when will decisions be made in Tier 3?

SUMMARY: ASSESSING MTSS READINESS

In this chapter, we focused on school readiness for MTSS. Readiness involves collaboration among campus leaders, the MTSS Leadership Team, and those responsible for assessment and instruction. Readiness also encompasses a commitment to professional learning for all colleagues involved in the design and implementation of MTSS. We also presented a sample timeline for implementation of MTSS and emphasized that a feasible MTSS implementation timeline occurs over a span of several years.

CHAPTER 16

Collaboration as the Foundation for Implementing MTSS

Throughout much of this book, we have focused on your actions as a teacher, including everything from how to design your instruction to meet all students' needs to how to use assessment data to guide your instructional planning decisions. Even though we have focused on your classroom, MTSS cannot be effectively implemented in only one teacher's classroom. It is a systems-level initiative that requires the involvement of many people within a school, school district, and sometimes within the state education agency to effectively support all students' needs to positively affect student outcomes. Some of the many examples of collaboration in an MTSS framework include the following:

- General education teachers and special education teachers work together to design and deliver multi-tiered systems of instruction.

- School psychologists work together with administrators to select and implement technically adequate systems of assessment.

- Math intervention specialists work with general education and special education teachers to support their understanding of the structure of language and differentiated strategies to support content area reading.

These and other examples highlight the importance of collaboration among a variety of educational professionals to effectively implement MTSS.

In this chapter, we discuss collaboration within an MTSS framework. We answer the following questions:

- What is collaboration within this framework?

- Why is collaboration important for MTSS? Why is it especially important in mathematics?

- What does effective collaboration look like?

- What are the steps to effective collaboration?

- How can you use an inventory of assets to support effective collaboration?

WHAT IS COLLABORATION?

Suppose you are working with another teacher from your grade-level team to plan a field trip to the science and nature museum. You and your colleague meet to divide up the tasks that need to get done before the field trip (e.g., copying the permission slips, arranging the buses). You enjoy working with your colleague and find that working together increases your efficiency and saves your department money. Is this an example of collaboration? Although you are working with a colleague to accomplish a task, this is an example of teamwork or cooperation, not collaboration.

Collaboration is different from other forms of collegial interactions in several important ways. Collaboration is a deliberate process in which individuals purposefully come together with a shared long-term goal. Although teamwork and cooperation may involve people working together, collaboration goes beyond teamwork or cooperation because it is an intentional and ongoing process that involves shared responsibility and authority for decision making (Hord, 1986).

Collaboration is an essential component of MTSS. As we've talked about throughout this book, MTSS includes an integrated system of instruction and assessment that is implemented with the purpose of supporting students' mathematics achievement. For all of these pieces to come together to support positive student outcomes, those involved must collaborate.

WHY IS COLLABORATION IMPORTANT FOR MTSS—ESPECIALLY IN MATHEMATICS?

We all know that working together to solve a problem can sometimes take longer than if we solved it on our own. However, we also all know that when we work together, the solutions are usually much better. Working together to solve a problem brings new perspectives and knowledge, helps us see gaps in our thinking, challenges our beliefs, and is usually more fun. All of these outcomes are needed when implementing MTSS.

At the heart of MTSS is the goal of supporting positive outcomes—mathematics achievement—for all students. To realize this goal, many people are involved in delivering services and providing resources, as depicted in Figure 16.1. The purpose of collaboration among all of these people is to provide a coherent educational program (Ketterlin-Geller, Baumer, & Lichon, 2015). To create a coherent educational program that is aligned with students' needs, educational service providers and other stakeholders need to work together to administer assessments and interpret data, design and deliver evidence-based instruction, and coordinate additional services. Collaboration is not the intended outcome, but it is a means of achieving this goal.

Collaboration supports the implementation of MTSS by not only helping to create coherence but also bringing together stakeholders with various strengths and talents that can support the success of all students. In inclusive settings, for example, collaboration between general education teachers and special education teachers has been the hallmark of many service delivery models, such as co-teaching. In these contexts, general and special education teachers contribute their unique expertise to plan and deliver instruction that meets the needs of students with disabilities. With MTSS, this collaboration is extended to include a broader range of stakeholders to support all students being served in the school building. Each stakeholder brings specialized skills and knowledge that contributes to the overall educational programming. In Chapter 17, Nicole, a district RTI coordinator, highlights the importance

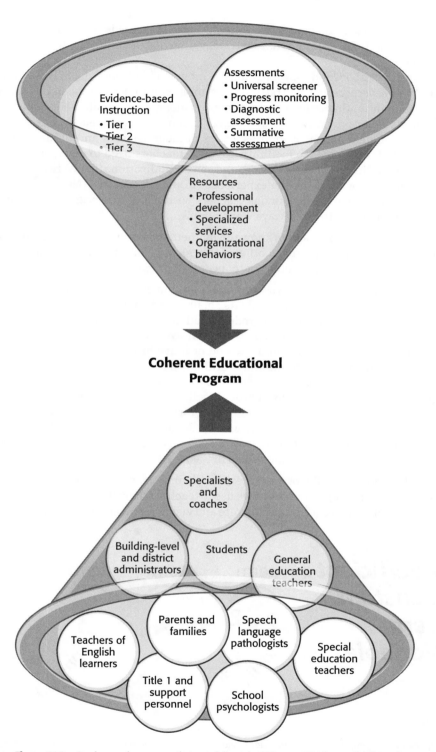

Figure 16.1.   Services and resources that are delivered within an MTSS framework by various stakeholders.

of and challenges associated with bringing these stakeholders together to support implementation of MTSS, and shares strategies her district implemented to overcome these barriers.

Why is collaboration especially important when implementing MTSS in mathematics? For several reasons. First, students' understanding of mathematics concepts and fluency in mathematics procedures grow along a continuum. New learning is added to students' previous understanding of the concept or procedure to deepen their knowledge and extend their abilities across number systems and to new contexts, concepts, and principles. To facilitate learning, teachers need to elicit, build on, and refine students' initial understandings and conceptualizations that were developed in prior grades and/or through prior experiences in and out of school (National Research Council, 2010). Collaboration among teachers within and across grades can directly support new learning in many ways. For example,

- With collaboration, teachers know the mathematics concepts and skills that were taught in earlier grades (or in other settings) and can activate the students' prior knowledge before introducing new concepts or procedures.

- With collaboration, teachers have a shared understanding of the mathematics terminology and vocabulary students should know and be able to use within and across grades. For example, in grade 6, students are typically expected to extend their understanding of number to the full system of rational numbers, which includes negative rational numbers and negative integers, and apply this knowledge to number line diagrams and coordinate axes. Through collaboration, teachers can establish common expectations for both teachers' and students' use of precise mathematical terms. Through collaboration, teachers can also discuss whether both teachers are using the same formal mathematical language instead of one teacher using formal language and the other using informal language—for example, using *coefficient* instead of *number* or *variable* instead of *x* when working through problems like the one shown in Figure 16.2.

A second reason why collaboration is especially important in mathematics is related to the instructional representations we use to teach mathematics concepts and procedures. As discussed in Section II, concrete and visual representations of mathematics

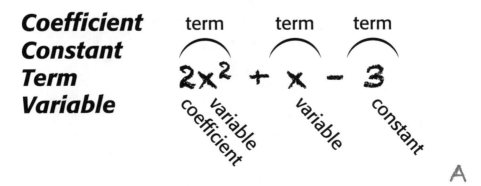

Figure 16.2. Example of correct terminology used to label a mathematics equation. (Reprinted with permission from Powell, S. R., Stevens, E. A., & Hughes, E. M. Math language in middle school: Be more specific. *Teaching Exceptional Children.* Copyright © 2018. SAGE Journals. DOI: 10.1177/0040059918808762.)

concepts and procedures, as well as representations of problem structures, can enhance students' understanding of mathematics concepts and procedures. These representations, like mathematical language, are most effective if they are used consistently within and across grades and are appropriately extended as the concepts and procedures increase in complexity. For example, area models are effective for introducing the concept of multiplication and division of whole numbers. If students become proficient in using these models with this concept, these same models can be used when discussing the concept of multiplication and division of fractions. Similarly, consistently using schemas to represent common problem structures (see Chapter 6) can help reinforce underlying problem structures and demystify word problems for many students. Collaboration within and across grades can facilitate consistent use of these representations and, ultimately, support student learning.

Collaboration not only improves coherence in the educational program, but also builds capacity across stakeholders. We each have areas in which we have particular expertise, and other areas where we could use support—both in our content knowledge and in our pedagogical knowledge. For example, one teacher might excel in working with statistics and probability. For this teacher, creating engaging lessons and meaningful tasks around topics such as sampling distributions and comparing mean differences in two samples of the population comes easily. Another teacher may have similar ease when preparing lessons and tasks that engage students in constructing and examining the relationships among geometric figures using scale drawings. By collaborating, these teachers can leverage their collective expertise to provide enhanced learning opportunities for their students across topics. Similarly, one teacher may be most comfortable using concrete objects to model a ratio relationship between two quantities, whereas another teacher prefers to use a double number line to model the same ratio relationship. By collaborating, these teachers expand the repertoire of representations they can use to model ratio relationships with their students.

WHAT DOES EFFECTIVE COLLABORATION LOOK LIKE?

You can spot effective collaboration when you see all stakeholders within the MTSS system working together toward a common goal—in our case, the common goal is for all students to succeed in mathematics. Although this sounds straightforward, several key assumptions underlie this statement.

First, the phrase *working together* means sharing information, resources, and time. It means building trusting, collegial, and respectful relationships. It means breaking out of our silos of departments or grade-level teams or traditional service delivery models. Working together means communicating and problem solving, and being flexible when implementing solutions. It means dropping the notion that some teachers only work with certain populations of students (e.g., special education teachers only work with students with disabilities). Finally, working together likely means creating common planning time and rearranging schedules to ensure regular meetings among all stakeholders.

Second, the phrase *all stakeholders within the system* is intentionally inclusive of all people who make decisions that directly or indirectly support student learning. In a school system, the stakeholders include those people who typically

- Deliver instruction (e.g., teachers, interventionists)

- Lead aspects of the organization (e.g., administrators, instructional coaches)

- Provide specialized services to specific groups of students (e.g., speech-language pathologists, reading specialists)

- Care for students' needs (e.g., parents and families, community organizations)

and many others. Because MTSS is implemented at the systems level, all stakeholders must be focused on the same goals to realize the benefits.

Third, setting our sights on "success in mathematics for all students" requires a commitment from all stakeholders to meet all students' needs. All stakeholders must believe that all students can learn mathematics. Also, to perceive that all students can learn mathematics, all stakeholders must believe that they, too, can learn mathematics. It is common in our culture to hear adults saying, "I'm not a math person." When we hold this belief about ourselves, we implicitly give the message that some people are or are not "math people." This message can undermine the beliefs that all students can learn and be successful in mathematics.

In a school with effective collaboration in mathematics, you should see

- All service providers working together to support all students' success in mathematics (regardless of eligibility or classification)

- All service providers planning together and sharing resources

- All service providers analyzing assessment data to determine students' learning needs

- All service providers talking about evidence-based instructional practices, planning lessons and units to optimize student learning, sharing resources

WHAT ARE THE STEPS TO EFFECTIVE COLLABORATION?

Effective collaboration can be cultivated in any organization through intentional and thoughtful effort. Figure 16.3 highlights several key ingredients that are needed to facilitate effective collaboration. The next subsections discuss the steps educators must take to ensure these ingredients are in place.

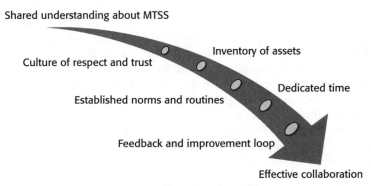

Figure 16.3. Key ingredients needed for effective collaboration.

Develop a Shared Understanding About MTSS

To support effective collaboration, all stakeholders in your school should have a shared understanding about MTSS, including the goals and components, the common and specialized vocabulary, and the roles and responsibilities of various stakeholders. This will likely start with developing a common understanding of the goals and tenets, as well as of why your school decided to implement MTSS. In a series of case studies of five schools that implemented MTSS, a common reason for doing so was the reflection that the current organizational structures and processes in place in each school were not supporting students' academic or behavioral needs (Tackett, Roberts, Baker, & Scammaca, 2009). Sharing students' mathematics performance data with stakeholders and your hypotheses about why the current organizational structures and/or processes are affecting student success may help shape people's understanding about the need for MTSS. As we noted in Chapter 15, an example of an organizational structure that might affect students' success in mathematics is having dedicated time to provide supplemental instructional support (either at Tier 2 or Tier 3) to students who are underperforming. Having a regularly scheduled, common meeting time to review students' mathematics performance data is another example of an organizational process that might affect students' success.

Through this process of discussing the purpose, core components, and rationale for implementing MTSS, a shared vocabulary can be developed. This shared vocabulary is essential for effective and respectful communication and lays the groundwork for meaningful collaboration. A good starting place is to develop a common understanding about the core components of MTSS. This book is intended to support your understanding of these components and can be a good resource for developing a shared vocabulary. However, some terms may need to be revised based on your context. For example, some vendors may refer to universal screeners as "benchmark assessments" or to Tier 1 instruction as "core instruction." Your team will need to decide which terms you want to use and then use them consistently.

To support collaboration among general education and special education teachers, Da Fonte and Barton-Arwood (2017) recommend creating information sheets. Special education teachers can create information sheets that describe student characteristics based on disability category and define key terms such as *accommodations* and *modifications* (defined in Chapter 3 of this book). General education teachers can create information sheets that provide details about the content standards and instructional approaches. These information-sharing tools can help minimize gaps in understanding among collaborators. You may find it useful to update the MTSS implementation framework with the terms your team decides to use. Recording this information can help reinforce the group decisions and may provide new stakeholders with a reference point for learning the terms.

In addition to having this shared understanding of core components, it is also important to develop common language about less obvious terms. Because those involved in MTSS represent multiple professional paradigms, it cannot be taken for granted that all stakeholders will have the same understanding of terms such as *success, inclusion,* and *struggling.* Similarly, some professions have technical terminology that is unique to the field and will likely be new to other stakeholders. These terms might not feel particularly technical to one person but may be overwhelming to another. For example, some general educators may not be aware of terminology or concepts used in special education (e.g., applied behavioral analysis, augmentative and alternative communication device, least restrictive environment, transition planning). Some special educators may not be aware of specific mathematics instructional strategies, approaches, or tools (e.g., number talks, adaptive reasoning, algebra tiles). Combined, some general and special education teachers may not be aware of terms used by speech-language pathologists (e.g., phonation, expressive aphasia, prosody). Without demystifying these terms, some stakeholders may feel excluded from conversations. To avoid confusion and promote communication, your school will need to establish a common language and, as important, a respectful culture that is conducive to seeking and providing clarification about terminology. This will likely be an ongoing process that requires intentional support to develop and nurture.

As stakeholders engage in discussions to develop shared understandings and beliefs about MTSS, they need to understand the roles and responsibilities that various stakeholders will play while implementing MTSS in your school. Some roles and responsibilities (such as delivering Tier 1 instruction) may already be well established, but others will be newly established and/or newly assigned to specific stakeholders. Still others will be reduced or shared. Defining these roles and responsibilities and then distributing them among the stakeholders should be accomplished with respect, sensitivity, and adherence to the policy and procedural guidelines provided by the school district.

Conduct an Inventory of Assets

An important component of collaboration is determining the areas of expertise within your team from which you can draw. Most important for the work we have been discussing is expertise related to 1) designing and delivering evidence-based mathematics instruction across the tiers of support and 2) interpreting and taking action from assessment data. By finding the pockets of expertise on your team, you can leverage the knowledge and skills across multiple stakeholders to improve the educational programming for all students.

One strategy for making these pockets of expertise visible is to conduct an inventory of assets. In simple terms, an inventory of assets is a survey administered to all stakeholders that helps identify each person's level of knowledge and skills in specific areas. However, it is as much a process as it is a product. It is an opportunity for all stakeholders to come together to discuss the types of expertise needed to implement MTSS in mathematics, determine which stakeholders may have unique and specialized knowledge and skills, and engage in conversations about how to leverage those skills to support all stakeholders in reaching the shared goal of supporting all students' success in mathematics. Some professional development resources might refer to this process as a needs assessment; however, we use the term *inventory of assets* to highlight the areas of existing expertise as opposed to areas of need. That said, the outcome of both processes is the same: a comprehensive understanding of the expertise that exists within your team and the areas in which to focus professional development efforts.

When conducting an inventory of assets, it is important to be clear about the knowledge and skills needed to effectively support all students within an MTSS framework. In the sample shown in Figure 16.4, we highlighted essential knowledge and skills across the core MTSS components. (This inventory of assets form is also available with the downloadable materials for this book.) We ask stakeholders to respond to statements about their knowledge of specific core components and

Inventory of Assets for Implementing MTSS								
	How much do you know about . . .?				How confident are you in implementing . . .?			
	I know a lot about this topic.	I know about this topic.	I know a few things about this topic.	I don't know very much about this topic.	I am very confident.	I am mostly confident.	I am somewhat confident.	I am not confident.
Designing explicit and systematic instruction	4	3	2	1	4	3	2	1
Designing guided and independent practice opportunities	4	3	2	1	4	3	2	1
Using multiple representations (concrete, visual, abstract) to teach concepts or procedures	4	3	2	1	4	3	2	1
Using problem-solving strategies	4	3	2	1	4	3	2	1
Designing opportunities for students to develop fact and computational fluency	4	3	2	1	4	3	2	1
Posing varied questions to elicit students' thinking (why, when, how)	4	3	2	1	4	3	2	1
Providing opportunities for students to talk about math	4	3	2	1	4	3	2	1
Interpreting results from universal screeners	4	3	2	1	4	3	2	1
Using results from universal screeners to make instructional decisions	4	3	2	1	4	3	2	1
Graphing progress monitoring data	4	3	2	1	4	3	2	1
Interpreting progress monitoring data to evaluate how students are responding to instruction	4	3	2	1	4	3	2	1
Implementing diagnostic assessments	4	3	2	1	4	3	2	1
Using results from diagnostic assessments to design interventions based on students' needs	4	3	2	1	4	3	2	1

Figure 16.4. Inventory of assets for implementing MTSS.

their confidence in implementing those same components. By asking about a person's knowledge and confidence, you may better understand the depth of his or her experience with each core component, from which you can determine the level of support he or she needs to implement it within the MTSS framework. For example, someone who is very knowledgeable but not very confident in using manipulatives and visual representations during instruction may benefit from peer observations with someone who is both knowledgeable and confident in using both. You may find that some of the statements in the sample inventory of assets are more or less relevant in your context, and you may also need expertise in different areas. As such, you can use this inventory as a starting point from which to design your own inventory of assets.

Foster a Culture of Respect and Trust

Underlying much of our conversation about implementing MTSS is the fact that many people within the educational system will be required to do things differently than before. Although their functional role (e.g., general education teacher, speech-language pathologist) may remain the same, they will necessarily be doing things differently, such as administering formative assessments, working with stakeholders with whom they have not previously worked, and engaging with colleagues to learn about and implement evidence-based instructional practices. An organization that is conducive to change can flexibly solve problems and has a culture of respect and trust.

As an example, conducting the inventory of assets requires a culture of respect and trust. For stakeholders to honestly reflect on their knowledge and confidence implementing the core MTSS components, they will need to know that the information gathered through this process will not be used to evaluate their performance or otherwise negatively affect their position. In interviews with 26 preservice teacher candidates, Da Fonte and Barton-Arwood (2017) found that although all teachers noted a willingness to learn from their future colleagues, they expressed anxiety about having a lack of specialized knowledge and skills to support collaboration. For example, preservice special education teachers noted that they felt unprepared on content-specific knowledge to work with their general education peers.

Also, productively discussing students' performance data requires a culture of respect and trust. Discussing your students' mathematics performance can be anxiety-provoking and cause some people to get defensive or accusatory. However, within an MTSS framework, we need to talk about data to improve our practices and change the instructional opportunities we provide our students. Nonjudgment is needed to have these honest conversations that lead to effective collaboration.

Arrange for Dedicated Collaboration Time

There is nothing more frustrating than trying to find time to get together with someone—a friend, colleague, or even a relative—only to discover that both of your calendars are booked for weeks. In the end, you either plan to meet later than expected or cancel a previous engagement, depending on your priorities. In MTSS, getting together with stakeholders is an integral part of the implementation process and cannot be left to chance openings in your calendar. Time must be intentionally organized to facilitate effective collaboration and must be safeguarded from competing priorities.

Collaboration time is needed to accomplish many goals within the MTSS framework. Time is needed to plan together, learn together, review and discuss data together, and design instructional opportunities together (see Figure 16.5 for some of the collaborative tasks that require time). Most important, stakeholders need to use collaboration time to analyze data and identify and address the mathematics difficulties the students are currently facing, with the intention of constructively offering solutions that will lead to improved outcomes.

Time is one of our most precious assets: We never seem to have enough of it, and what we do have is pulled by many priorities. Because of these reasons, we must carefully organize our time and invest it where our priorities lay. In that way, some tasks that are associated with initiatives that have lower priority should get less of our time.

Some ways in which MTSS teams and administrators can arrange time for collaboration, described in detail next, include common planning time, professional learning communities, a floating planning period, and periodic data dives.

Common planning time. Arranging the master schedule to include time during the school day in which to collaborate can be an effective way to facilitate collaboration. One possible arrangement is to have a common planning time for the mathematics instructional team by grade level, including those teachers providing Tier 1 instruction as well as Tier 2 and 3 interventions. This dedicated time can be used to

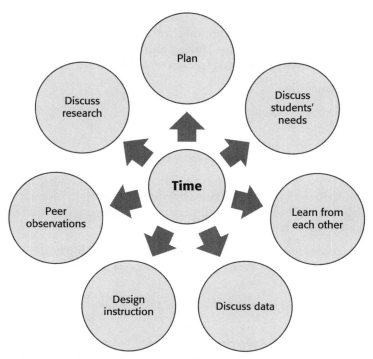

Figure 16.5. Collaborative tasks in MTSS.

graph and analyze students' progress monitoring data and design upcoming lessons to address students' needs.

Professional learning communities. If your school has dedicated time for stakeholders to come together in a professional learning community, these meetings can be used for collaboration. For example, professional learning community meetings can be used to provide targeted professional development on MTSS components across a broad range of stakeholders.

Floating planning period. Some stakeholders (e.g., special education teacher, speech-language pathologist) may need to meet with multiple teachers or teams. For these stakeholders to effectively collaborate with others, they may need a planning period that is scheduled at different times throughout the week.

Periodic data dives. At least three times per year, you will be awash with data from all students on the universal screener. Some schools find it valuable to set aside a block of time after each testing window to interpret, analyze, and make decisions from these data (Tackett et al., 2009).

Because time is scarce, we need to intentionally schedule time for collaboration and protect it. In some instances, protecting time will be more difficult than scheduling it. Situations arise in which we are faced with a choice about how to spend our time. It is essential that the time that is set aside for collaboration is used for collaboration.

Establish Norms and Routines

If time is being prioritized for collaboration, then collaboration needs to be the priority during that time. We all know how easy it is to lapse into conversations about challenging situations in the classroom, lessons that went awry, or upcoming week-end plans. Although this type of communication can support relationship building, it may derail the goals of collaboration. Having norms and an established routine may help you stay focused. We recommend that stakeholders follow these guidelines:

1. Set some ground rules.

2. Pick a location.

3. Set an agenda.

4. Take notes and follow up.

Set some ground rules. As you begin working with a new group of stakeholders, it is helpful to talk through the ground rules by which you want to interact. These rules or expectations should be created by the group and represent a shared set of norms that everyone agrees to live by. Some topics to consider are

- Communication: How will you manage questions or "off-topic" items? What does active listening look like? What type of behavior is acceptable for interjecting a point?

- Decision making: Will you make decisions by consensus, majority, or do you need unanimous support?

- Facilitation and record keeping: Who will facilitate the meeting by getting it started and keeping everyone on track? Who will be the record keeper to send the agenda and take notes? Will people share this role or will one person assume this responsibility?

- Etiquette: Will cell phones be on or off? Will there be food (will everyone bring their own or will someone be in charge of bringing snacks)? How will you notify people if you are running late?

Pick a location. Find a location that will allow you to concentrate on the goals of your meeting without competing distractions. Meeting in your classroom may be con-venient, but if you have students coming in for make-up assignments or are distracted by the piles of papers on your desk, you may want to look for another location such as the library, a conference room, or another teacher's empty classroom.

Set an agenda. Collaboration time needs to be focused on high-priority tasks. It is helpful to set an agenda that includes the meeting start and stop times, specific topics that will be discussed, and approximate time allocations for each agenda item. Because the purpose of these meetings is to collaborate around MTSS imple-mentation, the agenda should focus on analyzing data to identify and address math-ematics difficulties that students are currently facing. Instructional design and delivery decisions should focus on evidence-based practices. Figure 16.6 shows a thumbnail of a sample form to use for setting the meeting agenda. (You may obtain a full-size, photocopiable version of this form online with the downloadable materials for this book.)

Take notes and follow up. An important part of communication is establishing a protocol for recording decisions and major discussion points. It is important that someone take notes during the meeting and make these available for others to ref-erence. These notes should also include a list of any "action items" that people have

MTSS in Mathematics Collaboration Team Meeting
Agenda for [insert date here]

Confirmed attending:

1. ______________________
2. ______________________
3. ______________________
4. ______________________

Start time: ______________________ Stop time: ______________________

Agenda topic (in order of priority)	Time allocation

Figure 16.6. A sample form to use for setting meeting agendas.

agreed to complete before the next meeting. A thumbnail of a sample form to use for notetaking is shown in Figure 16.7. (A full-size, photocopiable version online is available with the downloadable materials for this book.)

Create a Feedback and Improvement Loop

Just as we evaluate the progress students are making in response to our instruction, we need to evaluate the progress of collaborative teams. Although the data might look different, it is important to reflect on successes and challenges of the process and

MTSS in Mathematics Collaboration Team Meeting
Minutes for [insert date here]

Attended:

1. ______________________
2. ______________________
3. ______________________
4. ______________________

Start time: ______________________ Stop time: ______________________

Agenda topic	Discussion

Action items	By whom	When

Next meeting:

Date: ______________________ Time: ______________________

Figure 16.7. A sample form to use for notetaking.

Key ingredient for effective collaboration	Successes		Challenges		
	What is working well?	What should we keep doing?	What are some challenges?	What should we do differently?	By when?
Shared understanding about MTSS					
Inventory of assets					
Culture of respect and trust					
Dedicated time					
Established norms and routines					
Feedback and improvement loop					

Figure 16.8.   A sample form to use for seeking feedback.

outcomes of collaboration. Because the goal of collaboration is to work together to create a coherent educational program that is aligned with students' needs, we need to determine if the processes we have put in place to facilitate collaboration are helping us reach this goal.

One way of gathering feedback and making improvements to the processes you have put in place to support collaboration is to periodically ask for input on the key ingredients for effective collaboration we discussed in this chapter. Because we want to keep what is working and change what isn't, it is useful to ask for feedback on the strengths and challenges that stakeholders are encountering. You may find it useful to structure the feedback such that you can identify what is working—and should be kept—and what isn't working. The template shown in Figure 16.8 may support the process of seeking feedback. (You may obtain a full-size, photocopiable version of this template online with the other downloadable materials for this book.)

As the collaborative team reviews the data that are gathered, you can celebrate the successes and reflect on the challenges. From the list of what isn't working, you can collectively discuss what changes might be possible to improve upon the current processes. If changes are agreed upon, it is helpful to have a timeline for implementing these changes.

SUMMARY: EFFECTIVE COLLABORATION

The goal of implementing MTSS is to support mathematics success for all students. To effectively implement MTSS, you will have many opportunities to collaborate with colleagues from across your school. In this chapter, we provided you with resources and tools to help facilitate meaningful collaboration. By working together to support student learning, you can more effectively help realize the goals of MTSS.

Implementing MTSS:
Voices From the Field

As you begin reading this last chapter, your mind is likely swirling with new information and techniques to improve all students' mathematics knowledge using an MTSS framework. However, it is also highly probable that you have many questions about how to effectively implement MTSS in your classroom and school. In this book, we have walked through the core components of this framework, including instruction and assessment. We presented numerous strategies to help improve the effectiveness of mathematics instruction, including evidence-based practices for intervention and problem solving. We also provided information on the types and purposes of assessments that can be used to assist in decision making and monitoring progress, and on how to choose an assessment based on the decision you are trying to make. Implementing one strategy, such as administering a universal screener or using schemas to support students' learning and success with word problems, may seem attainable; however, it may be difficult to picture how to simultaneously implement all of the components within an MTSS framework. Similarly, it may be challenging to conceptualize how to manage all of the data you will be collecting. Luckily, MTSS does not have to be a juggling act.

In this chapter, we hope to provide a few glimpses into real classrooms and schools from teachers and leaders who have been successful implementers of MTSS. It is our hope that, in learning from these educators, you utilize their advice and tips but also recognize that successful implementation never looks exactly the same for everyone. Every situation, every school, and every child is different, and we must stay flexible and creative as we work together to support all students in their mathematics learning. Echoing the previous chapter's focus on collaboration, we've included multiple voices from the field, including teachers, school leaders, and district leaders. All stakeholders must work together to effectively implement MTSS, and each stakeholder has a unique role and contribution in this process.

The format of this chapter is question and answer. The questions are organized around two primary topics: preventing roadblocks and seeing success. Before diving into our contributors' responses, read a bit of background information about each contributor and their expertise. Because these are real educational professionals working in real schools, their titles reflect the current usage of the terms RTI or MTSS in their schools or districts. Which contributor has a position or situation like yours?

Voices From the Field: About Our Contributors

Kellie, RTI Seventh-Grade Mathematics Teacher. Kellie is currently an RTI math teacher for seventh-grade math. For the past 6 years, she has been teaching a double-blocked math class for which she identifies and fills in gaps in student understanding in addition to teaching grade-level standards. Previously, she spent 5 years teaching math learners who struggle in a single-block class, separate from their on grade-level math class. She has been implementing RTI strategies in various ways over the last 11 years. She works in a large suburban school district.

Matthew, RTI Eighth-Grade Mathematics Teacher. Matthew teaches intervention classes for RTI and regular grade 8 mathematics. The intervention class he teaches helps students fill in gaps and gives them extra time for math. He has been implementing RTI for more than 14 years. He works in a large suburban school district.

Nicole, District RTI Coordinator. Nicole focuses on districtwide math intervention. Before holding this position, she provided state-level training and technical assistance supporting schools and districts in building their MTSS, including 5 years on a school personnel development grant funded by Office of Special Education Programs. While at the state level, she was also a coach for the National Center on Intensive Intervention and ran pilot work in middle school math intervention across five middle schools. She has been implementing RTI for about 10 years. She currently works in a suburban school district that serves about 4,500 students.

Brent, Senior Administrator of Special Education. Brent has been working in education for 13 years. He was a high school science special education teacher for 6 years. He is currently a special education administrator for a large urban city school district and has been working to support citywide RTI work over the past 4 years.

Melanie, Senior Director of Curriculum and Instruction. Melanie has held multiple positions within education. As senior director for curriculum and instruction at a large, suburban school district, she currently manages all core content areas, languages other than English, gifted and talented, professional development, and RTI. Previously, she was a middle school principal at a large urban middle school. Melanie has also served as an associate and assistant principal and an elementary school teacher. She has been implementing RTI for more than 7 years.

PREVENTING ROADBLOCKS

In interviewing the educators who contributed to this chapter, we sought to identify common roadblocks to implementing MTSS and to learn how teachers and administrators address them. We asked about how they manage the component pieces of MTSS, what they had personally found most challenging about implementation, and what actions they took to prevent roadblocks. We also asked what advice they would give to educators who are new to implementing MTSS. Because the various school systems in which our contributors work use different combinations of MTSS and RTI, we use the combined term MTSS/RTI in our questions. Our contributors' responses are only minimally edited for length and clarity.

Question 1: How do you balance and manage all of pieces within MTSS/RTI?

Kellie, RTI Seventh-Grade Mathematics Teacher: The biggest key to success in order to balance and manage all the pieces of RTI is to keep classes small and to allow time to document and reflect, which often is dictated by administration. My administration limits all my RTI math classes to 12 students or less. With small classes, I can effectively work with students individually or in small groups. In RTI classes of more than 12, documentation and intervention become extremely burdensome and ineffective. My administration has also provided me with additional time for documentation. For example, since I focus solely on teaching RTI math classes, I am not required to attend as many meetings as my colleagues. Instead I can spend that time documenting, analyzing, and reflecting on my students and their needs.

Brent, Senior Administrator of Special Education: We balance the pieces by ensuring that a core team of leaders, including both administrators and teachers, are collaborating with one another. This ensures consistency and allows the team to serve as thought-partners for all school staff throughout the year.

Melanie, Senior Director of Curriculum and Instruction: Having a team approach really assists in managing all of the RTI pieces. No one person should be in charge of all of it. Each person should be responsible for different pieces and for following up on those pieces. Teachers must be responsible for collecting the initial data when they want to recommend a student to the RTI committee. Teachers must also must be in charge of monitoring students' progress.

Question 2: What has been the most challenging aspect of implementing MTSS/RTI in your classroom, campus, or district?

Kellie, RTI Seventh-Grade Mathematics Teacher: The most challenging part of implementing RTI is identifying gaps in student learning. I've been teaching seventh-grade math for my entire career, so I am an expert on seventh-grade–math standards and how to scaffold appropriately to build a strong understanding of concepts. However, students in my RTI math class often have different educational gaps due to a variety of reasons. The question I started asking myself was "How can I identify those gaps and what can I do to fill them?" The district created a curriculum writing team to help solve that problem. As a part of that team, we created a "checkpoint" system that helps us identify learning gaps and provides resources to bridge those gaps and support the teacher and student.

Nicole, District RTI Coordinator: The most difficult aspect of implementing RTI in a district is that the framework touches all other bodies of work (e.g., core instruction, comprehensive assessment systems, special education), and often those other bodies of work are led by different leaders. This complexity leads to obstacles of establishing a common vision for RTI, common goals, aligned action plans, and communication. This is an immense coordination and communication task even if all the people involved are "on the same page." To overcome this challenge, first—district and school leaders need to truly believe all students can learn and expect the education system to produce growth in all students. Philosophical approaches, such as the "bubble kids" mentality (i.e., the idea that we should target kids closest to proficiency to increase the likelihood of moving test scores as the primary goal) versus the idea that all students, including the most challenged, deserve our attention, can be profoundly different and can sabotage the work. It is all about culture. I believe we can work together and ensure all students learn—it doesn't need to be an either/or. It is up to a district leader to set the expectation for all administrators in the system that all students matter and that it is unethical to make some students matter more than others. Next, extensive time needs to be devoted to the early planning stages, and any early implementation should be in small pilots to identify areas of misalignment early on and keep problem solving manageable.

Brent, Senior Administrator of Special Education: The most challenging aspect of implementing RTI has been supporting schools in establishing an RTI protocol that is inclusive of a dynamic set of assessments, diagnostics, and intervention tools and strategies, especially for schools with grades 6–12. It is also difficult to ensure schools keep consistent to this cycle. To overcome these challenges, our department has had a resurgence of RTI trainings (inclusive of some data-based individualization [DBI] learning series in ELA [English language arts] and math) for both school and district leaders. Anecdotally, having attended many of the DBI learning series, school leaders and teachers in those cohorts have expressed a real interest in this more "clinical" approach, especially for the most struggling students. Many expressed that PD (professional development) over the past decade in this urban school district has not presented this type of an approach as a viable intervention strategy for Tier 3.

Melanie, Senior Director of Curriculum and Instruction: The most challenging part is figuring out what to do next when a student is struggling with a certain concept. It is much easier to diagnose a student and their learning gaps than it is to design an intervention. Teachers rarely receive training on how to design interventions, and many times, general education teachers have never learned how to intervene on concepts that are below grade level. We need to strategically think about how our teacher certification programs and districts are equipping our teachers to design interventions to support students.

Question 3: How have you prevented roadblocks?

Matthew, RTI Eighth-Grade Mathematics Teacher: There will always be roadblocks in your classes, but [the key factor] is the willingness and effort of the teacher to make sure that *all* students can and will learn. Teachers must stay persistent and use a variety of strategies to help struggling learners.

Nicole, District RTI Coordinator: Attending to the "should we do it?" or consensus-building stage of systems change is critical. Time needs to be dedicated to fully understanding the context. What do data tell us about the issue? Are we struggling in some places more than others (what are the "others" doing?)? What other work is happening and how does this work fit with it? Much of the early work is auditing, collecting information, listening, and most importantly—communicating and fostering relationships. We have to start slow even though the need before us may be so urgent. It is a framework, not a magic recipe that we can just take from somewhere else and implement.

Melanie, Senior Director of Curriculum and Instruction: The biggest roadblock is effective Tier 1 instruction. Before moving a student to Tier 2, we must do some detective work to see what Tier 1 instruction looks like. We can't say that a student needs to be moved to Tier 2 if we don't see differentiation and progress monitoring with multiple sources of data. Another way to prevent roadblocks is to help teachers and administrators see that RTI does not determine a permanent placement for a student. RTI is not a magic bullet, and we must understand that the responsibility is on all of us (e.g., general education teacher, intervention teacher, administrators, etc.) to help all students succeed.

Question 4: What advice would you give a teacher or leader who is new to MTSS/RTI?

Matthew, RTI Eighth-Grade Mathematics Teacher: First, I would learn all you can about your students. This does not mean about how they behave, but instead, how they learn best. Doing this enables you to understand where your students are and how you can help then. Secondly, I would say "be flexible," because you might have to change your curriculum and the methods you use to teach your students. Utilizing different ways of teaching a mathematical concept (e.g., small groups, extra practice, visuals, etc.) is very important. Third, and quite possibly the most important, I would make sure that you understand all aspects of your subject. If you understand everything about your subject, then you can teach the concepts in many different ways to help your students. Last, I believe if a student trusts and respect you, then they will work hard for you.

Nicole, District RTI Coordinator: Everyone has an opinion about what RTI is/is not. I would advise someone new to the work to unify all stakeholders around what the research says, using What Works Clearinghouse Practice Guides, Institute of Education Science (IES) Guides, IRIS Modules from Vanderbilt University, etc. Research and practice are often disconnected, and the resources from these clearinghouses help bridge this gap. Also, always embed social emotional skills and positive behavior approaches in all academic instruction and intervention. Students who struggle academically develop avoidance behaviors and often struggle with self-regulation and other social skills. We need to stop looking at these pieces in discrete silos and use a whole-child approach.

Brent, Senior Administrator of Special Education: Work with your school leadership team (or department leadership team) to establish a valid and reliable universal screening system. Ensure that there aren't gaps across or between grade levels with the core curriculum and use of the normed screener. Also, look for patterns across the school and classrooms on screeners and discuss implications for instructional shifts, and/or the need to integrate diagnostic practices into your teaching.

Melanie, Senior Director of Curriculum and Instruction: A principal's leadership is key to successful implementation of RTI. If your principal is not fully invested in RTI, it is hard to make RTI happen on a campus. When I was a middle school principal, I developed and implemented an RTI committee. A team of us, made up of mathematics teachers, English language arts teachers, counselors, and administrators, would meet every three weeks to discuss our students. Math and ELAR (English language arts and reading) would rotate in based on grade level during their professional development planning period. We would discuss each individual student, including those who had previously been identified as struggling plus those who had not previously been identified. When we first started this, no one had any data to share.

People would say, "This child is doing fine," but they would not have data or artifacts to back up that statement. We had to help teachers learn how to track what students are doing. What data are you really using to say a student is or is not making progress? This method of thinking about each students' progress prevented us from missing any students that might need additional support. This process must be regular, ongoing, and built into the schedule. As a principal, it allowed me to really understand and help manage the support students needed.

There will inevitably be roadblocks as you and your campus implement MTSS/RTI. However, these teachers and leaders have highlighted multiple ways to prevent roadblocks from happening in the first place. Their feedback centers around two primary actionable ideas:

1. Work to identify and learn the best methods for diagnosing students' needs and selecting interventions based on students' needs.

2. Ensure that all stakeholders, including teachers and leaders at all levels, are fully invested in MTSS/RTI and willing to collaborate together in order for it to be successful.

One of the key premises of the MTSS/RTI model centers on being able to identify which students are struggling and what mathematical content they are struggling with. Identifying these learning gaps can be challenging; however, multiple tools are available to assist you in making screening and diagnostic decisions (see Chapters 10 and 13 in Section III, respectively). Assessments should be selected based on the decision you are trying to make and should have adequate validity and reliability evidence. Using screening and diagnostic tools, along with additional formative and summative assessments, can help you learn more about your students and their needs. Many times, students need differentiation or interventions within Tier 1 instruction, and improving Tier 1 instruction will help all students improve. However, some students may need more strategic or intensive intervention in Tier 2. Learning more about best practices in mathematics instruction and intervention (see Section II) will help you load your toolkit full with promising interventions and a variety of strategies. Also, deeply knowing your content area will assist you in designing high-quality Tier 1 instruction and more targeted interventions for Tiers 2 and 3.

Although much of MTSS/RTI happens in the classroom through instruction and intervention, it is a collaborative effort. The teachers and leaders interviewed for this chapter noted that it must be a team approach, because no one person can do it all. All stakeholders must have a shared understanding regarding practices and expectations. Getting teachers and leaders on the same page about MTSS/RTI promotes a positive campus culture centered on helping all students succeed in mathematics. This type of collaboration also makes it possible for teachers and leaders to discuss the types of resources or support teachers may need to provide their students with the instruction and intervention they need. For example, teachers may need additional time to document students' progress or plan interventions. If regular conversations are happening between leaders and teachers, this type of request will be easy to make and will likely be something foreseen by campus administrators. (See Chapter 16 for additional information on collaboration.) The information shared by these teachers and leaders is sure to help you prevent roadblocks and set your students up for success.

SEEING SUCCESS

Additional questions we asked Kellie, Matthew, Nicole, Brent, and Melanie focused on understanding how these educators define *success* and what concrete evidence of success they saw after implementing MTSS/RTI. We asked how they defined success in MTSS/RTI, what improvements they had observed in their own setting, what role assessment played in successful implementation, and what instructions and interventions had been most effective.

Question 1: What does *success* mean when thinking about MTSS/RTI?

Matthew, RTI Eighth-Grade Mathematics Teacher: First, I think of success as progress in students' learning. Tests can be an effective way of seeing progress and success, but tests are not all we should look at. I look beyond grades to students' confidence level in math. The confidence level is a key piece to success, because if they feel confident in what they are doing, then they will work harder. While students would like to pass the state standardized test, we should not only consider these scores as a measure of success. At the end of the year, I look at how much students have progressed from the previous year.

Nicole, District RTI Coordinator: Success is when we have a system that is ensuring that most students' needs are effectively being met academically, behaviorally, and social-emotionally to the degree that for the one or two that still need more, we have the resources (e.g., time, personnel, etc.) to intensify for those few until we can ultimately find success.

Brent, Senior Administrator of Special Education: Success is when schools can minimize the amount of time a student spends in a classroom (or smaller intervention setting) not responding to instruction.

Melanie, Senior Director of Curriculum and Instruction: Success with RTI is twofold: success with students and success with adults. For students, success is moving off of a tier. For example, it is a great achievement to have a student move from Tier 2 to Tier 1 or from Tier 3 to Tier 2. This demonstrates that the interventions are working. With adults, success is shifting mindsets about RTI. Placement on a tier is not a permanent life condition, and teachers should believe that they really can help all students succeed.

Question 2: In what ways have you seen success from implementing MTSS/RTI in your classroom, campus, or district?

Matthew, RTI Eighth-Grade Mathematics Teacher: Over the past few years, I have seen a lot success in my Target Classes. These classes include the students that didn't do well on the state standardized test the previous year and are for students who are on Tier 2 or 3. Implementing a lot of different teaching methods and using data has helped me help all of my students. Almost 100% of my students passed the state standardized test.

Nicole, District RTI Coordinator: I have seen success in many ways! I have seen large-scale data (screening, grades, and state accountability) show that interventions are effective and also student and teacher feedback. Nothing beats when a student who struggled for years in math writes "I am smart" on their math work in intervention, and a general education teacher reports he is engaging and participating with growing confidence every day. That is what it is all about.

Question 3: How has the use of assessment (e.g., universal screeners, diagnostic assessments) data assisted in understanding which students need support and the types of support they need?

Kellie, RTI Seventh-Grade Mathematics Teacher: There are two ways in which this is done. First, assessment data are used to determine which students are placed in the RTI math class, which provides additional instruction beyond their regular math class. Second, data are used to identify concepts and skills students are struggling with. The process of selecting the RTI students begins with analyzing three main data points. The RTI committee on my campus looks at District Assessment averages, scores from standardized universal screeners, and state standardized test scores for each student. When a student is performing below average in all three categories, they are immediately flagged for RTI and the RTI math class. If a student is performing low in one or two of those areas, the committee discusses the best options for that student. Is an RTI math class the best option? Is tutoring a better option? Is a certain teacher going to interact more effectively with this student? Once students have been placed in an RTI math class, the RTI teacher uses a systematic way of identifying learning gaps and works to bridge those areas of weakness. If a student is not in the RTI math class, then the regular math teacher will provide extra support during the school day during an "intervention" time, which is in between two class periods. It is a 30-minute block of time in which teachers can work with struggling students.

Nicole, District RTI Coordinator: Oddly, assessment has potentially been the greatest obstacle within our RTI work. Repeatedly, I see that we don't have enough training or knowledge on psychometric properties to understand what the data is useful for and what it is not (be it screening, progress monitoring, or diagnostic). General education data, often teacher-made or textbook tests, are often valued over RTI assessment data when in reality, all of these data should factor into an effective problem-solving process to determine students' needs. Training teachers and administrators in data literacy and a systematized process of data use is a critical early step.

Melanie, Senior Director of Curriculum and Instruction: Using assessment data from a variety of sources is sometimes a challenge in secondary settings because most teachers and leaders are accustomed to heavily weighting state standardized test data within their RTI decision-making process. Oftentimes, the assessments used are very global and force teachers to make very global decisions. For example, most state or district assessments are not diagnostic and do not help identify learning gaps; these assessments just provide information about whether they learned the material or not. Therefore, it is important to use a variety of assessments, both summative and formative, to collect the data necessary for informed RTI decision making. To help encourage the use of formative assessments, we are starting to design common formative assessments within professional learning communities. Teachers identify a few common standards, design the formative assessment, give it to their students, and analyze the data. This process helps us think through what mastery looks like and what errors and misconceptions may surface.

Question 4: In terms of instructional intervention, what methods have been most successful?

Kellie, RTI Seventh-Grade Mathematics Teacher: The biggest, most important intervention is small-group instruction. It is absolutely imperative to work with a small group of students in order to monitor work closely and identify and correct misconceptions early and quickly. Another component I have found to be effective is technology and computer programs. I believe that in grades 6 and 7, fact fluency plays an important role in overall mathematical success, and there are many online programs that help with fluency. I also use the computer to make videos of lessons or concepts that my students may struggle with, and the students can watch these videos, pausing when needed to process, and complete an assignment while they are watching the video. All of these computer components help students work independently while I may be working with another group of students on a specific skill. Lastly, a word wall is very important to help with academic vocabulary in math. I have a word wall posted in the front of my room for all current academic vocabulary for that unit. Once a unit is over, I move those words to the back of the room so they are still posted and can be referred to in the future.

Matthew, RTI Eighth-Grade Mathematics Teacher: I use small groups frequently and scaffolding within lessons. Small groups allow for more time with each student in a smaller environment. Scaffolding shows me where the students have gaps and how I can help them more.

Nicole, District RTI Coordinator: After years of pilot work across different schools and districts, the most successful math interventions target what research says about struggling math learners. First, many students simply need more practice than we typically give for mastering math facts and committing the learning to long term memory with high degrees of fluency. Adding strategy instruction to that practice with self-regulation, like in Peer Assisted Learning Strategies (PALS Math), is effective. In addition, students struggle with word problems, and intervention that is effective here is twofold: 1) students should be taught word problem schemas, and 2) math academic vocabulary needs to be explicitly taught and reinforced.

Implementing MTSS/RTI can assist you and your school in improving mathematics instruction and subsequently, student achievement, but what does success look like and what tools are critical to success? Our contributors noted that success is really twofold: success with students, and success with adults. Success for students centers on minimizing educational gaps and minimizing time in the classroom during which students are not responding to instruction. Students' progress can be seen by examining a variety of student scores, such as those from state tests, universal screeners, and report cards. However, our contributors noted that scores should not be the only indicator of student success. We want students to enjoy and be confident with mathematics, and our contributors have seen these results with their students. In addition, moving a student along tier levels (e.g., from Tier 3 to Tier 2) is also a sign of success; this movement demonstrates that students are responding to instruction and that they are steadily improving.

Although MTSS/RTI is designed to assist students, success is dependent on and affects adults. MTSS/RTI has the potential of changing teachers' mindsets about students. For example, teachers may have had previous notions about students who struggle mathematically, even believing that some students "don't have the math gene." However, all students can be successful in mathematics, and implementing MTSS/RTI and seeing all students succeed in mathematics can shift these harmful mindsets.

Assessment and instructional interventions should be used strategically within MTSS/RTI to see these types of successes. With assessment, our contributors noted that multiple pieces of data should be used in order to make decisions about students' risk status and their progress over time. Screening and diagnostic tools can be used to determine who needs additional support and the mathematical concepts they struggle with (see Chapters 10 and 11 for more information about screening and diagnostic assessments). An assessment should be chosen to match the type of decision you are trying to make. For example, using a state standardized test score may not be the best choice if you are trying to determine what content a student struggles with. Most state tests are not designed to provide diagnostic results and only provide very global interpretations about students' performance. See Chapter 9 for more information on choosing assessments based on the decision you need to make.

Once you know which students are struggling and what they may be struggling with, evidence-based interventions and practices should be designed and implemented. Our contributors noted the importance of small group instruction and positive outcomes they observed when implementing evidence-based strategies, such as peer-tutoring and teaching students' schemas to help them with word problems. They also referenced the value of focusing instruction on academic vocabulary and differentiating their instruction. You can read more about evidence-based interventions and practices throughout Section II of this book.

SUMMARY: HELPING ALL STUDENTS SUCCEED

Woven throughout the information shared by our five contributors from the field are the underlying ideas that all students can succeed with the right amount of intervention and support. These educators emphasized that MTSS is a shared responsibility. Whatever your position is within your school or district, you have an important role to play within MTSS.

Implementation can be strengthened by collaborating with others, learning about evidence-based practices, understanding assessment use, continuously monitoring students' progress, and regularly evaluating the overall effectiveness of the implementation.

References

Allsopp, D. H., Lovin, L. H., & van Ingen, S. (2018). *Teaching mathematics meaningfully: Solutions for reaching struggling learners* (2nd ed.). Baltimore, MD: Paul H. Brookes Publishing Co.

Archer, A. L., & Hughes, C. A. (2011). *Explicit instruction: Effective and efficient teaching*. New York, NY: Guilford Press.

Ashcraft, M. H., & Moore, A. M. (2009). Mathematics anxiety and the affective drop in performance. *Journal of Psychoeducational Assessment, 27,* 197–205. https://doi.org/10.1177/0734282908330580

Ashlock, R. B. (1994). *Error Patterns in Computation, 6th Edition*. Englewood Cliffs, NJ: Prentice Hall.

Bailey, D. H., Siegler, R. S., & Geary, D. C. (2014). Early predictors of middle school fraction knowledge. *Developmental Science, 17*(5), 775–785. https://doi.org/10.1111/desc12155

Ball, D. L., Thames, M. H., & Phelps, G. (2008). Content knowledge for teaching: What makes it special? *Journal of Teacher Education, 59,* 389–407. https://doi.org/10.1177/0022487108324554

Baroody, A. J., & Ginsburg, H. P. (1983). The effects of instruction on children's understanding of the "equals" sign. *Elementary School Journal, 84*(2), 198–212. https://doi.org/10.1086/461356

Blackburn, B. R., & Witzel, B. S. (2018). *Rigor in the RTI and MTSS classroom: Practical tools and strategies*. New York, NY: Routledge.

Bottge, B. A. (1999). Effects of contextualized math instruction on problem solving of average and below-average achieving students. *Journal of Special Education, 33,* 81–92. https://doi.org/10.1177/002246699903300202

Bottge, B. A., Rueda, E., LaRoque, P. T., Serlin, R. C., & Kwon, J. (2007). Integrating reform-oriented math instruction in special education settings. *Learning Disabilities Research and Practice, 22,* 96–109. https://doi.org/10.1111/j.1540-5826.2007.00234.x

Bouck, E. C., & Cosby, M. D. (2017). Tier 2 response to intervention in secondary mathematics education. *Preventing School Failure, 61,* 239–247. https://doi.org/10.1080/1045988X.2016.1266595

Butler, F. M., Miller, S. P., Crehan, K., Babbitt, B., & Pierce, T. (2003). Fraction instruction for students with mathematics disabilities: Comparing two teaching sequences. *Learning Disabilities Research and Practice, 18,* 99–111. https://doi.org/10.1111/1540-5826.00066

Cerasoli, C. P., & Ford, M. T. (2014). Intrinsic motivation, performance, and the mediating role of mastery goal orientation: A test of self-determination theory. *Journal of Psychology, 148,* 267–286. https://doi.org/10.1080/00223980.2013.783778

Common Core State Standards Initiative. (2010). *Standards for mathematics practice*. Retrieved from http://www.corestandards.org/Math/Practice/

Cook, B. G., Buysse, V., Klingner, J., Landrum, T. J., McWilliam, R. A., Tankersley, M., & Test, D. W. (2015). CEC's standards for classifying the evidence base of practices in special education. *Remedial and Special Education, 36,* 220–234. https://doi.org/10.1177/0741932514557271

Cook, B. G., & Cook, S. C. (2013). Unraveling evidence-based practices in special education. *Journal of Special Education, 47,* 71–82. https://doi.org/10.1177/0022466911420877

Cuenca-Carlino, Y., Freeman-Green, S., Stephenson, G. W., & Hauth, C. (2016). Self-regulated strategy development instruction for teaching multi-step equations to middle school students struggling in math. *Journal of Special Education, 50,* 75–85. https://doi.org/10.1177/0022466915622021

Da Fonte, M. A., & Barton-Arwood, S. M. (2017). Collaboration of general and special education teachers: Perspectives and strategies. *Intervention in School and Clinic, 53*(2), 99–106. https://doi.org/10.1177/105345127693370

Dennis, M. S., Sharp, E., Chovanes, J., Thomas, A., Burns, R. M., Custer, B., & Park, J. (2016). A meta-analysis of empirical research on teaching students with mathematics learning difficulties. *Learning Disabilities Research and Practice, 31,* 156–168. https://doi.org/10.1111/ldrp.12107

Dowker, A., Sarkar, A., & Looi, C. Y. (2016). Mathematics anxiety: What have we learned in 60 years? *Frontiers in Psychology, 7*(508), 1–16. https://doi.org/10.3389/fpsyg.2016.00508

Ersoy, E., & Oksuz, C. (2015). Primary school mathematics motivation scale. *European Scientific Journal, 11,* 37–50.

Every Student Succeeds Act of 2015, PL 114-95, 20 U.S.C. §§ 6301 *et seq.*

Flores, M. M., Hinton, V., & Strozier, S. D. (2014). Teaching subtraction and multiplication with regrouping using the concrete-representational-abstract sequence and strategic instruction model. *Learning Disabilities Research and Practice, 29,* 75–88. https://doi.org/10.1111/ldrp.12032

Fuchs, D., Fuchs, L. S., & Compton, D. L. (2012). Smart RTI: A next-generation approach to multilevel prevention. *Exceptional Children, 78,* 263–279. https://doi.org/10.1177/001440291207800301

Fuchs, L. S., Fuchs, D., & Compton, D. L. (2010). Rethinking response to intervention at middle and high school. *School Psychology Review, 39,* 22–28.

Fuchs, L. S., Fuchs, D., Hamlett, C. L., Phillips, N. B., Karns, K., & Dutka, S. (1997). Enhancing students' helping behavior during peer-mediated instruction with mathematical explanations. *Elementary School Journal, 97,* 223–249. https://doi.org/10.1086/461863

Fuchs, L. S., Fuchs, D., Hamlett, C. L., Walz, L., et al. (1993). Formative evaluation of academic progress: How much growth can we expect? *School Psychology Review, 22*(1), 27–48.

Fuchs, L. S., Fuchs, D., & Malone, A. S. (2017). The taxonomy of intervention intensity. *Teaching Exceptional Children, 50*(1), 35–43. doi:10.1177/0040059917703962

Fuchs, L. S., Fuchs, D., Powell, S. R., Seethaler, P. M., Cirino, P. T., & Fletcher, J. M. (2008). Intensive intervention for students with mathematics disabilities: Seven principles of effective practice. *Learning Disability Quarterly, 31,* 79–92. https://doi.org/10.2307/20528819

Fuchs, L. S., Fuchs, D., & Prentice, K. (2004). Responsiveness to mathematical problem-solving instruction: Comparing students at risk of mathematics disability with and without risk of reading disability. *Journal of Learning Disabilities, 37,* 293–306. https://doi.org/10.1177/00222194040370040201

Fuchs, L. S., Hamlett, C. L., & Fuchs, D. (n.d.). *Monitoring Basic Skills Progress* [Sample page]. Austin, TX: PRO-ED. Retrieved from http://www.proedinc.com/Downloads/8551sample.pdf

Fuchs, L. S., Powell, S. R., Cirino, P. T., Schumacher, R. F., Marrin, S., Hamlett, C. L., ... Changas, P. (2014). Does calculation or word-problem instruction provide a stronger route to prealgebraic knowledge? *Journal of Educational Psychology, 106,* 990–1006. https://doi.org/10.1037/a0036793

Fuchs, L. S., Seethaler, P. M., Powell, S. R., Fuchs, D., Hamlett, C. L., & Fletcher, J. M. (2008). Effects of preventative tutoring on the mathematical problem solving of third-grade students with math and reading difficulties. *Exceptional Children, 74,* 155–173. https://doi.org/10.1177/001440291807400202

Gagnon, J. C., & Maccini, P. (2001). Preparing students with disabilities for algebra. *Teaching Exceptional Children, 34*(1), 8-15. https://doi.org/10.1177/004005990103400101

Garet, M. J., Porter, A. C., Desimone, L., Birman, B. F., & Yoon, K. S. (2001). What makes professional development effective? Results from a national sample of teachers. *American Educational Research Journal, 38,* 915–945. https://doi.org/10.3102/00028312038004915

Geary, D. C. (2004). Mathematics and learning disabilities. *Journal of Learning Disabilities, 37,* 4–15. https://doi.org/10.1177/00222194040370010201

Gersten, R., Beckmann, S., Clarke, B., Foegen, A., Marsh, L., Star, J. R., & Witzel, B. (2009). *Assisting students struggling with mathematics: Response to intervention (RtI) for elementary and middle schools* (NCEE 2009-4060). Washington, DC: National Center for Education Evaluation and Regional Assistance, Institute of Education Sciences, U.S. Department of Education. Retrieved from https://ies.ed.gov/ncee/wwc/Docs/PracticeGuide/rti_math_pg_042109.pdf

Gersten, R., & Chard, D. (1999). Number sense: Rethinking arithmetic instruction for students with mathematical disabilities. *Journal of Special Education, 33*(1), 18–28. https://doi.org/10.1177/002246699903300102

Gersten, R., Chard, D. J., Jayanthi, M., Baker, S. K., Morphy, P., & Flojo, J. (2009). Mathematics instruction for students with learning disabilities: A meta-analysis of instructional components. *Review of Educational Research, 79,* 1202–1242. https://doi.org/10.3102/0034654309334431

Gersten, R., Dimino, J. A., & Haymond, K. (2011). Universal screening for students in mathematics for the primary grades. In R. Gersten & R. Newman-Gonchar (Eds.), *Understanding RTI in mathematics.* Baltimore, MD: Paul H. Brookes Publishing Co.

Ginsburg, H. (1987). How to assess number facts, calculation, and understanding. In D. D. Hammill (Ed.), *Assessing the abilities and instructional needs of students.* Austin, TX: ProEd.

Griffin, C. & Jitendra, A. (2009). Word problem-solving instruction in inclusive third-grade mathematics classrooms. *Educational Psychology, 102,* 187–201. https://doi.org/10.3200/joer.102.3.187-202

Hall, T. (2002). *Differentiated instruction.* Wakefield, MA: National Center on Accessing the General Curriculum. Retrieved from www.cast.org/udlcourse/DifferInstruct.doc

Hallett, D., Nunes, T., & Bryant, P. (2010). Individual differences in conceptual and procedural knowledge when learning fractions. *Journal of Educational Psychology, 102*(2), 395–406.

Hamilton, L., Halverson, R., Jackson, S., Mandinach, E., Supovitz, J., & Wayman, J. (2009). *Using student achievement data to support instructional decision making* (NCEE 2009-4067). Washington, DC: National Center for Education Evaluation and Regional Assistance, Institute of Education Sciences, U.S. Department of Education. Retrieved from https://ies.ed.gov/ncee/wwc/Docs/PracticeGuide/dddm_pg_092909.pdf

Hecht, S. A. (1998). Toward an information processing account of individual differences in fraction skills. *Journal of Educational Psychology, 90,* 545–559. https://doi.org/10.1037/0022-0663.90.3.545

Hecht, S. A., Close, L., & Santisi, M. (2003). Sources of individual differences in fraction skills. *Journal of Experimental Child Psychology, 86*(4), 277–302. https://doi.org/10.1016/j.jecp.2003.08.003

Hill, H. C., Rowan, B., & Ball, D. L. (2005). Effects of teachers' mathematical knowledge for teaching of student achievement. *American Educational Research Journal, 42,* 371–406. https://doi.org/10.3102/00028312042002371

Hord, S.M. (1986). A synthesis of research on organizational collaboration. *Educational Leadership, 43*(5), 22–26.

Hudson, P., Miller, S. P., & Butler, F. (2006). Adapting and merging explicit instruction with reform based mathematics classrooms. *American Secondary Education, 35,* 19–32.

Hughes, E. M., Powell, S. R., & Lee, T.-Y. (in press). Development and psychometric report of a middle school mathematics vocabulary measure. *Assessment for Effective Intervention.* https://doi.org/10.1177/1534508418820116

Hughes, E. M., Powell, S. R., Lemke, E. S., & Riley-Tillman, C. (2016). Taking the guesswork out of locating evidence-based mathematics practices for diverse learners. *Learning Disabilities Research and Practice, 31,* 130–141. https://doi.org/10.1111/ldrp12103

Hunt, J. H., & Vasquez III, E. (2014). Effects of ratio strategies intervention on knowledge of ratio equivalence for students with learning disability. *Journal of Special Education, 48,* 180–190. https://doi.org/10.1177/0033466912474102

Individuals with Disabilities Educational Improvement Act (IDEA) of 2004, PL 108-446, 20 U.S.C. §§ 1400 *et seq.*

Janney, R., & Snell, M.E. (2006). *Modifying schoolwork: Teachers' guides to inclusive practices* (3rd ed.). Baltimore, MD: Paul H. Brookes Publishing Co.

Jitendra, A. K. (2013). Understanding and accessing standards-based mathematics for students with mathematics difficulties. *Learning Disability Quarterly, 36,* 4–8. https://doi.org/10.1177/0731948712455337

Jitendra, A., DiPipi, C. M., & Perron-Jones, N. (2002). An exploratory study of schema-based word-problem-solving instruction for middle school students with learning disabilities: An emphasis on conceptual and procedural understanding. *Journal of Special Education, 36,* 23–38. https://doi.org/10.1177/00224669020360010301

Jitendra, A. K., Griffin, C. C., Deatline-Buchman, A., & Sczesniak, E. (2007) Mathematical word problem solving in third-grade classrooms. *Journal of Educational Research, 100,* 283–302. https://doi.org/10.3200/JOER.100.5.283-302

Jitendra A. K., Griffin C. C., Haria P., Leh J., Adams A., & Kaduvettoor A. (2007). A comparison of single and multiple strategy instruction on third-grade students' mathematical problem solving. *Journal of Educational Psychology, 99,* 115–127. https://doi.org/10.1037/0022-0663 .99.1.115

Jitendra, A. K., Lein, A. E., Im, S., Alghamdi, A. A., Hefte, S. B., & Mouanoutoua, J. (2018). Mathematical interventions for secondary students with learning disabilities and mathematics difficulties: A meta-analysis. *Exceptional Children, 84,* 177–196. https://doi.org/10.1177 /0014402917737467

Jitendra, A. K., & Star, J. R. (2011). Meeting the needs of students with learning disabilities in inclusive mathematics classrooms: The role of schema-based instruction on mathematical problem-solving. *Theory Into Practice, 50,* 12–19. https://doi.org/10.1080 /00405841.2011.534912

Jitendra, A. K., & Star, J. R. (2012). An exploratory study contrasting high- and low-achieving students' percent word problem solving. *Learning and Individual Differences, 22,* 151–158. https://doi.org/10.106/j.lindif.2011.11.003

Jitendra, A. K., Star, J. R., Dupuis, D. N., & Rodriguez, M. C. (2013). Effectiveness of schema-based instruction for improving seventh-grade students' proportional reasoning: A randomized experiment. *Journal of Research on Educational Effectiveness, 6,* 114–136. https://doi.org /10.1080/19345747.2012.725804

Johnson, E. S., & Smith, L. A. (2011). Response to intervention in middle school: A case story. *Middle School Journal, 42*(3), 24–32. https://doi.org/10.1080/00940771.2011.11461762

Kena, G., Hussar W., McFarland J., de Brey C., Musu-Gillette, L., Wang, X., Zhang, J., Rathbun, A., Wilkinson- Flicker, S., Diliberti M., Barmer, A., Bullock Mann, F., and Dunlop Velez, E. (2016). *The Condition of Education 2016* (NCES 2016-144). U.S. Department of Education, National Center for Education Statistics. Washington, DC. Retrieved from http://nces.ed.gov/pubsearch

Ketterlin-Geller, L. R., Baumer, P., & Lichon, K. (2015). Administrators as advocates for teacher collaboration. *Intervention in School and Clinic, 51*(1), 51–57. https://doi.org/10.1177 /1053451214542044

Ketterlin-Geller, L. R., & Chard, D. J. (2011). Algebra readiness for students with learning difficulties in grades 4–8: Support through the study of number. *Australasian Journal of Learning Disabilities, 16*(1), 65–78. https://doi.org/10.1177/1053451214542044

Ketterlin-Geller, L. R., Gifford, D. B., & Perry, L. (2015). Measuring middle school students' algebra readiness: Examining validity evidence for three experimental measures. *Assessment for Effective Intervention, 41,* 28–40. https://doi.org/10.1177/15345008415586545

Ketterlin-Geller, L. R., & Jamgochian, E. M. (2011). Instructional accommodations and modifications that support learning. In S. N. Elliott, R. J. Kettler, P. A. Beddow, & A. Kurz (Eds.), *The handbook of accessible achievement tests for all students: Bridging the gap between research, practice, and policy* (pp. 131–146). New York, NY: Springer.

Kingsdorf, S., & Krawec, J. (2012). Error analysis of mathematical word problem solving across students with and without learning disabilities. *Learning Disabilities Research and Practice, 29,* 66–74. https://doi.org/10.1111/ldrp.12029

Kintsch, W., & Greeno, J. G. (1985). Understanding and solving word arithmetic problems. *Psychological Review, 92,* 109–120. https://doi.org/10.1037//0033-295x.92.1.109

Krawec, J. L. (2014). Problem representation and mathematical problem solving of students of varying math ability. *Journal of Learning Disabilities, 47,* 103–115. https://doi.org /10.1177/0022219412436976

Krawec, J., Huang, J., Montague, M., Kressler, B., & de Alba, A. M. (2012). The effects of cognitive strategy instruction on knowledge of math problem-solving processes of middle school students with learning disabilities. *Learning Disability Quarterly, 36,* 80–92. https://doi.org/10.1177/0731948712463368

Lembke, E. S., Garman, C., Deno, S. L., & Stecker, P. M. (2010). One elementary school's implementation of response to intervention (RTI). *Reading and Writing Quarterly, 26,* 361–373. https://doi.org/10.1080/10573569.2010.500266

Lembke, E. S., Strickland, T. K., & Powell, S. R. (2016). Monitoring student progress to determine instructional effectiveness. In B. S. Witzel (Ed.), *Bridging the gap between arithmetic and algebra* (pp. 139–155). Arlington, VA: Council for Exceptional Children.

Manalo, E., Bunnell, J. K., & Stillman, J. A. (2000). The use of process mnemonics in teaching students with mathematics learning disabilities. *Learning Disability Quarterly, 23,* 137–156. https://doi.org/10.2307/1511142

Meece, J. L., Blumenfeld, P. C., & Hoyle, R. H. (1988). Students' goal orientations and cognitive engagement in classroom activities. *Journal of Educational Psychology, 80,* 514–523. https://doi.org/10.1037/0022-0663.80.4.514

Miller, S. P., & Hudson, P. J. (2006). Helping students with disabilities understand what mathematics means. *Teaching Exceptional Children, 39*(1), 28–35. https://doi.org/10.1177/004005990603900105

Montague, M. (2008). Self-regulation strategies to improve mathematical problem solving for students with learning disabilities. *Learning Disability Quarterly, 31,* 37–44. https://doi.org/10.2307/30035524

Mulcahy, C. A., Krezmien, M. P., & Travers, J. (2016). Improving mathematics performance among secondary students with EBD: A methodological review. *Remedial and Special Education, 37,* 113–128. https://doi.org/10.177/0741932515579275

National Assessment of Educational Progress. (2017). *NAEP mathematics report card.* Retrieved from https://www.nationsreportcard.gov/math_2017/nation/achievement/?grade=8

National Center on Intensive Intervention. (2017). *Academic progress monitoring tools chart rating rubric.* Retrieved from https://intensiveintervention.org/sites/default/files/NCII_APM_RatingRubric_Oct2017.pdf

National Council of Teachers of Mathematics. (2006). *Curriculum focal points for prekindergarten through grade 8 mathematics.* Reston, VA: Author.

National Council of Teachers of Mathematics. (2014). *Principles to actions.* Reston, VA: Author.

National Governors Association Center for Best Practices, & Council of Chief State School Officers. (2010). *Common Core State Standards mathematics.* Washington, DC: Authors.

National Mathematics Advisory Panel. (2008.) *Foundations for Success: The Final Report of the National Mathematics Advisory Panel.* Washington, DC: U.S. Department of Education.

National Research Council. (2001). *Adding it up: Helping children learn mathematics.* Washington, DC: National Academies Press.

National Research Council. (2010). *Preparing teachers: Building evidence for sound policy.* Committee on the Study of Teacher Preparation Programs in the United States, Center for Education, Division of Behavioral and Social Sciences and Education. Washington, DC: National Academies Press.

Nelson, G., & Powell, S. R. (2018). A systematic review of longitudinal studies of mathematics difficulty. *Journal of Learning Disabilities, 51*(6), 523–539. https://doi.org/10.1177/0022219417714773

Ni, Y., & Zhou, Y.-D. (2005). Teaching and learning fraction and rational numbers: The origins and implications of whole number bias. *Educational Psychologist, 40,* 27–52. https://doi.org/10.1207/s15326985ep4001_3

No Child Left Behind Act of 2001, PL 107-110, 20 U.S.C. §§ 6301 *et seq.*

Park, D., Gunderson, E. A., Tsukayama, T., Levine, S. C., & Beilock, S. L. (2016). Young children's motivational frameworks and math achievement: Relation to teacher-reported instructional practices, but not teacher theory of intelligence. *Journal of Educational Psychology, 108,* 300–313. https://doi.org/10.1037/edu0000064

Partnership for Assessment of Readiness for College and Careers. (2015). *Math Spring Operational 2015: Grade 8 end of year released items.* Washington, DC: PARCC Assessment Consortia. Retrieved from https://parcc-assessment.org/content/uploads/released_materials/02/8th_grade_Math_EOY_Item_Set_8-30-16.pdf

Pólya, G. (1945). *How to solve it.* Princeton, NJ: Princeton University Press.

Porter, A., McMaken, J., Hwang, J., & Yang, R. (2011). Common Core standards: The new U.S. intended curriculum. *Educational Research, 40,* 103–116. https://doi.org/10.3102/0013189X11405038

Powell, S. R. (2011). Solving word problems using schemas: A review of the literature. *Learning Disabilities Research and Practice, 26*(2), 94–108. https://doi:10.111/j.1540-5826.2011.00329.x

Powell, S. R., & Fuchs, L. S. (2015). Intensive intervention in mathematics. *Learning Disabilities Research and Practice, 30,* 182–192. https://doi.org/10.1111/ldrp.12087

Powell, S. R., Fuchs, L. S., & Fuchs, D. (2013). Reaching the mountaintop: Addressing the Common Core Standards in mathematics for students with mathematics difficulties. *Learning Disabilities Research and Practice, 28,* 38–48. https://doi.org/10.1111/ldrp.12001

Powell, S. R., & Stecker, P. M. (2014). Using data-based individualization to intensify mathematics intervention for students with disabilities. *Teaching Exceptional Children, 46*(4), 31–37. https://doi.org/10.1177/0040059914523735

Powell, S. R., Stevens, E. A., & Hughes, E. M. (2019). Math language in middle school: Be more specific. *Teaching Exceptional Children, 51,* 286–295. https://doi.org/10.11770040059918808762

Ramirez, G., Chang, H., Maloney, E. A., Levine, S. C., & Beilock, S. L. (2016). On the relationship between math anxiety and math achievement in early elementary school: The role of problem solving strategies. *Journal of Experimental Child Psychology, 141,* 83–100. https://doi.org/10.1016/j.jecp.2015.07.014

Riccomini, P. J., Smith, G. W., Hughes, E. M., & Fries, K. M. (2015). The language of mathematics: The importance of teaching and learning mathematical vocabulary. *Reading and Writing Quarterly, 31,* 235–252. https://doi.org/10.1080/10573569.2015.1030995

Regan, K. S., Berkeley, S. L., Hughes, M., & Brady, K. K. (2015). Understanding practitioner perceptions of responsiveness to intervention. *Learning Disability Quarterly, 38,* 234–247. https://doi.org/10.1177/0731948715580437

Rittle-Johnson, B., Schnieder, M., & Star, J. R. (2015). Not a one-way street: Bidirectional relations between procedural and conceptual knowledge of mathematics. *Educational Psychology Review, 27,* 587–597. https://doi.org/10.1007/s106048-015-9302-x

Rubenstein, R. N., & Thompson, D. R. (2002). Understanding and supporting children's mathematical vocabulary development. *Teaching Children Mathematics, 9,* 107–112.

Russell, M., & Masters, J. (2009). *Formative Diagnostic Assessment in Algebra and Geometry.* Paper presented at the Annual Meeting of the American Education Research Association, San Diego, CA.

Scarlato, M. C., & Burr, W. A. (2002). Teaching fractions to middle school students. *Journal of Direct Instruction, 2*(1), 23–38.

Schenke, K., Ruzek, R., Lam, A. C., Karabenick, S. A., & Eccles, J. S. (2018). To the means and beyond: Understanding variation in students' perceptions of teacher emotional support. *Learning and Instruction, 55,* 13–21. https://doi.org/10.1016/j.learninstruc.2018.02.003

Schleppegrell, M. J. (2012). Academic language in teaching and learning. *Elementary School Journal, 112,* 409–418. https://doi.org/10.1086/663297

Schumacher, R. F., & Malone, A. S. (2017). Error patterns with fraction calculations at fourth grade as a function of students' mathematics achievement status. *Elementary School Journal, 118,* 105–127. https://doi.org/10.1086/692914

Siegler, R., Carpenter, T., Fennell, F., Geary, D., Lewis, J., Okamoto, Y., . . . Wray, J. (2010). *Developing effective fractions instruction in kindergarten through 8th grade: A practice guide* (NCEE #2010-4039). Washington, DC: National Center for Education Evaluation and Regional Assistance, Institute of Education Sciences, U.S. Department of Education.

Simzar, R. M., Martinez, M., Rutherford, T., Domina, T., & Conley, A. M. (2015). Raising the stakes: How students' motivation for mathematics associates with high- and low-stakes test achievement. *Learning and Individual Differences, 39,* 49–63. https://doi.org/10.1016/j.lindif.2015.03.002

Star, J. R., Caronongan, P., Foegen, A., Furgeson, J., Keating, B., Larson, M. R., . . . Zbiek, R. M. (2015). *Teaching strategies for improving algebra knowledge in middle and high school students* (NCEE #2014-4333). Washington, DC: National Center for Education Evaluation and Regional Assistance, Institute of Education Sciences, U.S. Department of Education.

Stecker, P. M., Lembke, E. S., & Foegen, A. (2008). Using progress-monitoring data to improve instructional decision making. *Preventing School Failure, 52,* 48–58. https://doi.org/10.3200/PSFL.52.2.48-58

Stein, M., Carnine, D., & Dixon, R. (1998). Direct Instruction: Integrating curriculum design and effective teaching practice. *Intervention in School and Clinic, 33,* 227–233. https://doi.org/10.1177/105345129803300405

Stevens, E. A., Rodgers, M. A., & Powell, S. R. (2018). Mathematics interventions for upper elementary and secondary students: A meta-analysis of research. *Remedial and Special Education, 39*(6), 327–340. https://doi.org/10.1177/0741932517731887

Tackett, K. K., Roberts, G., Baker, S., & Scammaca, N. (2009). *Implementing response to intervention: Practices and perspectives from five schools. Frequently asked questions.* Portsmouth, NH: RMC Research, Center on Instruction.

Templeton, T. N., Neel, R. S., & Blood, E. (2008). Meta-analysis of math interventions for students with emotional and behavioral disorders. *Behavioral Disorders, 16,* 226–239. https://doi.org/10.1177/1063426608321691

Thompson, A. (2013). Interventions at Windy Pines: Is RTI the answer or the problem? *Journal of Cases in Educational Leadership, 16,* 49–55. https://doi.org/10.1177.1555458913478423

Thompson, S. J. (2005). An introduction to instructional accommodations. *Special Connections.* Retrieved from http://www.specialconnections.ku.edu/~kucrl/cgi-bin/drupal/?q=instruction/instructional_accommodations

Tomlinson, C.A. (1999). *How to differentiate instruction in mixed-ability classrooms.* Alexandria, VA: ASCD.

Turse, K. A., & Albrecht, S. F. (2015). The ABCs of RTI: An introduction to the building blocks of response to intervention. *Preventing School Failure, 59,* 83–89. https://doi.org/10.1080/1045988X.2013.837813

Van de Walle, J. A., Karp, K. S., & Bay-Williams, J. M. (2013). *Elementary and middle school mathematics: Teaching developmentally* (8th ed.). Boston, MA: Pearson.

Van de Walle, J. A., Karp, K. S., & Bay-Williams, J. M. (2015). *Elementary and middle school mathematics: Teaching developmentally.* New York, NY: Pearson.

van Garderen, D. (2007). Teaching students with LD to use diagrams to solve mathematical problems. *Journal of Learning Disabilities, 40,* 540–553. https://doi.org/10.1177/00222194070400060501

van Garderen, D., Scheuermann, A., & Jackson, C. (2012). Developing representational ability in mathematics for students with learning disabilities: A content analysis of grades 6 and 7 textbooks. *Learning Disability Quarterly, 35,* 24–38. https://doi.org/10.1177/0731948711429726

van Garderen, D., Thomas, C. N., Stormont, M., & Lembke, E. S. (2013). An overview of principles for special educators to guide mathematics instruction. *Intervention in School and Clinic, 48,* 131–141. https://doi.org/10.1177/1053451212454006

Walker, D. W., & Poteet, J. A. (1990). A comparison of two methods of teaching mathematics story problem-solving with learning disabled students. *National Forum of Special Education Journal, 1,* 44–51.

Watt, S. J., & Therrien, W. J. (2016). Examining a preteaching framework to improve fraction computation outcomes among struggling learners. *Preventing School Failure, 60,* 311–319. https://doi.org/10.1080/1045988X.2016.1147011

Wei, X., Lenz, K. B., & Blackorby, J. (2013). Math growth trajectories of students with disabilities: Disability category, gender, racial, and socioeconomic status differences from ages 7 to 17. *Remedial and Special Education, 34,* 154–165. https://doi.org/10.1177700741932512448253

Witzel, B. S. (2005). Using CRA to teach algebra to students with math difficulties in inclusive settings. *Learning Disabilities: A Contemporary Journal, 3*(2), 49–60.

Witzel, B. S., Mercer, C. D., & Miller, M. D. (2003). Teaching algebra to students with learning difficulties: An investigation of an explicit instruction model. *Learning Disabilities Research and Practice, 18,* 121–131. https://doi.org/10.1111/1540-5826.00068

Witzel, B. S., Riccomini, P. J., & Schneider, E. (2008). Implementing CRA with secondary students with learning disabilities in mathematics. *Intervention in School and Clinic, 43,* 270–276. https://doi.org/10.1177/1053451208314734

Woodward, J., Beckmann, S., Driscoll, M., Franke, M., Herzig, P., Jitendra, A., . . . Ogbuehi, P. (2012). *Improving mathematical problem solving in grade 4 through 8: A practice guide* (NCEE #2012-4055). Washington, DC: National Center for Education Evaluation and Regional Assistance, Institute of Education Sciences, U.S. Department of Education.

Xin, Y. P., Jitendra, A. K., & Deatline-Buchman, A. (2005). Effects of mathematical word problem solving instruction on middle school students with learning problems. *Journal of Special Education, 39,* 181–192. https://doi.org/10.1177/00224669050390030501

Xin, Y. P., & Zhang, D. (2009). Exploring a conceptual model-based approach to teaching situated word problems. *Journal of Educational Research, 102,* 427–441. doi:10.3200/joer.102.6.427-442

Index

References to tables and figures are indicated with a *t* and *f* respectively.